Zionism through Christian Lenses

Zionism
through Christian Lenses

Ecumenical Perspectives on the Promised Land

Edited by
CAROLE MONICA BURNETT

Foreword by
NAIM S. ATEEK

Contributors:
Carole Monica Burnett   David W. Good
Daryl P. Domning   Beverly Eileen Mitchell
Stephen H. France   Bernard Sabella
Paul H. Verduin

◆PICKWICK *Publications* · Eugene, Oregon

ZIONISM THROUGH CHRISTIAN LENSES
Ecumenical Perspectives on the Promised Land

Copyright © 2013 Wipf and Stock Publishers. All rights reserved. Except for brief quotations in critical publications or reviews, no part of this book may be reproduced in any manner without prior written permission from the publisher. Write: Permissions. Wipf and Stock Publishers, 199 W. 8th Ave., Suite 3, Eugene, OR 97401.

Pickwick Publications
An Imprint of Wipf and Stock Publishers
199 W. 8th Ave., Suite 3
Eugene, OR 97401

www.wipfandstock.com

ISBN 13: 978-1-61097-771-5

Cataloguing-in-Publication Data

Zionism through Christian lenses : edited by Carole Monica Burnett, with a foreword by Naim S. Ateek.

xxvi + 202 p.; 23 cm. Includes bibliographical references.

ISBN 13: 978-1-61097-771-5

1. Christian Zionism. 2. Arab-Israeli conflict—Religious aspects—Christianity. 3. Palestine in Christianity. 4. Social justice—Religious aspects—Christianity. I. Burnett, Carole Monica. II. Ateek, Naim Stifan, 1937–. III. Title.

DS119.76 B985 2012

Manufactured in the U.S.A.

All song lyrics, hymn lyrics, and poetry printed in this book are in the public domain.

The hymns "Jerusalem, the Golden" and "O Holy City, Seen of John" are transcribed by permission from *The Pilgrim Hymnal*, published by The Pilgrim Press. Proper academic credit is given in the documentation accompanying the essay by David W. Good.

Scripture texts in the essay by Daryl P. Domning are taken from the *New American Bible, revised edition* © 2010, 1991, 1986, 1970, Confraternity of Christian Doctrine, Washington, D.C., and are used by permission of the copyright owner. All Rights Reserved. No part of the New American Bible may be reproduced in any form without permission in writing from the copyright owner.

Scripture texts in the essay by Stephen H. France are taken from the HOLY BIBLE, NEW INTERNATIONAL VERSION©. Copyright © 1973, 1978, 1984 by International Bible Society. Used by permission of Zondervan. All rights reserved.

Scripture texts in the essay by David W. Good and the essay by Carole Monica Burnett are taken from Revised Standard Version of the Bible, copyright 1952 [2nd edition, 1971] by the Division of Christian Education of the National Council of the Churches of Christ in the United States of America. Used by permission. All rights reserved.

Scripture texts in the essay by Beverly Eileen Mitchell and the Foreword by Naim S. Ateek are taken from the New Revised Standard Version Bible, copyright 1989, Division of Christian Education of the National Council of the Churches of Christ in the United States of America. Used by permission. All rights reserved.

Contents

Foreword by Naim S. Ateek | ix
Preface | xix
Acknowledgments | xxiii
Contributors | xxv

Zionism and the Scriptures

1. How Should the People and Land of Israel be Understood in the Light of the Covenant?
   DARYL P. DOMNING | 3

2. Not Like the Nations: Zionism's Biblical Dilemma
   STEPHEN H. FRANCE | 25

Zionism and Ancient Christianity

3. Early Christians: Belonging Everywhere and Nowhere
   CAROLE MONICA BURNETT | 69

Zionism and Modern Christianity

4. "Why the Caged Bird Sings": Faithfulness in Exile
   BEVERLY EILEEN MITCHELL | 109

5. Praiseworthy Intentions, Unintended Consequences: Why Krister Stendahl's Quest for "Healthy Relations" between Jews and Christians Ended Tragically
   PAUL H. VERDUIN | 132

6. Catholic Social Teaching and Vatican Relations
with Israelis and Palestinians
Bernard Sabella | 162

7. The New Jerusalem: A Personal Perspective
David W. Good | 186

Foreword

NAIM S. ATEEK

The Rev. Dr. Naim S. Ateek, a Palestinian Anglican priest who has served as Canon of St. George's Cathedral in Jerusalem, is the founder and director of the Sabeel Ecumenical Liberation Theology Center, whose main office is located in Jerusalem. He is the author of two books, *Justice and Only Justice: A Palestinian Theology of Liberation* and *A Palestinian Christian Cry for Reconciliation*, as well as numerous articles.

I AM THANKFUL TO Dr. Carole Monica Burnett for assembling an outstanding ecumenical group of conscientious Christian thinkers to reflect on the phenomenon of Zionism and how it has impacted and impeded the achievement of a just peace in Palestine-Israel.

The background to this project is a conference in Portland where I mentioned that the heart of the conflict over Palestine has to do with one's perspective on the land of Palestine. Basically, the conflict boils down to one thing, the land: whose land is it? Does it belong to the Palestinian people or the Jewish people? Is it possible for the two claimants to share it? Can we find a just solution for this seemingly intractable conflict? Often at conferences I ask the biblical scholars, theologians, and other concerned attendees to address this issue from various perspectives. I was, therefore, delighted when Dr. Burnett volunteered to edit a volume on this topic.

There are seven contributors belonging to the three major categories of Christian churches, namely, the Orthodox, Catholic, and Protestant. They are all concerned about the Palestine-Israel issue and have been active in various ways, whether academically or pragmatically, in the search for a just peace. One of the contributors and I are Palestinians living in Jerusalem; the rest are Americans resident in the United States.

Foreword

The contributors have approached the topic from their faith perspective and their area of expertise, as well as their personal knowledge and experience of visiting the area. I believe that they provide a valuable contribution to the ongoing discussion of the cumulative endeavors of many people who continue to work for justice and peace for the people of Palestine and Israel, regardless of their ethnic or religious background, so that all can live in peace, freedom, and human dignity.

In light of the title of the book, *Zionism through Christian Lenses*, it is important to introduce the reader to the phenomenon of Zionism, though very briefly. To begin with, Zionism was the name given to the national movement that started among a group of Jews at the end of the nineteenth century in Europe. Its aim was the ingathering of the Jewish people in Palestine to establish a Jewish state there.[1] The name itself is derived from the word "Zion," which is a biblical name for a small mountain in Jerusalem. Subsequently it has come to represent the city of Jerusalem and even the whole land.

Generally speaking, there are three major types or trends of Zionism. The first is the Zionism of Theodor Herzl (1860–1904). This is the original political Zionism that officially began in 1897 in Basel, Switzerland. In this first Zionist Congress, around two hundred people from seventeen countries gathered at Herzl's invitation.[2] Herzl is credited as being the father of Political Zionism. He made it clear that "[t]he aim of Zionism is to create for the Jewish people a home in 'EretzIsrael' secured by law."[3] Herzl's Zionism envisaged the expulsion of the indigenous people of Palestine across the border and the establishment of a Jewish state.[4]

Herzl had come to recognize that the pervasiveness of anti-Semitism made it impossible for Jews to enjoy equal rights and full citizenship in Europe. It was clear to him that even in France, where the French Revolution (1789) was based on the motto "Liberty, Equality, and Fraternity," anti-Semitism was rife, as indicated by the Dreyfus affair. Alfred Dreyfus was a French army officer who was charged with espionage. Although

---

1. "Zionism," Jewish Virtual Library. See http://www.jewishvirtuallibrary.org/jsource/Zionism/zionism.html; accessed on Feb 29, 2012.

2. Kamal and Mahdy, "Requiem for Palestine." Pressenza International Press Agency. See http://pressenza.com/npermalink/requiem-for-palestine-xixx-a-conflict-born-with-a-solution; accessed on Feb 29, 2012.

3. "The First Zionist Congress and the Basel Program," Jewish Virtual Library. See http://www.jewishvirtuallibrary.org/jsource/Zionism/First_Cong_&_Basel_Program.html; accessed on Feb 29, 2012.

4. Mulhall, *America and the Founding of Israel*, 49.

Foreword

innocent, he was indicted because he was Jewish. Herzl believed that since such an incident was possible in France, full emancipation would not come to the Jewish people, and that the only way out for Jews would be to live in their own state away from European anti-Semitism.

Herzl was a secular Jew, and religion did not play any role in his upbringing. Neither he nor his Zionist friends could anticipate a future in Europe where full emancipation and democratic principles would make it possible for all people including Jews to be equal under the law. In order for the Zionist project to materialize, Herzl started to look for a European sponsor.

Although there were a number of setbacks at finding a sponsor, ultimately it was the British government that supported the Zionist project.[5] The Balfour Declaration of 1917, just before the end of World War I, stated Britain's willingness to establish in Palestine a national home for the Jewish people.[6]

Zionism spread in Jewish communities throughout Europe and North America and attracted a number of sympathizers and supporters. It is important to point out, however, that a substantial movement within Judaism, consisting primarily of Orthodox and Reform Jews, rejected Zionism and considered it a religious aberration.[7]

Despite its being shunned by the religious, Zionism became a formidable movement. After World War I, when Palestine came under the British Mandate, the Zionists were considered the official representatives of the interests of Jews worldwide. Moreover, the Zionists were able to form and build the organizational, political, and military infrastructure that made it possible to establish the State of Israel in 1948. This was the political Zionism that was successful in achieving the recognition and respect of the western countries. All the successive Israeli governments from 1948 to 1977 belonged to the political party that was based on the ideology and political Zionism of Theodor Herzl.

5. Ibid., 60–63.

6. In a November 2, 1917, letter to Lord Rothschild, what came to be known as "The Balfour Declaration" reads as follows: "His Majesty's government view with favour the establishment in Palestine of a national home for the Jewish people, and will use their best endeavours to facilitate the achievement of this object, it being clearly understood that nothing shall be done which may prejudice the civil and religious rights of existing non-Jewish communities in Palestine, or the rights and political status enjoyed by Jews in any other country." Schneer, *The Balfour Declaration*, 341–42.

7. Kolsky, *Jews Against Zionism*. The entire book documents Jewish resistance to Zionism in the first half of the twentieth century. For the composition of Jewish anti-Zionist movements in Europe and North America, see p. 28.

Foreword

The second trend of Zionism is religious Zionism. The 1967 war was the watershed that further changed the political map of the region. At the end of the 1948–49 war, the Zionists had been able to establish the State of Israel on 78 percent of Palestine, approximately 20 percent more than the United Nations partition plan of 1947 had allotted them. During the 1967 war, the government of Israel was able to expand its territory over the rest of Palestine; that is, the 22 percent that constitutes the West Bank, including East Jerusalem, and the Gaza Strip. In addition, the Israeli army was able to take possession of the Sinai Peninsula from Egypt, the Golan Heights from Syria, and smaller areas of land from Jordan.

What is ideologically significant is that the 1967 war marked the beginning of a gradual shift from a secular form of Zionism into a religious form. For most religious Jews in the three major Jewish denominations, the success of the 1967 war was perceived as miraculous. The war was a blitzkrieg; within six days the Israeli military was able to destroy the military capability of three Arab armies and occupy the ancient Jewish "homeland" and, most significantly, East Jerusalem.

The stage was now set for the religious ideology to take over slowly. There was euphoria among religious Jews after the war. Though hesitant at the beginning, they later determinedly expressed their ideology in settlement-building throughout the West Bank and around Jerusalem. All the successive Israeli governments, whether Labor or Likud, secular or religious, were committed to building new settlements on Palestinian land, referring to the West Bank by its biblical name of Judea and Samaria.

Slowly, secular Zionism began to wane while religious Zionism began to grow stronger. Zionism had a new lease on life with the backing of the religious. There was a new impetus that was different from the building of the state nineteen years before. In 1948, the strongest justification for the establishment of the state was the Nazi Holocaust. The state was born from the ashes of the Holocaust, and the Western countries, recognizing Israel with jubilation, did not compel the new Israeli state to implement U.N. resolutions. After the 1967 war, however, the primary justification was no longer the Holocaust, but the reclamation of a lost ancient inheritance. The land was no longer seen as the gift of the victorious Western powers after World War II, but the gift of "God" given to them thousands of years ago. The Zionist claim was no longer based on the promise of Lord Balfour, but on the promise of the Lord God. For some religious Zionists, the events of 1967 were a reprise of Joshua's conquest of the land of Canaan. In fact, a Western Christian Zionist theologian, Paul van Buren, wrote that

Foreword

God was fighting against the Palestinians on the side of Jews as in the time of Joshua.[8]

Indeed, the 1967 war initiated a new revival that swept across the Jewish community throughout the world. If the Holocaust had given a strong rationalization for the establishment of the state in 1948, the Hebrew Scriptures were considered to be the title deed to the land. Many religious Jews turned to Zionism, believing that, although the state was established by secular people and not by the Messiah, God was using the Zionists to bring about redemption. To many religious Jews, such a belief constituted a solemn divine call to take back the land from the Palestinians, whom some regarded as successors of the Amalekites, and to settle it.[9]

I hope it is clear to the reader that the introduction of the religious factor into the political conflict has enormously complicated the pursuit of peace. If secular Zionism was and is difficult to deal with, religious Zionism exacerbated the issue for Palestinians. When religion is invoked and involved in violent conflict, the problems and difficulties increase exponentially. It has become, therefore, an extremely thorny task to penetrate the emotions since the Bible and God are invoked. Tragically, religious sentiments have a greater potency to perpetuate and inflame conflicts than most secular ideologies. In the Israel-Palestine conflict, the abuse of the Bible has had severe implications.

We are cognizant today that the most obstinate questions that prevent the pursuit of peace are those that relate to settlement-building because they are heavily founded and rationalized on the bases of biblical texts.

The third trend of Zionism is Christian Zionism. What do we mean by this oxymoronic expression? Donald Wagner provides us with a straightforward definition: "Christian Zionism is a movement within Protestant fundamentalism that understands the modern State of Israel as the fulfillment of biblical prophecy and thus deserving of political, financial, and religious support."[10] In other words, we are speaking about Christians who have espoused the theology and ideology of Zionism. There are generally two types. One group, militant and growing in number, is "associated with more fundamentalist forms of Protestant Christianity."[11] The second type is made up of Christians belonging to mainline churches—Presbyterians,

8. Ateek, *Justice and Only Justice*, 63.
9. Ibid., 85.
10. Wagner, "A Christian Zionist Primer," *Cornerstone* 31:12. See http://www.sabeel.org/datadir/en-events/ev49/files/CornerStone31.pdf; accessed on Mar 24, 2012. Quoted in Ateek, *A Palestinian Christian Cry*, 79.
11. Ruether, "Christian Zionism and Main Line Western Christians," 155.

Methodists, Episcopalians, Lutherans, United Church of Christ, and others, as well as some Catholics and Orthodox—who blindly support the State of Israel, and refrain from criticizing its policies. The perspective of the Western mainline churches is significantly shaped by a desire to atone for past Christian anti-Semitism, even though the Palestinians are paying the price.[12]

It is important to point out that the early Christian Zionists of the nineteenth century were known as Christian Restorationists. They believed that before Jesus' Second Coming, Jews must return to Palestine, and that Christians should advocate for them to be able to do so. This early form pre-dated the political Zionism of Herzl by more than seventy years.[13] It is also true to say that throughout its development Christian Zionism has contained various theological shades. At its basis, it had to do with a literal reading, study, and a futurist biblical interpretation of the Bible, especially the texts that have to do with the end-times and the Second Coming of Christ. One of its prominent exponents was John Nelson Darby (1800–1882), who is credited as being the father of Dispensationalism.[14] This theory became wildly popular among certain Protestant and Evangelical Christians during the nineteenth and twentieth centuries, but is nearly defunct theologically among mainline churches today. It is still alive, however, among right-wing conservative and evangelical Christian groups.

At its beginning, this type or form of Bible study and spiritual reflection was confined within the group itself. It became more dangerous when it was translated into a political agenda. For example, Lord Shaftesbury in the 1840s lobbied the British government to promote the return of Jews to Palestine in order to hasten the Second Coming of Christ. William Blackstone lobbied U.S. President Harrison in 1891 to promote the migration of American Jews to Palestine. Both of these Christian activists were busy promoting their theological ideas before Herzl established the Zionist Movement in 1897.

It is worth mentioning that at the first Jewish Zionist Congress in Basel, the Rev. William H. Hechler (1845–1931), an Anglican clergyman, was one of the very few non-Jews to attend, at the invitation of Herzl himself. In fact, Herzl named Hechler the first Christian Zionist.[15]

---

12. Ibid.
13. Ruether and Ruether, *Wrath of Jonah*, 72–78.
14. Ibid., 77.
15. Klinger, "Rev. William Hechler and Theodor Herzl." Herzl wrote in his journal,

Foreword

Most of the early Christian Zionist leaders were interested primarily in the end of the world and the Second Coming of Christ. They surmised that, before that can happen, Jews must return to Palestine. But people like Rev. Hechler were also interested in promoting the immigration of Jews with a political agenda in mind. In fact, it is Lord Shaftesbury who is credited with the phrase, "a country without a nation for a nation without a country," which the Zionists rearranged to read, "a land of no people for a people with no land." This interplay between religious faith and political expediency increased among Christian Zionists after the establishment of the Zionist Movement. Christian Zionism influenced both British Foreign Secretary Lord Balfour and Prime Minister Lloyd George. They played a significant role in the issuance of the Balfour Declaration in 1917, which gave the first formal impetus to the Zionists.[16] Subsequently Zionism became a relentless force that influenced political events and eventually led to the establishment of the State of Israel in 1948. It is worth noting that this Christian Zionism was increasing in determination and strength and was active among Western Christians (especially Protestants). In fact, it had no counterpart, at the time, on the Jewish religious side, since most of the Jewish religious were anti-Zionist.

The political and diplomatic support that Christian Zionists have given for the establishment of the State of Israel has been quite extensive. For many years, Christian Zionists were working independently and discretely. After the 1967 war, with the rise of the Religious Right in the United States and Religious Zionism in Israel, Christian Zionists cautiously began to align themselves with Jewish Zionist groups. Today there is a strong bond between some Western Christian organizations and Israeli Jewish religious Zionists. Due to Christian Zionist beliefs that the land of Israel has been given by God as an eternal inheritance to the Jewish people and that the Palestinians have no share in it, and due to their staunch support of the settler movement, the activities of the Christian Zionists are one of the main obstacles to peace, especially in light of their relatively robust political clout in the United States.

I hope that this brief introduction can help the reader to realize the immensity of the problem we face. These three types of Zionism (Jewish—secular and religious—and Christian) are still with us. They form three

"Hechler declares my movement to be a 'Biblical' one, even though I proceed rationally in all points." This shows part of the different perspectives of the two men. See http://www.ourjerusalem.com/history/story/rev-william-hechler-theodor-herzl.html; accessed on Feb 29, 2012.

16. Tuchman, *The Bible and the Sword*, 324.

historical links that contribute both to the conflict itself as well as to the complications and obstacles that have stood in the way of peace. Each of these three types plays a role in aggravating the conflict. The original sin, however, remains that in the mind of Herzl and his friends the indigenous people of Palestine were dispensable. This premise was supported, rationalized, and justified by a certain reading of the Bible that became the strongest alibi for the theft of Palestine.

Today, the weakest link of the three is the original political Zionism of Herzl. Although it is still the foundational form, it has given way to the more formidable power and potent ideas of militant religious Zionism.

In my ongoing biblical research, I am convinced that both Jewish and Christian Zionism have done and continue to do a great disservice to the Bible. The reason is that they emphasize exclusive texts that reflect a tribal and narrow understanding of God. The texts that talk about the land promises (such as Gen 15, 17, 28, 35, and others) as well as God's command to drive out and/or annihilate the indigenous people of the land (see Num 33:50–56 and Deut 20:16–18) are critiqued within the Old Testament itself by other Old Testament writers also claiming the authority of God (see, for example, Ezek 47:21–23 and Isa 56:1–7, among others). I have found many examples that reflect this religious thought development.

Let me give one illustration. In the books of Ezra and Nehemiah it is easy to detect sentiments against non-Jews in the land after the period of the exile. In fact, Ezra the priest led the people into ritual acts of repentance because they sinned against God by marrying foreign wives and having children and breaking the law of God. After much prayer, Ezra demanded that Jewish husbands abandon their non-Jewish wives and even their children, and separate themselves from the strangers and foreigners (Ezra 9–10; Neh 9:2). The aim was to preserve a purely ethnic Jewish community (Ezra 9:2). One of the strong critics of this position was a "liberation theologian" whom we know only as "Third Isaiah." Claiming the authority of God he condemns what Ezra and Nehemiah are doing and presents an impressively inclusive picture of God:

> Do not let the foreigner joined to the LORD say, "The LORD will surely separate me from his people"; and do not let the eunuch say, "I am just a dry tree." . . . And the foreigners who join themselves to the LORD, to minister to him, to love the name of the LORD, and to be his servants, all who keep the Sabbath, and do not profane it, and hold fast my covenant—these I will bring to my holy mountain, and make them joyful in my house of prayer; their burnt offerings and their sacrifices will be accepted

on my altar; for my house shall be called a house of prayer for all peoples (Isa 56:3, 6–7).[17]

Instead of a theology that presents God as being against foreigners and strangers, this writer sees God as a God who embraces all people and welcomes their inclusion in prayer and worship: "my house shall be called a house of prayer for all peoples."

The exclusive is critiqued and replaced by the inclusive. This religious revolution within Hebrew Scripture itself has not been adequately considered by Jewish and Christian Zionists. Their present position is still antagonistic to and exclusive of the Palestinians, and they use God as corroborator. What is important to emphasize is that the witness of the Bible is not about a bigoted and a racist god, but the creative, faithful God who loves and cares for all people.

This revolution that started in the Hebrew Bible continued in the ministry and teachings of Jesus. This is the Christian lens that helps me critique Zionism, whether in its secular or religious garbs, Jewish or Christian. Zionism needs to be critiqued and rejected because it does injustice to the human being. Secular Zionism, while aiming to protect and support Jews, has totally negated the Palestinians and deemed them dispensable. As for the Jewish and Christian forms of religious Zionism, instead of starting with the more noble and developed understanding of an inclusive God that lies at the heart of the biblical message, they have regressed to primitive and exclusive concepts that some Old Testament writers had already critiqued and shed. The damage that has been done to both Judaism and Christianity has been immense.[18]

I believe that the contributors to this volume are aware of these negative religious forces as impeding the pursuit of a just peace. In the midst of the dilemma and crisis of the quest for peace, each contributor is using his or her lens to analyze the problem and offer helpful suggestions to promote a solution that can be based on the demands of international law as well as a solution that is worthy of a faith in the God who loves all and cares for all people equally and who works through us to include rather than to exclude the other.

My hope and prayer is that this book will make a substantial contribution to the endeavors for a just peace and will open the eyes and minds of many people to become actively involved in the pursuit of an enduring peace for all our people.

17. See also Howard-Brook, *Come Out My People*, 244–68.
18. Rabkin, *A Threat from Within*, especially 150–51, 225–28.

Foreword

It is time to listen to the voices of these seven insightful contributors.

BIBLIOGRAPHY

All quotations from the Bible are drawn from the New Revised Standard Version.

Ateek, Naim Stifan. *Justice and Only Justice: A Palestinian Theology of Liberation.* Foreword by Rosemary Radford Ruether. Maryknoll, NY: Orbis, 1989.
———. *A Palestinian Christian Cry for Reconciliation.* Foreword by Archbishop Desmond Tutu. Maryknoll, NY: Orbis, 2008.
"The First Zionist Congress and the Basel Program." Jewish Virtual Library. At http://www.jewishvirtuallibrary.org/jsource/Zionism/First_Cong_&_Basel_Program.html. Accessed on Feb 29, 2012.
Holy Bible. New Revised Standard Version. Grand Rapids: Zondervan, 1989.
Howard-Brook, Wes. *Come Out My People: God's Call Out of Empire in the Bible and Beyond.* Maryknoll, NY: Orbis, 2010.
Kamal, Baher, and Farred Mahdy. "Requiem for Palestine (1): A Conflict Born With a Solution." Human Wrongs Watch via Pressenza International Press Agency, Sept 4, 2011. At http://pressenza.com/npermalink/requiem-for-palestine-xixx-a-conflict-born-with-a-solution. Accessed on Feb 29, 2012.
Klinger, Jerry. "Rev. William Hechler & Theodor Herzl: A Zionist Debt Fulfilled." At *Our Jerusalem,* http://www.ourjerusalem.com/history/story/rev-william-hechler-theodor-herzl.html. Accessed on Feb 29, 2012.
Kolsky, Thomas A. *Jews Against Zionism: The American Council for Judaism 1942–1948.* Philadelphia: Temple University Press, 1990.
Mulhall, John W. *America and the Founding of Israel.* Los Angeles: Deshon, 1995.
Rabkin, Yakov M. *A Threat from Within: A Century of Jewish Opposition to Zionism.* London: Zed, 2006.
Ruether, Rosemary Radford. "Christian Zionism and Main Line Western Christians." In *Challenging Christian Zionism: Theology, Politics, and the Israel-Palestine Conflict,* edited by Naim Ateek, Cedar Duaybis, and Maurine Tobin, 154–62. London: Melisende, 2005.
Ruether, Rosemary Radford, and Herman J. Ruether. *The Wrath of Jonah: The Crisis of Religious Nationalism in the Israeli-Palestinian Conflict.* 2nd ed. Minneapolis: Fortress, 2002.
Schneer, Jonathan. *The Balfour Declaration: The Origins of the Arab-Israeli Conflict.* New York: Random House, 2010.
Tuchman, Barbara. *The Bible and the Sword: England and Palestine from the Bronze Age to Balfour.* New York: Ballantine, 1984.
Wagner, Donald. "A Christian Zionist Primer, Part II: Defining Christian Zionism." *Cornerstone* 31 (Winter 2003) 12–13. At http://www.sabeel.org/datadir/en-events/ev49/files/CornerStone31.pdf. Accessed on Mar 24, 2012.
"Zionism," Jewish Virtual Library. At http://www.jewishvirtuallibrary.org/jsource/Zionism/zionism.html. Accessed on Feb 29, 2012.

Preface

How is a Christian to perceive the modern State of Israel—specifically, Israel's theological claims not only to its own land but also to the West Bank ("Judea and Samaria," in the Zionist lexicon) with its natural resources, as well as to the control of the Gaza Strip? Biblically-based claims to the land have resulted in chaos, suffering, and death for Israelis and Palestinians (including both Christian and Muslim Palestinians), causing some religious believers to wonder whether the Zionist initiatives of the past century have been entirely in accord either with sound biblical interpretation or with God's will.

Although Christian academics in the past two decades have contributed penetrating biblical exegesis and moral analysis to the theological discourse on Zionism, significant numbers of American Christians apparently belong to either of the following two categories: (1) those who, seemingly driven by the horrors of the Holocaust and by collective guilt for centuries of cruel Christian anti-Semitism, extend unreserved support to the policies of Israel's government; (2) those who embrace Christian Zionism with its eschatological scenario of a restored Old Testament kingdom in the Holy Land as a prerequisite for the Second Coming. But are these the only two options? Are not other perspectives possible—perspectives that grieve for the sickening tragedy of the Holocaust without either wrapping Israel's government in a mantle of perpetually innocent victimhood or casting the State of Israel in the role of indispensable catalyst for the fulfillment of God's ultimate plan for humankind?

The ecumenical team that created this book has presented alternative approaches for thoughtful Christians to consider. Each writer has brought his or her own emphases, grounded upon her or his own formation in the Christian faith, to bear on the theological issues raised by Zionist claims.

Preface

Here is a preview of some of the themes prevalent in the diverse but harmonious segments of our book:

- What is Zionism? In the book's Foreword, a Palestinian Christian clergyman provides a sketch of Zionism's inception, development, and consequences.
- How can we assess the relationship between the Old Testament and the State of Israel, which was pioneered by secular Zionists but bases its territorial claims on the Hebrew Scriptures? Twenty-first-century Christians can urge modern Israel to hold itself accountable to the mission and moral standards enjoined upon ancient Israel by its sacred Covenant, as recorded in the Scriptures that are shared by Jews and Christians alike.
- Who are Abraham's true descendants? Both Scripture and tradition speak to this question.
- In its first few centuries the Christian church, in dealing with both external threats and internal disputes and in setting the boundaries of its own identity, gleaned valuable insights from the Old and New Testaments; in so doing, its theologians expounded the concepts of homeland in general and of the promised land in particular.
- Contemplating the colonial era and its aftermath, we can gain inspiration from the African-American endurance of exile, that is, of forcible removal from the African homeland, an experience that bears certain points of contact with the displacement and domination suffered by Palestinians. It was the Spirit-filled faith of the oppressed African-American people that enabled them to survive.
- The biblical exegesis and activism of a renowned Swedish Lutheran theologian of the late twentieth century, who was recoiling in horror from the blood-stained centuries of anti-Semitism in the West and especially from the Holocaust, provide a fruitful resource for understanding the disastrous impact of the Holocaust on Christian theology.
- The modern social teachings of the Roman Catholic Church, as well as recent statements by popes and bishops, have offered biblically based approaches, shaped by tradition yet attuned to the "facts on the ground," for resolving the ongoing crisis of Palestine and Israel—approaches that uphold the dignity and promote the welfare of every human being.

Preface

- As the capstone to this book, a pastor reflects informally on his own Puritan tradition as well as on Scripture, the Crusades, and his personal experiences in the Holy Land.

The writers of these essays have come from a variety of personal backgrounds, church affiliations, and livelihoods. Of the seven contributors (not including the author of the Foreword), four are professional academics pursuing different areas of study, and only one is an ordained clergyperson in pastoral ministry. The remaining two are professionally qualified in their own fields. All are reading, thinking church members actively concerned about human suffering. Diverse among ourselves, we have addressed our thoughts to a broad, diverse spectrum of Christian believers, both lay and clergy, of many denominations. We hope that the ecumenical composition of our writing team, as well as the non-specialist nature of our essays, will attract a wide audience, and that the insights stimulated in each of us by our research will nourish the thought of many Christian readers in formulating a response to the deeply troubling situation gripping the Holy Land and its people in our time.

Carole Monica Burnett

Acknowledgments

GRATITUDE IS OWED TO Pickwick Publications for their acceptance of a multi-author work in spite of the current conventional wisdom. Robin Parry's editorial expertise and cordial manner have been a blessing. Charlie Collier and Christian Amondson have been cheerfully supportive and a delight to work with.

Bernard Sabella offers his thanks to His Beatitude Monsignor Michel Sabbah, Emeritus Latin Patriarch of Jerusalem, who kindly commented on the first draft of Dr. Sabella's essay.

Daryl Domning would like to thank Fr. Joseph F. Wimmer, OSA, for assistance with sources and helpful comments on a draft of Dr. Domning's paper.

Carole Monica Burnett is grateful to Dr. Michael J. Gorman, of the Ecumenical Institute of Theology in Baltimore, for his advice and support during the search for a publisher. She would also like to thank the Rev. Dr. Naim S. Ateek for his lucid, informative Foreword.

Contributors

CAROLE MONICA BURNETT is a member of the Antiochian Orthodox Church. The author of journal articles and book chapters in the academic field of Early Christian Studies, she teaches ancient Greek and Latin in a Catholic graduate school of theology and edits a series of translated patristic texts for a Catholic publisher in Washington, DC. She also participates in the activities of Sabeel-DC Metro, which is affiliated with Friends of Sabeel North America (FOSNA), an outgrowth of Sabeel, the Jerusalem-based organization founded by the Rev. Dr. Naim S. Ateek.

DARYL P. DOMNING, a Roman Catholic, is a Professor of Anatomy at Howard University in Washington, DC. A co-author of the book *Original Selfishness: Original Sin and Evil in the Light of Evolution* (with the late theologian Monika K. Hellwig), he is a paleontologist with an interest in the theological implications of evolution.

STEPHEN H. FRANCE is a lawyer and journalist. An Episcopalian and a graduate of the Education for Ministry program of the School of Theology of the University of the South, he serves on the Leadership Council of Sabeel-DC Metro, a grass-roots organization affiliated with Friends of Sabeel North America and with Sabeel, a Jerusalem-based ecumenical theological center promoting justice and peace.

DAVID W. GOOD is the Senior Minister of the First Congregational Church in Old Lyme, Connecticut. The founder of the Tree of Life Educational Fund (an organization dedicated to peace and justice), he leads annual trips to Palestine and Israel.

Contributors

BEVERLY EILEEN MITCHELL is a Professor of Historical Theology at Wesley Theological Seminary in Washington, DC. An American Baptist who has been confirmed in the Episcopal Church, she is the author of two books: *Black Abolitionism: A Quest for Human Dignity* and *Plantations and Death Camps: Religion, Ideology, and Human Dignity.*

BERNARD SABELLA, a Roman Catholic, is a retired Associate Professor of Sociology from the Pontifical University of Bethlehem in the Palestinian Territories. Since 2006 he has served as an elected member on one of the six Christian quota seats in the Palestinian Legislative Council representing Jerusalem, and he is active in the Department of Service to Palestinian Refugees of the Middle East Council of Churches.

PAUL H. VERDUIN is Co-Coordinator of Sabeel-DC Metro, the Washington metropolitan area's local affiliate with Friends of Sabeel North America and with the Sabeel Ecumenical Liberation Theology Center in Jerusalem. He is active in the Presbyterian Church USA's Israel Palestine Mission Network as well as the Evangelical Lutheran Church in America's national Peace Not Walls advocacy group. He recently participated in the *Kairos USA* drafting conference, and has traveled throughout Palestine-Israel three times since 2008.

Zionism and the Scriptures

1

How Should the People and Land of Israel be Understood in the Light of the Covenant?

Daryl P. Domning

Zionism, whether Jewish or Christian, looks to the return of the people of Israel to the Near Eastern land they occupied in biblical times. Zionism as a modern social, political, and religious phenomenon is inescapably based on theological rationales; and to understand these rationales it is necessary to examine their biblical roots in the idea of God's covenant with Israel and the importance of the land in the context of that covenant.

In brief, the particular covenant with Israel as described in the Bible was first instituted as an agreement between two parties, God and Abraham. Each wanted something out of this agreement: Abraham wanted progeny, and God wished to formalize a fellowship with human beings. Abraham soon got what he wanted; the entire remainder of salvation history has been the working out of whether and to what extent he and his descendants would deliver on his pledge of allegiance to God. A persistent issue in this drama has been the seemingly divergent ways in which God and human beings have understood the role played in that pledge by the *land* of Israel itself.

In interpreting this history I draw on what will no doubt appear as a novel and unexpected source of insight: evolutionary biology. I have argued elsewhere[1] that the theology of human nature, and human sinfulness, can be properly viewed only through the lens of human evolution. In our present, Neo-Darwinian understanding of evolution, survival and adaptation of species come about through the interplay of mutation and natural selection; and natural selection ensures that all living organisms give first priority to their own survival and reproduction. This self-centered orientation must be seen by believers as part of the creative process and of the creation that God pronounced "very good" (Gen 1:31). But on the human level (where genetically programmed behavior is supplemented and often reinforced by learned behavior, culture, and free will) it also makes possible (indeed, statistically inevitable) the sinfulness that has been part of human nature from its beginning. Much of human history, including the Bible story, is just what evolutionary theory would have predicted; and against this contrasting background, the parts that it would *not* have predicted stand out all the more sharply.

I should also note that in the following discussion, I do not take a position on whether particular biblical passages (such as the story of Abraham) are strictly historical in all respects. Rather, it suffices that the biblical writers viewed their *lessons* as normative for the believing community for whom they wrote. It is our task here to discern what those lessons are, for them and for us.

THE COVENANT WITH ISRAEL

The earliest expressions of Israel's belief in the divine covenant which gave the nation being are found in the stories collected in the book of Genesis. These are commonly accepted as having been assembled and edited into their present form around the time of the Babylonian captivity (585–539 BCE), when return to their previous homeland was understandably a preoccupation of the Hebrew people. Throughout Genesis and the remainder of the Hebrew (and Christian) Scriptures, there is, I think, a consistent (albeit developing) portrayal of how the covenant was viewed by its initiator: God.

The Israelites understood that God, by exercise of sovereign power, created (*bara'*) the world, with the intention of bringing into being humans

---

1. Domning and Hellwig, *Original Selfishness*.

who would then enjoy fellowship with God (Gen 1–2). This fellowship is variously described metaphorically by Genesis as the Garden of Eden, by Isaiah as a peaceable kingdom, and by Jesus as the reign of God. Although human sinfulness was and is an obstacle to this fellowship, throughout salvation history God has held out to humanity the promise of its attainment.

The first expressions of this promise are portrayed as covenants with all humanity, symbolized by Adam (Gen 1–2) and by Noah (Gen 8:21–22). The next step in the establishment of this fellowship was God's creation, as it were out of nothing, of a particular people that had not existed before as a distinct group. (The same word *bara'* used in Genesis for God's creation of the world is also used, for example in Isa 43:1, for God's creation of Israel.)[2] As the story is presented, God's chosen instrument for this creation was Abram (Abraham), out of whom God promised to "make a great nation"—though not for that nation's exclusive benefit, but as a means of blessing the entire human race (Gen 12:2–3; 18:18; 22:18; cf. Isa 49:6). In terms of New Testament imagery (Matt 13:33; Luke 13:21), it was to act like yeast in the world.

It is natural for human beings, as for all living things (thanks to Darwinian natural selection, as noted above), to seek to reproduce themselves. Abram was no exception: like every man of his time, his standing in his own eyes, in society, and even (though unconsciously) in evolutionary history itself, depended on the number of his offspring. This natural state of affairs provided the opening for the initiative God wished to take: since Abram's wife Sarai was barren (Gen 11:30), God's promise of progeny was the answer to his deepest prayer (Gen 15:2), so he was ready to respond to God's gratuitous proposal of an explicit covenant (Gen 12:1–4).

This promise of progeny was renewed repeatedly (Gen 13:14–17; 15:1–5; 17:2–7, 16–21; 18:9–15); and to it was added, in the most solemn fashion, that of possession of the land of Canaan, where Abram then resided (Gen 12:7; 15:7–21; 17:8)—territory and its resources, of course, being the necessary Darwinian means of supporting one's offspring. Abram up till then had been a nomad who had left his extended family in Haran (Gen 11:27—12:5) and had no real estate or grazing rights to call his own, but only what he could acquire by diplomacy, trade, or conquest (Gen 12–14). So the promise of land was as existentially vital to him as that of offspring.

---

2. Schmidt, in *Theologisches Handwörterbuch*, 336–39. This word is used in the Hebrew Scriptures exclusively to describe the creative activity of God.

Zionism and the Scriptures

In due course, God added a significant proviso to what had hitherto been a one-sided promise—stating, in fact, what had been God's intent all along: "I will maintain my covenant with you and your descendants after you throughout the ages as an everlasting pact, *to be your God and the God of your descendants after you*. I will give to you and to your descendants after you the land in which you are now staying . . . as a permanent possession; *and I will be their God*. . . . On your part, you and your descendants after you *must keep my covenant throughout the ages*" (Gen 17:7–9; emphasis added).

Thus, the fully-stated agreement took the form of a so-called "vassal" (or "ruler") covenant; it called for God to provide protection and other benefits (descendants and land), and for Abram and his descendants (the vassals) to provide *hesed* (love, loyalty, and obedience).[3] What God wanted from the bargain, it turned out, was the allegiance of the newly created nation, so that it might carry out God's plans for human salvation—and do so specifically through their *ethical behavior*: "I have singled [Abraham] out that he may direct his sons and his posterity to keep the way of the Lord *by doing what is right and just,* so that the Lord may carry into effect for Abraham the promises he made about him" (Gen 18:19; emphasis added). Thus the promises were conditioned on the nation's *doing justice*. This requirement of reciprocity was solemnized by the rule of circumcision, as well as by renaming the couple Abraham and Sarah (Gen 17:5, 9–15).

Since Sarah still remained childless, however, they both came to doubt this promise of progeny, which indeed was not fulfilled for many years. They even resorted to the natural expedient of surrogate motherhood (in its ancient form), resulting in the birth of Ishmael (Gen 16:1–16). But at length Isaac was born to them, fulfilling God's pledge to give Abraham offspring through Sarah (Gen 21:1–8).

---

3. Powell and Self, *Holy Murder,* 155. It is not necessary here to tarry over whether, or at what stage, the covenant was a conditional covenant or a promissory (unconditional) one. As D. J. McCarthy, *Old Testament Covenant,* 81, notes, "the Old Testament had no single necessary form for expressing or making covenants. The essential thing seems to have been that an obligatory relationship was formed. . . . Surely a promise from God was a firm basis for obligation, a fixed relationship we may still call covenant. So also of a divine command: it put an obligatory relationship upon the one commanded."

THE TEST

Then there comes a crucial turn in the story. God's good faith has been demonstrated by the birth of Isaac; now it is Abraham's turn to show his own good faith. He was doubtless grateful to God for the gift of his son; but in his eagerness for offspring he had pledged more than mere gratitude. He had sworn permanent allegiance and exclusive loyalty to one single deity; and that deity proved to be "a jealous God" who required that nothing else take priority in the follower's mind (Exod 20:3–6)—not other gods, not the follower's own present needs or even his future "Darwinian fitness" (that is, descendants). It could not be otherwise, because God's plan was going to make unprecedented, even "unnatural" demands on human beings, asking them precisely to turn away from the genetic ties of family and nationhood enforced by natural selection, and instead to join a voluntary spiritual community founded on altruism.[4]

The episode of the *Akedah*, the near-sacrifice of Isaac (Gen 22:1–18), has occasioned almost as much of a crisis of faith for readers of the Bible (Jewish, Christian, and Muslim, in their different ways)[5] as it must have for Abraham himself. Indeed, Laurence Kant admits that the rabbinical tradition has not done a good job of responding to the ethical challenges of this scriptural passage. (Nor has the Christian tradition done better.) How, and why, could God have asked Abraham to sacrifice his longed-for son? What kind of heartless God could this be? What kind of father would do it? Should he have loved his son more than he loved God?

The answers proposed have been endless: that the story aimed to justify a ban on child sacrifice; that it serves as a horrible example of family dynamics (even being a Jewish version of the Oedipus story); that Abraham had to atone for the expulsion of Hagar and Ishmael; that Isaac agreed to his own slaughter, and even bound himself (!); that Isaac was really slain but then resurrected (or Abraham had faith that he would be); that Abraham was really testing *God's* morality; that Abraham had misunderstood God's instruction merely to *bring* Isaac up the mountain, not kill him; that God's instruction was ambiguous, maybe even intentionally; that it symbolizes the "binding" of every Jewish child to the fate of the Jewish people; and on and on.[6] Commentators have subjected the *Ake-*

---

4. Domning and Hellwig, *Original Selfishness*.

5. Cf. Kant, "Restorative Thoughts." Indeed, Kessler, *Bound by the Bible*, 182, emphasizes that "[n]either Jewish nor Christian interpretations [of the *Akedah*] can be understood properly without reference to the other."

6. For a sampling of such interpretations, see (among many others) Levenson,

dah to every imaginable, anachronistic sort of midrash, psychoanalysis, numerology, and contortion of grammar, stressing above all its ambiguity. Some, like Laurence Kant,[7] would seem to make this very ambiguity a virtue. But in the end, this just makes God out to be a poor communicator; and if the message is fundamentally unclear, then no particular interpretation is binding, least of all that of the Binding itself.

But it seems to me that the *Akedah* has a simple and clear meaning, and one perfectly in line with the overall theme of the covenant that is central to the Hebrew Scriptures. It also fits with evolutionary theology, especially if we accept the suggestion[8] that the *Akedah*, as Abraham's act of self-denial *par excellence*, counteracted the "sin of Adam and Eve" (which I have elsewhere identified with evolutionary selfishness)[9] and put the people of God on a different track right from the start.

In its context as laid out above, the story is not about Isaac, or Ishmael, or Sarah, or the ram, or child sacrifice, or the *Shoah*, or any of the other characters, customs, or subsequent history that have been invoked, but only about the two protagonists—God and Abraham—and the terms of their bargain.[10] Nor was it simply a test of Abraham's vague faith that God had something reasonable in mind, or would somehow make things right in the end: it was more sharply drawn than that. To repeat, Abraham

---

Death and Resurrection; Berman, *Akedah;* Moltz, "God and Abraham"; Noort and Tigchelaar, *Sacrifice of Isaac;* Kant, "Restorative Thoughts"; Kessler, *Bound by the Bible;* Sherwood, "Binding-Unbinding"; and Powell and Self, *Holy Murder.* I follow Westermann, *Genesis 12–36*, in regarding the theme of child sacrifice in particular as *not* central to this narrative. I suspect that most of the agonizing over the ethical implications of the *Akedah* comes out of a mindset more modern than that of the story's time of origin, when (even if children were not normally sacrificed) men held the power of life and death over their women and children, whose opinions did not count for much and were not necessarily solicited—as exemplified here in the roles played by Sarah and Isaac. Although the *Akedah* may have served later as a proof-text against child sacrifice, I doubt that was its meaning at the time the story originated (and let us keep in mind that the text we have is a *human* impression, many times re-told and re-edited, of whatever it was that happened; we do not really get to hear God's side of the story!). I also agree with Levenson, *Death and Resurrection,* that it is wrong to "spiritualize" the *Akedah*: it is Abraham's readiness to *act,* and not his faith alone, that is crucial to his passing the test.

7. Kant, "Restorative Thoughts."
8. Levenson, *Death and Resurrection,* 140.
9. Domning and Hellwig, *Original Selfishness.*

10. I have been interested to learn, subsequent to thinking of this interpretation, that it is also in line with the traditional Christian exegesis of Gen 22 (in contrast to Jewish exegesis, which typically emphasizes the role of Isaac rather than Abraham; Kessler, *Bound by the Bible,* 181). Why this difference arose, I leave to others to explain.

had gotten his wish for progeny in exchange for a pledge of perpetual loyalty to God. God had made good on the bargain; now it only remained for Abraham to do his part. The question to be answered was: How would he choose between his own Darwinian fitness—his hope of posterity—and God's sovereign will? Fidelity to the One who made the promise, or idolatry of the promise itself?[11]

The choice could not have been more neatly, or starkly, posed. The God of Abraham was the same[12] as the God of Moses, who was in deadly earnest that *nothing* in the sky, on the earth, beneath the earth, or in the human heart should come before God's self—not a golden idol, not "mammon," certainly not any of God's own gifts to humankind. The God who gave could also take away, and then restore: so the believer, like Job, was asked to trust. And God's trustworthiness had already been demonstrated to Abraham, in the person of Isaac himself. But gifts or no gifts, God was always supreme and to be acknowledged as such.

Abraham passed the test; and God once again proved trustworthy, by not requiring the life of Isaac after all (Gen 22:11–12). The covenant was reconfirmed (Gen 22:15–18; 26:1–5)—and most especially to Moses following the exodus from Egypt (Exod 24:1–9). The people of Israel lived ever after, though not always happily—because God's promise of the land was conditioned on the people's remaining as loyal to God as Abraham himself had been (Exod 19:3–8; Lev 26; Deut 28). And for centuries thereafter, their chronicles recorded reverse after reverse, including exile from the land, whenever they abandoned the way of the Lord and resorted to false gods.

A NATION LIKE OTHER NATIONS?

But now we must note the nature of this new people. Beginning with Abraham, through his and his descendants' voluntary acceptance of God's covenant down through the exodus and beyond, God did not simply *choose* an existing human community, but *created* (*bara'*) one where there had been none before. God thus "chose" this people like a leader individually

---

11. Also subsequent to writing the above, I have found this same idea expressed by another Catholic writer, Dianne Bergant ("Binding of Isaac," 33), in a response to Kessler; as well as by a Jewish author, Jon Levenson (*Death and Resurrection*, 126–28).

12. Strictly speaking, Abraham is said (Gen 17:1) to have worshiped "El Shaddai," usually translated as "God Almighty," but which actually means "the god of the city of Shaddai," identified subsequently with the Israelite god YHWH (Exod 6:2–3; Mendenhall, *Ancient Israel's Faith and History*, 117–18, 121). For YHWH, see note 22.

choosing picked men for a new mission, creating a new unit that had no previous existence. According to George Mendenhall, "[t]he oldest biblical sources say nothing at all about Israel being Yahweh's *'chosen'* people; instead, as in Exodus 15 and Deuteronomy 32, they refer to it as Yahweh's *'created'* people."[13] As Isa 43:19–21 has it, "See, I am doing something new! Now it springs forth, do you not perceive it? . . . For I put water in the desert . . . for my chosen people . . . the people whom I formed for myself. . . .'" Enlistment in this new outfit, furthermore, was open to volunteers, as was the case much later (John 1:12): "Any who did accept him he empowered to become children of God."

In the biblical account, the Hebrews enslaved in Egypt were the descendants of Jacob (= Israel), whose family had found refuge there during a famine. It is, however, scarcely plausible that only one clan out of all those living in the drought-stricken lands east of Egypt would have sought and obtained relief in the valley of the Nile. More likely, the Hebrews living in Egypt at the time of the exodus were derived from a motley assortment of Semitic tribes and bands that had straggled into Egypt as refugees or for other reasons (not least the invasion of the Semitic Hyksos). Indeed, the Bible admits that when the Israelites left Egypt, "a crowd of mixed ancestry also went up with them" (Exod 12:38; cf. Num 11:4). This mixture reflects in part the intermarriage of Israelites and Egyptians (cf. Lev 24:10), but perhaps also a more deep-seated diversity.

This picture also squares well with the derivation of the name "Hebrew," which many scholars equate with the word *habiru* or *'apiru*, known from many contemporary records. But whereas "Hebrew" has come to refer to a specific ethnic group, *habiru* seems to have originally meant something like "transgressor," and denoted a socioeconomic or politico-legal category, made up variously of semi-nomadic tribes, poor villagers, landless peasants, outlaws, insurrectionists, guerillas in the hills—in general, marginalized and disaffected people living on the fringes of urban civilization, perhaps having renounced any allegiance to organized polities, and more or less regarded (by urbanites) as the dregs of society. Although these people, like the Palestinian city-dwellers from whom they were distinguished (and maybe alienated), all shared a broadly Semitic ethnic identity (like Jews and Arabs today), the term *habiru* was apparently not in itself an ethnic label.[14]

---

13. Mendenhall, *Ancient Israel's Faith and History*, 90; emphasis original.
14. Mendenhall, "Hebrew Conquest," 105–6; *Ancient Israel's Faith and History*, 31.

It follows (at least in the view of some scholars) that the Hebrews in Egypt were originally united only by their identity as Semitic foreigners and refugees who, as people of the lowest status, were eventually put to forced labor by the Egyptians. This insight lends enormous significance to the statement of God that "Israel is my first-born son" (Exod 4:22; cf. Isa 1:2; Jer 31:9; Hos 11:1; Rom 9:4). Far from choosing any of the existing superpowers such as Egypt or Babylonia (which would surely have felt worthy of the honor), this God dramatically showed a "preferential option for the poor" by literally making a new nation from scratch, from the least promising material available (lacking even genealogical unity, let alone title to any real estate), and then adopting it as God's own. No selection of the "fittest" here.[15]

Here we pause to note the rupture this represented with the evolutionary "way of the world," according to which genetic ties and competitive superiority are paramount. Instead, we find in the Bible a consistent call to abandon these human, "tribal" values in favor of personal commitment to God and God's very different priorities, which naturally struck human beings as "unnatural." (In this light, Abraham's leaving his father's house, and the *Akedah*, emerge as examples of cutting genealogical ties with the past and future, respectively.)[16] For God to have created humanity by means of Darwinian processes including natural selection, and then to have flaunted this very law of nature from the beginning of salvation history, seems at first paradoxical (though I have argued for its moral necessity).[17] But God appears to have wanted a "nation" built not on the usual Darwinian genetics and power politics but on *ethics* such as justice, humility, and "fear of the Lord."

At any rate, all too soon this novel, heterogeneous conglomeration of humanity cast envious eyes on the nationhood of the nations around them. Besides worshiping foreign gods, another and significant way in which the people deviated[18] from the path recommended to them was their eventual insistence on having a king in place of the rule of the Judges. This desire for a king "as other nations have" amounted to a rejection of

---

15. This and the preceding three paragraphs are adapted from Domning and Hellwig, *Original Selfishness*, 130–31, where the evolutionary theme is developed more fully.

16. Fromm, *You Shall Be as Gods*, 72, quoted in Powell and Self, *Holy Murder*, 127–28, 156.

17. Domning and Hellwig, *Original Selfishness*.

18. This does not, however, exclude continuity between the pre-Davidic and Davidic *covenants*; see McCarthy, *Old Testament Covenant*, 82–85.

Zionism and the Scriptures

God as their king (1 Sam 8:4–7, 19–20). Mendenhall explains the religious importance of this:

> From its very beginnings, the Yahwistic faith transcended tribal religion, for it was intended and actually functioned in a way to create a community above the tribal level. It is only a subsequent period of religious history which made out of the faith a tribal religion, in which the function of the deity was regarded by blind nationalism as merely the protection of tribal-national political and economic interests....
>
> ... The religious community of early Israel created a contrast between the religious and the political aspects of human culture which had been inseparable in the idea of the "divine state" or the "divine kingship," because a complete identification of religious with political authority and obedience, so characteristic of ancient and modern paganism, became impossible....
>
> ... There can be nothing upon which the biblical traditions insist more strongly than the fact that "Israel" is specifically a *religious* community; the tradition that all the tribes were lineal descendants from a single ancestor is an attempt to give expression to a unity which was created by the religious factor, and is paralleled exactly by the attempt to express cultural relationships in ancient civilizations generally by the identical procedure.... Israel began as a specifically religious community; only in the course of time and historical calamity did the religious community come to rely largely upon biological continuity based upon endogamy and considerable resistance to the access of ethnic outsiders.... Early Israel was an ecumenical faith, a catholic religion in the best sense of the term, the very purpose of which was to create unity among a divided and warring humanity.... From a source of unity it became, like Islam and Christianity, a source of division and hostility.[19]

Another instance of this nationalistic overprint on Hebrew history is found in the stereotype of the wrathful, even murderous "Old Testament God."[20] Some of the most violent biblical passages, notably the description of the Israelites' genocidal "conquest" of Canaan (Josh 1–11), are apparently anachronistic misinterpretations and misrepresentations of the true history, read back into the record centuries after the fact by writers of the monarchic period who failed to grasp that pre-monarchic Israel had values and customs very different from their own violently nationalist

---

19. Mendenhall, "Hebrew Conquest," 108–9, 118–19; emphasis original.
20. Mendenhall, *Ancient Israel's Faith and History*, 147–48.

and imperialist state. This distortion "introduced terrible and tragic religious confusion into the biblical tradition, permanently etching in many people's minds the notion that Yahweh was, from the beginning, the god of one particular nation and one group of people."[21]

Instead, Mendenhall argues that the so-called twelve tribes of Israel sprang in large part from groups of Transjordanian and Palestinian villagers who remained in the land taken from local warlords by the Israelites (and who were initially put to forced labor by the Israelites; Judg 1:27–35), but who eventually joined the YHWHist community[22] that was descended from the slaves who had left Egypt. These new members, he says, "had little use for political power structures, great contempt for the value systems that necessitated them, and deep dissatisfaction with the old Bronze Age religious cults that legitimized them." So they made covenant with the newcomers and embraced their religious values and ethical system (Josh 24:14–15). But eventually, Israel itself succumbed to the temptations of power politics.[23]

With the passage of time, not only the nation but the covenant itself seems to have undergone a distortion of its original meaning. Whereas God's election of Israel originally was "an election to responsibility and obligation" and not "an act of favoritism," it has been suggested that it later (under the Davidic dynasty; 2 Sam 7:8–16, 23:5; 2 Chr 13:5) became in the popular mind "a false idea of privilege and security" that obligated God rather than Israel.[24]

A revival of the earlier concept of the covenant, recorded in Deuteronomy, probably inspired the prophet Jeremiah to envision a new, individualized covenantal relationship between God and the people:

> The days are coming, says the Lord, when I will make a new covenant with the house of Israel and the house of Judah. It will not be like the covenant I made with their fathers. . . . I will place my law within them, and write it upon their hearts. (Jer 31:31–33; cf. Deut 10:16; 30)

---

21. Mendenhall, *Ancient Israel's Faith and History*, 173; cf. Mendenhall, "Hebrew Conquest," 107.

22. The four letters YHWH comprise the Tetragrammaton, which signifies one of the most ancient Hebrew names for God. This sacred name is often pronounced by Christians as "Yahweh." See note 12.

23. Mendenhall, *Ancient Israel's Faith and History*, 73–100; quotation from p. 78. See also Dever, *Biblical Writers*, Chapter 4.

24. McKenzie, "Aspects," 750.

Also representative of this attitude is Ps 51:18–19, which affirms that God wants not sacrifice but "a broken, humbled heart." And yet again, after another great reverse (the Babylonian Exile), the priest Ezra reviewed the history of the people's infidelity, and yet again they reaffirmed their allegiance to God (Neh 9–10).

Thus it was clearly and repeatedly established that what God required of the people—individually as well as collectively—was "only to do the right and to love goodness, and to walk humbly with [their] God" (Mic 6:8). And thus they were given to understand that their tenure of the land was conditioned on obedience to this covenant—on fidelity to the One who made the promise of progeny and land, and not idolatry of the promise itself. That land, after all, was God's, and the Israelites were nothing but aliens who had become God's tenants (Lev 25:23).

> The Lord gave and the Lord has taken away; blessed be the name of the Lord! (Job 1:21)

ZIONISM AND PALESTINE

It is against this historical and theological background that I think we should view the present politics of Israel and Palestine, and the Zionist movement that created the present situation.[25] Modern Zionism began in the nineteenth century among secular European Jews, and became embodied in the State of Israel in 1948. To many Gentiles today, Zionism seems practically synonymous with Israel and even with Judaism itself; yet it has always been controversial among Jews, especially some of the most devout Jews, who see it as incompatible in various ways with the spiritual aspects of biblical Judaism.

The account of the covenant given above is consistent with this critique, as are at least some exegeses of the *Akedah*. Howard Moltz, for example, interprets the *Akedah* as ending in a mutual estrangement between God and Abraham: "Ironically, . . . the test that demanded the slaughter of the beloved son proved inconclusive, since it was a test of obedience and not of devotion[;] as such, it failed to address the question of whether Abraham remained in the covenant because of who God is or because of what God had promised."[26] Though I (and, seemingly, God; Gen 22:12)

---

25. For a detailed history of Zionism and the present conflict, see Ruether and Ruether, *The Wrath of Jonah*.
26. Moltz, "God and Abraham," 69.

disagree that the test of Abraham himself was inconclusive, the same perennial question can be asked of Israel today. Indeed, it is Abraham himself who poses to Zionism this challenge: Which actions to hold on to the land are licit, and which actions and policies place possession of the land before God's insistence on justice, indeed place it before God's self?

An example of how modern Israel's conflict with the Palestinians has violated the precepts of the Torah itself is seen in the routine destruction of Palestinian fruit trees and orchards by the Israeli government.

> When you are at war with a city and have to lay siege to it for a long time before you capture it, you shall not destroy its trees by putting an ax to them. You may eat their fruit, but you must not cut down the trees. After all, are the trees of the field men, that they should be included in your siege? (Deut 20:19)

War among men is sometimes unavoidable, but it should never extend to deliberate destruction of the land itself and its ability to support human life—especially in a land already as semi-arid and overstressed by human use as is Palestine. This is a violation of the original command "to cultivate and care for" the garden that is Earth (Gen 2:15).

As to the justice of Israel's treatment of the Palestinians themselves, many witnesses have spoken out in criticism. These include diverse and prominent Israelis such as Avraham Burg (Zionist and former Speaker of the Knesset), Uri Avnery (self-described "post-Zionist," former member of the Irgun and the Knesset, secular journalist and activist), Dan Meridor (Likud Deputy Prime Minister), Avishai Braverman (former Labor Minister of Minorities), and Adam Keller (army reservist who refused duty in the Occupied Territories), among others. Also many Jews outside Israel, for example in the USA, likewise disapprove of the occupation of Palestine.[27]

Today's world is divided into political states, so it is no doubt inevitable that a Jewish homeland in the twenty-first century be constituted as such a state, with a government "as other nations have." But that still leaves open the question of what sort of policies, indeed what sort of polity, should characterize this state. For Israel's right to exist is not premised merely on ethnic exclusivity or on a history of persecution (other nations can make similar claims), but on a unique relationship with God. By claiming the moral high ground—including, for many, fidelity to the Abrahamic covenant, with its intent that Israel should be a blessing to

---

27. E.g., Ben-Ami, *New Voice*.

all other nations—modern Israel sets a high standard by which its own behavior among nations is to be judged. Although political Zionism is a secular movement and Israel today is a largely secular society, with many non-Jewish citizens, and although many ultra-Orthodox Jews disapprove of modern political Zionism and the Jewish state itself—still the ultimate justification for the state's existence lies in the religious history of the Jews.

Of course, the Palestinians themselves and the neighboring Arab states have also committed countless crimes of violence in the course of their resistance to the Jewish state. Indeed, perhaps the greatest irony of the situation is that the Palestinians could have had their rights decades ago, and could be at peace with Israel today (either as part of it or in an independent state), if only they had followed the example of nonviolence set before them by Mohandas Gandhi, Martin Luther King, Jr., and Nelson Mandela. By claiming moral superiority, the Zionists made themselves easy targets for nonviolent resistance: they would have been even more helpless to refuse the Palestinians' legitimate demands than the British Raj was when confronted by Gandhi. Instead, under leaders like Yasser Arafat, the Palestinians copied the Irgun and other armed movements, and threw away a winning hand. Thus they are left stalemated today, with their moral claims stained by a history of terrorism, but with arms too weak to throw off the Israeli occupation.

There is never likely to be agreement on which of these sides threw the first punch; their lists of grievances each extend back to Bible times. The only practical question is: Which side has the power to resolve the present stalemate—and consequently the obligation to make the decisive move? Obviously, it is only Israel, with its overwhelming military superiority and its often-demonstrated power to lock down all of Palestinian society at any moment.

Therefore it is licit to ask how faithful Israeli policies are to the Jewish religious tradition. Appropriate questions might include the following:

1. If it is true that the ancient "Hebrews," before and after the exodus, were originally a socioeconomic rather than an ethnic group, finally united by a common religion; that once in Palestine their numbers were augmented by converts from local "tribes"; and that "descent" of the Israelites from Abraham, Isaac, and Jacob meant, in practice, primarily *spiritual* unity with them in the worship of the same God—then how theologically legitimate are the divisions among Jews and Arabs (both Christian and Muslim), all of whom are YHWHists, "brothers" as followers of "Abrahamic" religions?

2. Given that sibling rivalry is nonetheless natural, indeed Darwinian; that Jews today have a right to regard themselves as an ethnic group (having been treated as such through centuries of discrimination by Christians and Muslims), a right to self-determination, and a natural desire for a homeland; that every person and group has a right to self-defense; but also given that nuclear-armed Israel today is the dominant regional military power in the Near East, in no danger of annihilation by the Palestinians—what limits, if any, do Jewish religious precepts (for example, Mic 6:8: "to do the right and to love goodness, and to walk humbly with God") set to the allowable means of defense against the actual threat?

3. Given that possession of the land of Israel was originally conditioned on fidelity of the people to God, and not on the (Darwinian) right of conquest otherwise customary among nations—what are the implications for the theological legitimacy of land claims made by a largely secular movement and government and enforced unilaterally by grossly asymmetrical military means?

4. What might an alternative to the present conflict look like? Only in living memory have the Jewish people retaken possession of the promised land. Is it too late for them to ask for a do-over, and this time avoid the violent nationalism of the biblical monarchic period (and the present)? Organizationally, this need not mean a return to the time of the Judges, still less an oppressive theocracy; modern democracy can suffice, provided that a similarly "ecumenical" spirit prevails, with respect and political equality for all the "children of Abraham." Such a state would truly be a blessing to all the nations. But it is hard to see how it could at the same time remain, ethnically or religiously, a specifically "Jewish" state. A "YHWHist" state, at least, would seem more faithful to what God originally had in mind. For what else did Isaiah mean by the following words?

   > Thus says the Lord: Observe what is right, do what is just. . . . And the foreigners who join themselves to the Lord . . . them I will bring to my holy mountain . . . for my house shall be called a house of prayer for all peoples. Thus says the Lord God, who gathers the dispersed of Israel: Others will I gather to him, besides those already gathered. (Isa 56:1–8)

Zionism and the Scriptures

CHRISTIAN ZIONISM

Christian Zionism is the attitude, common since the Reformation,[28] of Christians (mainly evangelical and fundamentalist Protestants) who advocate the return of Jews to the Holy Land on the basis of messianic and end-time biblical prophecies, with or without expectation of their conversion to Christianity. In the USA today, it allies Jews with evangelicals by way of the Hebrew Bible and their shared opposition to leftist pro-Palestinian/anti-Israeli factions, though they do not necessarily share other political views.

More generally among Christians, this attitude finds little favor. In 2006, for example, the Catholic, Syrian Orthodox, Episcopal, and Evangelical Lutheran churches in the Holy Land proclaimed the *Jerusalem Declaration on Christian Zionism*,[29] which rejects Christian Zionism because it substitutes a political-military, often apocalyptic program in place of "living Christ's love and justice today." It said in part, "We categorically reject Christian Zionist doctrines as false teaching that corrupts the biblical message of love, justice, and reconciliation." This statement, of course, is analogous to the reasons why many religious Jews also oppose the policies of the Israeli government, as well as to the critiques that Isaiah, Jeremiah, and other prophets leveled at the ancient monarchy.

Likewise in the USA, the National Council of Churches resolved in 2007 that

> this theological stance [of Christian Zionism] adversely affects:
>
> - justice and peace in the Middle East, delaying the day when Israelis and Palestinians can live within secure borders
>
> - relationships with Middle Eastern Christians
>
> - relationships with Jews, since Jews are seen as mere pawns in an eschatological scheme
>
> - relationships with Muslims since it ignores the rights of Muslims

---

28. Ruether and Ruether explain that "a few maverick thinkers" of the sixteenth century pondered the concept of the restoration of the Jews to the promised land, an idea that gained momentum among seventeenth-century English Puritans and was revived in force in the middle of the nineteenth century, especially in England by the dispensationalist John Nelson Darby and by Anthony Ashley Cooper, the seventh Earl of Shaftesbury; *Wrath of Jonah*, 72–78.

29. http://www.voltairenet.org/article144310.html; accessed on Mar 17, 2011.

- interfaith dialogue, since it views the world in starkly dichotomous terms[30]

Similar statements have been made by the Reformed Church in America[31] and several other denominations. These statements are also consistent with the Catholic teaching of Vatican Council II in *Nostra Aetate* (1965) that God's covenant with the Jews is not abrogated or superseded. It is not the place of Christians to declare that any group of people is excluded from the people of God—least of all the Jews, whom God expressly chose.

As I will argue below, Christians have good reason to care about what happens in the Holy Land and to want to be a part of it. But this concern should not take the form of support for its domination by a particular ethnic group—especially considering that Christians themselves have been admitted to membership in God's people, not on account of ethnicity, but through faith (Gal 3:1–14). In their present forms, neither Christian nor Jewish Zionism offers a defensible solution to the current dilemma.

BACK TO THE FUTURE?

Rabbi Daniel F. Polish, in the Jesuit magazine *America*, responded eloquently to some Christian critiques of Israel. Christians, he says, need to understand that to believing Jews, even ones who themselves take issue with Israeli government policies, Israel plays a fundamentally emotional and spiritual role in their lives, and not just a social or political one. Jews feel at home there, "surrounded by people who bear the same label." At the same time, on a deeper level there is the collective awareness of surviving the Holocaust:

> Consciously or not, for all Jews Israel embodies the notion of resurrection. . . . The existence of Israel has changed what it means to be a Jew, whether one lives there or not. . . . [In cultural and political life,] [t]oday they feel a part, not apart. Israel possesses an incarnational dimension. . . . One might almost say that Israel functions for Jews in the same way that Communion functions for a Catholic. . . . [T]he leaders of the Soviet Union famously denigrated Jews as rootless cosmopolitans. The

---

30. "Response to Christian Zionism," http://www.ncccusa.org/NCCpolicies/christianzionism.htm; accessed on Mar 17, 2011.

31. "Position on Christian Zionism," https://www.rca.org/Page.aspx?pid=3839; accessed on Mar 17, 2011.

existence of Israel annuls any possibility of understanding Jews in that way again.³²

Polish goes on to specify the spiritual aspect of this newly-recovered rootedness. The philosopher Emil Fackenheim, he says, "implies that the existence of a Jewish state offers Jews the chance to apply the teachings of their tradition on a broader plain [sic] than they had when they were a marginal, pariah people. . . . It offers them the opportunity to be part of a people charged with expressing its culture in ever new forms, a living, dynamic organism rather than a static, petrified museum piece." "That call to re-enter history," says Polish,

> evokes and explains the pain many Jews feel when that state does not succeed in embodying the ideals of the inherited teaching, when its Jewishness is merely one of demography rather than character. . . . [T]he dream of Israel that animated those who built it and animates Jewish aspirations for it still, is not of a "normal" state like all the others, a state whose shortcomings are to be accepted as the "price" of realpolitik in a "dangerous neighborhood."
>
> Asher Ginzberg, who wrote under the pen name Achad Ha'Am, dreamed of a Jewish state that would embody the millennia-old values of the Jewish people. This state would be a light to the nations in the way it conducted its collective life, a state that offered a vision of what every state might be. That dream gives us permission to be pained by the distance between what Israel might be and what it is at this moment.³³

What form might this vision take, and what (beyond what is already written in the Hebrew Scriptures) might be its theological underpinning? A salutary lesson for Christians as well as Jews is drawn from the interpretation of the *Akedah* by Yehuda Gellman. Whereas Christian "supersessionism" traditionally viewed this story as an "inferior prefiguration" of the crucifixion, Gellman suggests a "postsupersessionist" interpretation more compatible with both faiths: that Christian events *repeat* patterns of God's opening to the world that are already *imaged* in the Hebrew Bible. The *Akedah* provides the paradigm: it and the crucifixion both required the "same openness to contradictory futures." Neither Abraham climbing Mount Moriah nor Jesus' disciples at Calvary had any reason to expect other than the final death of their beloved; but though shaken

32. Polish, "Spiritual Home," 14–15.
33. Ibid., 15.

and uncomprehending, still they kept faith in God. Both the reprieve of Isaac and the resurrection of Jesus were totally unexpected "contradictory futures" beyond their hoping or imagining. The repetition (in the Christ-event) of the original opening of God's self, however, is now "*widened* to the entire world," "repeated in a larger scope of application." "Thereafter, the structure of God's opening to the world continues in a two-fold manner: with God's opening to the Jewish people as its core, surrounded by the supplemental opening to the world, flowing out of that core."[34]

It might be hardly less "contradictory" for Jewish and Christian Zionists alike (as I suggested above) to look for a good future in an Israel that fully embraced non-Jewish citizens, in the way the Hebrews who first took possession of the promised land apparently came to accept many of its inhabitants (whose labor they had previously exploited) into their community. Polish thinks, to the contrary, that the Jew's spiritual and emotional engagement with Israel is "a relationship we cannot expect non-Jews to share."[35] But is this true?

The other Abrahamic religions certainly seem to have a strong spiritual and emotional engagement with "the Holy Land." Christians have felt so strongly attached to it that for centuries they crusaded to possess it; today they show concern over their fellow Christians' diaspora from it; and for Christian Zionists it is the centerpiece of their vision of a future apocalypse. As for Muslims, *Al-Haram al-Sharif* (to Jews, the Temple Mount) is the third most important site in Islam, after only the shrines of Mecca and Medina. To Muslims, Jerusalem itself is *Al-Quds al-Sharif*, The Holy Sanctuary; it preceded Mecca as the place toward which Muslims turn in prayer. While attachment to this land may have different rationales and intensities among and within the three communities, it is certainly not without prominence in their religious consciousnesses, and is therefore precious to them all.

This specifically *religious* focus of their attachment to this land makes it all the more unseemly that it has for centuries degenerated into a squabble over a piece of real estate. All three religions agree that their focus should be on God. So which is more essential: biological (or confessional) kinship with other people (and with it, emotional attachment to the land), or relationship with God? Of course it will be asked: How can Jews be expected to give up the idea of a specifically Jewish state? But by the same token: How could Abraham be expected to give up his beloved son?

34. Gellman, "*Akedah* and Covenant," 41; emphasis original.
35. Polish, "Spiritual Home," 15.

Zionism and the Scriptures

Recall that from the Darwinian perspective, the original promise of land was existentially vital precisely because land was necessary for the support and survival of the promised offspring. If, however, that land is equally vital for the survival of the Jewish people today, this is but a reflection of how little progress the human race has made beyond the law of the jungle, and no longer a reflection of God's desire for how humans are supposed to live at the present stage of our development. In practical reality, do not Jews today live more securely in (for example) the United States, as a small minority in a multicultural society, than they do as the dominant majority in Israel? Given that they should live in Israel as well, can it still be argued that their physical (or cultural) survival depends on that alone, or that their absolute ethnic and political dominance of that land is divinely justified?

This suggestion will no doubt give offense to some, to whom it will seem as though the Israelites just back from exile in Babylon were asked to welcome the Babylonians into the rebuilt Jerusalem. But what is the alternative: to become just another Babylon, equally pagan, under the flag of Israel? Is it not preferable to return to something recognizably like the community to which YHWH and the prophets—and now, it seems, Rabbi Polish himself—have been calling the people for centuries? In our century, an ideal "vision of what every state might be" is surely (among other things) a multi-ethnic, multi-religious state based on equality for all. Might this be the answer to what Polish envisions: an opportunity for the Jewish people to apply their traditional teachings on a broader plane and to express their culture "in ever new forms, a living, dynamic organism"—but one growing from something grander, more universal, than a merely Jewish state? Like yeast in humanity's dough, perhaps?

Nothing less than this sort of generous openness to the future, such a trusting leap of faith, would seem capable of imaging or repeating YHWH's own opening to the world. Our God is not only a God of promise, but of surprise: from Abraham's call to travel to a new land, to the gift of a child in his old age, to the exodus from Egypt and all the other astonishing turns of evolutionary and salvation history, we have seen enough to expect the unexpected in what God expects of us.[36] If Jewish Zionists, following the *Akedah*'s admittedly frightening example of self-abnegation, and Christian Zionists, following that of the crucifixion, would sacrifice the fetishes of ethnic and confessional homogeneity and let go of their possessiveness of that promised land they feel they cannot do without,

---

36. Johnson, *Quest for the Living God*, 191.

they might find that God is still a reliable partner who will give them all that was promised and more. In binding Isaac, Abraham bound the nation of Israel to a God of justice. Will today's Israel honor this commitment?[37]

BIBLIOGRAPHY

Scripture quotations are from *The New American Bible*.

Ben-Ami, Jeremy. *A New Voice for Israel: Fighting for the Survival of the Jewish Nation*. Basingstoke, UK: Palgrave Macmillan, 2011.
Bergant, Dianne. "The Binding of Isaac: Hermeneutical Reflections." In *Two Faiths, One Covenant? Jewish and Christian Identity in the Presence of the Other*, edited by Eugene B. Korn and John T. Pawlikowski, 29–34. Lanham, MD: Rowman and Littlefield, 2005.
Berman, Louis A. *The Akedah: The Binding of Isaac*. Northvale, NJ: Aronson, 1997.
Dever, William G. *What Did the Biblical Writers Know and When Did They Know It? What Archaeology Can Tell Us about the Reality of Ancient Israel*. Grand Rapids: Eerdmans, 2001.
Domning, Daryl P., and Monika K. Hellwig. *Original Selfishness: Original Sin and Evil in the Light of Evolution*. Aldershot, UK: Ashgate, 2006.
Fromm, Erich. *You Shall Be as Gods*. Greenwich, CT: Fawcett, 1966.
Gellman, Yehuda. "The *Akedah* and Covenant Today." In *Two Faiths, One Covenant? Jewish and Christian Identity in the Presence of the Other*, edited by Eugene B. Korn and John T. Pawlikowski, 35–42. Lanham, MD: Rowman and Littlefield, 2005.
Jerusalem Declaration on Christian Zionism. At http://www.voltairenet.org/article144310.html. Accessed on Mar 17, 2011.
Johnson, Elizabeth A. *Quest for the Living God: Mapping Frontiers in the Theology of God*. New York: Continuum, 2007.
Kant, Laurence. "Restorative Thoughts on an Agonizing Text: Abraham's Binding of Isaac and the Horror of Mt. Moriah (Genesis 22)." *Lexington Theological Quarterly* 38.2 (2003) 77–109; 38.3 (2003) 161–94.
Kessler, Edward. *Bound by the Bible: Jews, Christians, and the Sacrifice of Isaac*. Cambridge: Cambridge University Press, 2004.
Levenson, Jon D. *The Death and Resurrection of the Beloved Son: The Transformation of Child Sacrifice in Judaism and Christianity*. New Haven: Yale University Press, 1993.
Levering, Mathew. *Sacrifice and Community: Jewish Offering and Christian Eucharist*. Malden, MA: Blackwell, 2005.
McCarthy, Dennis J. *Old Testament Covenant: A Survey of Current Opinions*. Oxford: Blackwell, 1973.
McKenzie, John L. "Aspects of Old Testament Thought." In *The Jerome Biblical Commentary*, edited by Raymond E. Brown, Joseph A. Fitzmyer, and Roland E. Murphy, 736–67. Englewood Cliffs, NJ: Prentice-Hall, 1968.

---

37. I thank Joseph F. Wimmer, OSA, and Carole Monica Burnett for help with sources and helpful comments on a draft of this paper.

Zionism and the Scriptures

Mendenhall, George E. *Ancient Israel's Faith and History: An Introduction to the Bible in Context*. Edited by Gary A. Herion. Louisville, KY: Westminster John Knox, 2001.

———. "The Hebrew Conquest of Palestine." In *Biblical Archaeologist Reader* 3, edited by Edward F. Campbell, Jr., and David Noel Freedman, 100–120. Garden City, NY: Doubleday, 1970.

Moltz, Howard. "God and Abraham in the Binding of Isaac." *Journal for the Study of the Old Testament* 96 (2001) 59–69.

The New American Bible. Iowa Falls, IA: World Bible, 1987.

Noort, Edward, and Eibert J. C. Tigchelaar. *The Sacrifice of Isaac: The Aqedah (Genesis 22) and its Interpretations*. Leiden: Brill, 2002.

Polish, Daniel F. "A Spiritual Home: What Christians Should Know about Jewish Identity." *America* 204.12, whole no. 4929 (April 11, 2011) 12–15.

"Position on Christian Zionism." Reformed Church in America. At https://www.rca.org/Page.aspx?pid=3839. Accessed on Mar 17, 2011.

Powell, Larry, and William R. Self. *Holy Murder: Abraham, Isaac, and the Rhetoric of Sacrifice*. Lanham, MD: University Press of America, 2007.

"Response to Christian Zionism." National Council of Churches USA. Policy Statements, Resolutions, Messages and Documents. At http://www.ncccusa.org/NCCpolicies/christianzionism.htm. Accessed on Mar 17, 2011.

Ruether, Rosemary Radford, and Herman J. Ruether. *The Wrath of Jonah: The Crisis of Religious Nationalism in the Israeli-Palestinian Conflict*. 2nd ed. Minneapolis: Fortress, 2002.

Schmidt, Werner H. Article on the word *br'*. In *Theologisches Handwörterbuch zum Alten Testament. Band I*, edited by Ernst Jenni and Claus Westermann, 336–39. Munich: Kaiser, 1984.

Sherwood, Yvonne. "Binding-Unbinding: Divided Responses of Judaism, Christianity, and Islam to the 'Sacrifice' of Abraham's Beloved Son." *Journal of the American Academy of Religion* 72.4 (2004) 821–61.

Westermann, Claus. *Genesis 12–36: A Commentary*. Minneapolis: Augsburg, 1985.

2

Not Like the Nations
Zionism's Biblical Dilemma

STEPHEN H. FRANCE

The political divisions that are scarring the Holy Land are rooted in the religious imagination, and it is there that they must be combated and overcome.

SARI NUSSEIBEH[1]

Believing that a Jew could hold a purely secular vision of Palestine is, in the words of Marx, to forget the weight of the dead on the brains of the living.

GEORGES BENSOUSSAN[2]

---

1. *Once Upon a Country: A Palestinian Life*, 531.

2. Quoted in Rose, *The Question of Zion*, 34, citing Bensoussan, *Une histoire intellectuelle*, 498.

Zionism and the Scriptures

THE ANCIENT BIBLICAL STORY of God's promise of a land for the people of Israel is often invoked by modern Israel's defenders.[3] In fact, however, when taken in context, the biblical promise points away from nationalist domination and toward an ethos of sharing and consideration. Moreover, the history of the people of the promise confirms this view. For, since the beginning, the promised land has always been much more than mere land, the promise much more than a mere property claim, and the people of the promise much more than mere landowners.

The Zionist attempt to establish for the Jews a sovereign state "like the nations"[4] has represented a direct rejection of the master narrative of Jewish Scripture and tradition with predictably problematic consequences.[5] Zionism, however, manifestly has also drawn extraordinary energy from deep sources untapped by Orthodox, Reform, or secular Jewish groups in Europe.[6] Examination of Zionism's conflicted relationship to the God of the Bible and the Talmud shines a penetrating light on the deep crisis of Zionism, but also reveals a people positioned to rediscover God's justice and compassion and to carry out his will with unprecedented effect. How the Jewish "nation" decides to respond to God's offer of "a curse or a blessing" in the cauldron of today's Israel-Palestine will bring mighty curses or blessings to all the nations of the world.

A PARADOXICAL PROMISE

A belief that a land has been divinely provided to a divinely favored people has doubtless been common among tribes and nations throughout history. What is striking in the biblical land story is that Israel's self-understanding and self-justification from the beginning have a vaulting universalist

---

3. The State of Israel's Declaration of Establishment leads with a recounting of the Jews' transcendent attachment to their "ancient homeland." The text of the Declaration can be found at http://www.jewishvirtuallibrary.org/jsource/History/Dec_of_Indep.html; accessed on Mar 13, 2012.

4. See Ezek 20:32; also 1 Sam 8:20.

5. The Declaration of Establishment concludes its argument by stating that the right to establish the state "is the natural right of the Jewish people to be masters of their own fate, like all other nations, in their own sovereign State." This natural, Wilsonian right of self-determination is in tension with the particularist, transcendent warrant of the previously cited statement (see note 3) in the founding declaration—a tension that threads its way through all of Zionist-Israeli experience.

6. Non-European Jews played virtually no role in Zionism's formation although they have all been pulled in its train, especially Arab Jews. See Shiblak, *Iraqi Jews*.

element yoking the chosen people to obligations of holiness (love of God) and of service to all humankind (the nations).[7]

Called to the promised land to be "a kingdom of priests and a holy nation" (Exod 19:6), the chosen people of the Bible have experienced a profound tension between a unique sense of national identity and a unique sense of universal spiritual vocation; an extraordinary focus on one spot of land (Jerusalem and Palestine), coupled with a unique history of landlessness. Today, hunkered down on that land, the heirs of the promise should recall their universal vocation, invoke the hard-won gifts of exile, and let God lead them to a peace that truly fulfills the promise. They need to remember that the context of the story of the land is the whole of creation, and all of time since creation. The land functions as a microcosm. The promise and its history express the entire problem and promise of human existence.

The Bible shows the Hebrews as a landless people at the time of the exodus, formed by reference to the promised land. They went on to live a troubled existence in the land, were exiled to Babylon, partially returned, then were dispersed for a period longer than their entire previous history, and recently have imposed a "Jewish state" on the territory. Their return was intended to resolve their troubles, giving them an accepted place among the nations. But this bid for acceptance or "normalization," as Chaim Weizmann and other early Zionists put it, has resulted in a country singularly alienated from much of the rest of the world; witness numerous votes in the United Nations.[8]

---

7. The distinctive nature of the connection was stated by the founder of religious Zionism, Rabbi Abraham Kook (see note 88), as quoted in Martin Buber's 1944 lecture, published as *On Zion*: "The sacred association of Israel with its holy land is not like the natural tie which binds all peoples and tongues to their lands." Buber elaborates, "Everywhere else [but Israel] the connection is the result of history." *On Zion*, 148. Buber believed the gift of the land to Abraham's seed was unique. "[T]he heart of [Israel's] whole historical faith" is that it is "the one people that knows the truth [about] how it came into possession of its land." Ibid., 18–19. His own relationship to Zionism was highly conflicted. In 1921, he saw it as offering the Jews a way to "enter the sphere of world history once more, and become once more the standard bearer of their own fate." Quoted in Flohr, ed., *A Land of Two Peoples*, 61. But Buber was deeply disturbed as the attempt to make their own fate was "achieved at the expense of other people's rights." The secularization of the "sacred association" threatened to turn into a "profanation." Ibid., 183–84. See also Rose, *The Question of Zion*, 70–75.

8. Rose, *The Question of Zion*, 76, quoting Weizmann. Also p. 48, noting the contradiction of believing the fulfillment of a very particular history would consist of becoming normal.

Zionism and the Scriptures

The secularization of the promise into a simple territorial claim has severed many Jews from the ethical taproot of their religious tradition.[9] Others have been pulled into reviving a primitive, violent messianism not seen since Roman times. Still others are awakening from the nationalist illusion, realizing that their collective moral survival depends on loving—or at least respecting—their neighbor. Recognizing the danger of turning into "Pharaoh," they see that only in avoiding Pharaoh's "hardness of heart" can Israelis escape a wrathful fate. But simple abdication of all power and denial of nationhood or peoplehood would also miss the point.

A Different Destiny

The fundamental fact is that, for the Jews, it has always been different than for "the nations." In fact, to be "like the nations" was anathema to God's spokesmen, the prophets. The prophet Ezekiel, for one, relayed God's message: "You say, 'We want to be like the nations, like the peoples of the world, who serve wood and stone.' But what you have in mind will never happen" (Ezek 20:32).[10] In the book of Numbers, the prophet Balaam describes the people of Israel as "a people who live apart and do not consider themselves one of the nations" (Num 23:9).

How could Israel be a nation, but not "like the nations"? One might expect that God's chosen people, those to whom God first revealed himself as the Lord of all creation and of all peoples, would become exalted men and women, dispensing wisdom and holiness to the other peoples of the world. Or one might expect them to gain supremacy over the other peoples, to rule over them in God's name. Either destiny would lift them up above the normal lot of humanity. But neither destiny has been theirs. Instead, the story of God's people as told in the Bible and understood in subsequent Jewish religion is all-too-human, full of pathos and paradox and the grittiest human suffering. It is the story of people made of earth,

---

9. Contrast Buber, among other prophetic Zionist outliers, who rejected "all merely nationalistic, un-Messianic, anti-Messianic plans of restoring a Jewish Palestine as a state like other states, which deny the supranational task of the Jewish nation." Buber, *On Zion*, 117. Writing in 1944, he credits others, such as Moses Hess, Achad Ha'am, and A. D. Gordon, with similar visions of a Zionism fulfilling profound spiritual duties to humanity.

10. Expounding on this chapter of Ezekiel, Buber says, "If Israel reduces Zion to 'a Jewish community in Palestine,' it will not get the community. If it only wants to have a land like other lands, then the land will sink down under its feet just as the nation will melt away if it only wants to be a nation like other nations." *On Zion*, 145–46.

tied to the earth—but charged with restoring the earth by living in a godly way in "the land" or in hope of it.

The Bible depicts the people of Israel as a small, vulnerable people chosen by God, saved and spiritually formed as a special nation to serve as God's agent in rescuing his troubled creation. In the story, the people of Israel are forbidden from ever simply joining with or imitating other peoples. Countless commandments keep them apart from other peoples. To be God's agent the people of Israel must have a distinct and unassimilable identity. Yet, the story of their "peoplehood" has always been about the salvation of all humankind.[11] The God whom they serve is universal (the original universal God), and his purpose is universal. So the separation is not an end in itself. Nor is it based on the people of Israel being essentially different from other people. Rather, it is a paradoxical seed of unity: Only because the separation (holiness) of the people of Israel was expressly willed by God (and merely accepted by the people) to show forth God's glory can it serve God's ultimate desire to reconcile all the nations to himself and to each other. The people must be holy, and they must be priests. But priests are supposed to mediate between God and humans. Thus Israel is to serve as priest and exemplar to the nations. God must reign supreme in the land and in creation, but God is the God of all humans. This priestly role excludes tribalism or simply occupying and ruling territory in the same manner as the nations.[12]

Today it is Zionism, with all its grave tribalist faults, that has bestowed on the Jews the opportunity to realize their destiny to be "a light for the Gentiles" (Isa 49:6). Zionism gave the Jewish people back their existence as a nation among the nations, their power to make national choices. The opportunity to fulfill their destiny is slipping away, however. In ignoring God's intentions as conveyed in Scripture and tradition, the Zionists are not only depriving the Palestinian people of their human rights; they are trying to warp the soul of the Jewish people and consequently are sinking the world into hatred and strife.

It may not be too late to salvage Israel's unique mission. Through the failure of Zionism in practice to deliver peace, security, and happiness in

11. The "peoplehood" concept brings together religious and national identity, ethnicity and heritage, in a way meant to recognize commonality and downplay conflict among these categories. See Kopelowitz, ed., *Jewish Peoplehood: Change and Challenge*.

12. See Benamozegh, *Israel and Humanity*, 139–40, who in the nineteenth century stated, "For inasmuch as priests are ordained only for the sake of the laity, the priesthood of Jews presupposes a humankind in whose service the Jews have been placed by Providence"; quoted in Klinghoffer, *Why the Jews Rejected Jesus*, 219.

the land, it is now obvious that the moral survival of the Jewish people depends on blazing a new path of compassion and nonviolence that relates to the Palestinians not as enemies, nor as mere passive objects of benevolence, but rather as essential partners in peace. Small groups of Jews and Palestinians are already pioneering this path.[13] That partnership can impart a special light to all people, but the willingness to sacrifice and take risks is essential.

Of course, the Palestinians also face tough choices. While they truly are victims, they must avoid the flip side of a victim identity, which is self-pity, demonization of the "Other" (here the Israelis), and loss of creativity. Many who lecture Palestinians about their need to accept Israeli Jews are merely seeking an excuse for continued Israeli domination, but it is true that without a powerful commitment to reconciliation Palestinian liberation would be a grim affair.

A Long Story

From the very first pages of the Bible, humanity is linked to land, but land is only a medium for the relationship between God and humanity. The original promised land, of course, was the Garden of Eden.[14] In Gen 2–3, God creates the land before creating the Human Being, who is formed from the earth ("Adam" is from the Hebrew word for "earth," *adamah*) to take care of the Garden of Eden for God and with God. The garden is made for Adam and Eve, and they are made for the garden. This arrangement expresses God's loving nature. By living well in the garden, the humans are given a concrete way to love God back, just as God's gift of the garden is a concrete expression of his love for them. The garden is what brings the human beings and God together; it is what they share. Adam and Eve's most precious way of showing love for God is to respect God's prohibition against eating of the fruit of the tree of the knowledge of good and evil—to

---

13. Examples include the groups "Combatants for Peace," who are former Palestinian militants and Israeli soldiers "fighting together to break the cycle of violence and for a just two-state solution" (http://www.cfpeace.org/), and "Bereaved Parents Circle," which consists of Israelis and Palestinians who have lost family members in the conflict joining in a reconciliation mission for peace (http://www.theparentscircle.com/). Both websites accessed on Feb 20, 2012.

14. "The crimson thread that binds together the entire biblical story of the sojourn of Israel in Canaan . . . is the continual testing as to whether or not they abide by God's will . . . an expanded version of the sojourn of Adam in the Garden of Eden." Tarazi, *Land and Covenant*, 115.

share God's moral universe. The original sin is Adam and Eve's grasping, selfish attitude toward the land and its fruits. When they secretly eat of the forbidden fruit, they treat the garden simply as the object of their desires, rather than as the medium of a relationship of trust and transparency with God. The medium of their union with God becomes the medium of their alienation from God, from whom, in a final insult, they attempt to hide.

The first social sin, Cain's murder of his brother Abel, is framed by God as a sin against the land, and Cain's punishment is mediated through the land. In Gen 4:10–11, God states that Abel's blood "cries out to me from the ground," that Cain is "under a curse and driven from the ground," and that Cain's punishment consists in his alienation from the ground, both in his perpetual itinerancy and in the hardship of tilling infertile soil.

God's promise to Abraham of the land of Canaan is the central dynamic of the Hebrew Bible, but it is far from straightforward. It involves "all peoples on earth" (Gen 12:3), who God says will be blessed through Abraham. And, paradoxically, Abraham's original virtue is to give up his home and his nationality to live as a sojourner in a strange land. In Gen 12, Abram is called by YHWH as an individual to relinquish his home and relocate to a foreign land, where God promises he will become a great nation admired of all the peoples on earth and his name will be used by all in blessings (Gen 12:1–3). God pulls Abram away from his own people, and from people in general, to bestow on him a promise of land as a path to redeem humankind. After Abram arrives in Canaan, YHWH says he will give that land to Abram's progeny (who do not yet exist). Moreover, his progeny descended from Ishmael, his eldest son by Sarah's slave Hagar, will not be directly included in this promise, though God makes other provision for them. In all of this, Abram does not represent an ethnic group but the man whose faith in God is the seed of a new people who will leaven humankind. God never tells Abram that he is superior to other men in any way or that he will establish himself by his own efforts. His sole virtue is faithfulness.

It takes a major miracle for Abram (now Abraham, the "father of many nations," Gen 17:5) and Sarah even to have an heir. In Gen 17, God grants them a son (the seed of the promised particular nation of Israel) by a miracle in their barren old age, and in reward for Abraham's faithfulness (Gen 17:15). Then, to underscore the point that the object of the promise was not an end in itself, but wholly an expression of the beginning of a new relationship of trust between God and humanity, God demands that Abraham offer up that son, Isaac, the father-to-be of Israel (Gen 22:1–18).

Zionism and the Scriptures

In the offering and near-sacrifice of that heir, Isaac, Abraham proves his ultimate loyalty is to God, not to God's promise of land and progeny.

The enslavement of Abraham's descendants in Egypt appears to jeopardize the promise, but God leads the lowly Hebrew slaves out of Egypt in a deeply significant way. The point of the exodus from Egypt is to exalt God over Pharaoh (in Exod 14:17, God says, "I will gain glory through Pharaoh and all his army"), who represents the state—that is, the proud possession of land through might, wealth, and idolatry. The Hebrews do not and are not supposed to imitate or replace Pharaoh.[15] Their fatherly Pharaoh is God.

It is in complete, powerless, landless poverty in the wilderness that God forms the people by precept, providence, and harsh experience so that when they come into the land they will be free not just of Pharaoh but also of Pharaoh's ways.[16] As Old Testament scholar Walter Brueggemann

---

15. YHWH is the Anti-Pharaoh. The Hebrews begin to develop a sense of identity as a people while in bondage in Egypt, where they no longer are connected to the land. They are both fortunate and suffering, but their position is always different from the rest of humanity's. When Pharaoh's armies pursue the fleeing Hebrews, the people are not an army, nor do they win a military victory. Rather, God single-handedly intervenes to wipe out the danger. God, not weapons or skill, protects and forms Israel. Moses as a man is pointedly described as not up to the task of leading his people, except as a follower of God's commands.

As a matter of historical research, it is believed that the formation of the people of Israel involved several different groups coming together over an extended time from different parts of the region, including some coming from Egypt, but others not, and bonding around the shared belief in the God of the exodus, the God who cares and who acts and who transforms his people through their love and obedience. George E. Mendenhall theorizes that "Numbers 11:4 notes that Moses brought with him out of Egypt *'asaf-suf,* a pejorative label meaning 'mixed rabble,' . . . of diverse ethnic backgrounds" who bonded into one people through the Sinai covenant and who accepted YHWH as their king in opposition to Pharaoh and all the other "divine" monarchs of the time. See Mendenhall, *Ancient Israel's Faith and History,* 51–56. Of course, the degree to which the biblical narratives reflect the facts of history is very uncertain, though this is not important to the present discussion, which focuses on the message of the biblical narrative from a mythological beginning into historical times. Thus, for example, there is a scarcity of historical evidence for the exodus from Egypt. Moreover, it has been plausibly argued that the Pharaoh of exodus was actually modeled on autocratic King Solomon. In any event, Scripture offers both rulers as examples of human power in conflict with God's will. See Howard-Brook, *Come Out My People,* 98–100.

16. The long experience of Israel's landless learning in the wilderness—possessed of nothing but a promise—is what forms them as God's people, where through the Torah they are taught and trained to love God and each other. There, and then later, as the people of the promised land, they experience a series of misunderstandings and revelations about what it means to be God's chosen people. The essential point is that it is not about the people or their might, prosperity, and prestige in the world as

writes, the wilderness is "the arena of chaos that, like the darkness before creation, is 'formless and void.'" The people are shown that "life-giving resources do not come from land but from Yahweh."[17] Key testing-points include the people's loss of faith in the promise when they arrive at the border of the land (Num 13:21—14:35); the gift of manna from the heavens (Exod 16:2-31); the gift of drinking water at Massah and Meribah (Exod 15:23-25; 17:1-7); the gift of the Law at Mount Sinai (Exod 20); and the episode of the golden calf (Exod 32).

Finally the people reach their destination. Later, after many generations struggling in the land, the people feel lost in a new way and decide to establish a monarchy. God consents but issues a stark warning about how monarchs will create a state that will usurp the place of God and community.[18] The prophet Samuel warns the people of the perils of statehood and all the evil that kings do to their people (1 Sam 8:11-17), but they insist, "We want a king over us. Then we will be *like all the other nations*, with a king to lead us and to go out before us and fight our battles" (1 Sam 8:19-20; emphasis added).

Under David and Solomon such a state is established, with impressive results. But the pursuit of national power has deadly side effects, blinding and deafening a series of rulers to God's will as they violate the covenant commitment to justice and mercy.[19] This errant course brings on the destruction of the Northern Kingdom of Israel (722 BCE), and then the Babylonian Captivity of the Southern Kingdom of Judah (587-538 BCE). The great prophets cry out that God has chosen the Jews not because they are better and thus to be rewarded but so that in their very insignificance and suffering they may show a true faith that reveals God in a fully human

---

a nation among the nations. (Deut 7:7-10: Israel is "the fewest of all peoples"; it was only because YHWH loved them and stood by his promise that he brought them out of Egypt; but if they defy and reject his law he will repay them with destruction; see also Deut 9:5.)

17. Brueggemann, *The Land*, 28, 30.

18. God has told Samuel, "It is not you they have rejected, but they have rejected me as their king" (1 Sam 8:7).

19. Mendenhall, whose scholarship led the way to understanding the royal covenant form in the Late Bronze Age, the model for the Sinai covenant, notes that "for the Hebrews, God was a king—they were his vassal, and he was their *lord*," though not their dictator. Mendenhall, *Ancient Israel's Faith and History*, 58. Speaking of the covenant commands, he writes, "[W]hen people act on these *commitments*—all of which restrict self-interest—the rule of God becomes a tangible reality, establishing a religious basis (i.e., faith) on which human differences can be transcended and community achieved." Ibid., 61.

way through their obedience, their love of God, and their compassion and love of neighbor and stranger. This is a potent new expression of holiness—of showing God's truth and power in history and over the world.[20]

Chosen—But for What?

The biblical point is that to live as God's people is neither an ethereal, monkish pursuit nor a warrior's triumph. Relationship with God goes through the community, the land, and the human heart, with all its dark parts.[21] The story of the people chosen to live in the land is a story of earthly striving in passionate relationship with God. Over and over again, the message is, "Yes, I have truly chosen you, and for reasons that defy human calculations. But no, this does not authorize you to act like spoiled princes or to value the gifts more than the giver." Indeed, the entire calling of the chosen people can be seen as a massive "bait-and-switch." The people assume they are chosen for worldly success and gratifications, only to experience defeats and hardship on the path to a deeper understanding of God's redemptive plan. Thus, Amos tells the people, the Lord says, "You only have I chosen of all the families of the earth; therefore I will punish you for all your sins" (Amos 3:2).

Throughout all these events what is essential about the promised land is that it is God's gift, the medium of his love for Israel, and that it gives Israel the means to love back concretely by creating a just and intentional (holy) community. What is worst about exile is not the fact of living in Babylon or elsewhere than in Judea, but that the exile expresses God's alienation and anger with Israel for having broken its covenant obligations. Yet even this divine jealousy also expresses relationship.

Moreover, the classic period of possession of the land (from the death of Moses to the Babylonian Exile) featured fierce, radical rejection of Canaanite and Philistine earth-oriented fertility cults, as well as of socially oppressive, economic exploitation of the land through priestly and royal

---

20. God explains the consequences of selfishness: "Therefore I will make you an object of scorn to the nations and a laughingstock to all the countries. Those who are near and those who are far away will mock you, you infamous city, full of turmoil. See how each of the princes of Israel who are in you uses his power to shed blood. In you they have treated father and mother with contempt; in you they have oppressed the alien and mistreated the fatherless and the widow" (Ezek 22:4–7).

21. Deut 10:16: "Circumcise your hearts, therefore, and do not be stiff-necked any longer."

bureaucracies, including those of Jerusalem.[22] In other words, the spiritual leaders of the people of Israel believed there was an intense, highly tempting danger that the people would have an abusive relationship to the land that would feed into abusive social relations.

Viewed in this light, it appears that the cult of the promised land has functioned on the one hand as a barrier to prevent the people from bonding closely with any other land, and on the other as a reminder of their creaturely nature in God's good creation. Because they had been promised one particular land, they could not be fully at home in any other land. Moreover, the onerous religious code made clear that any physical relationship with the promised land had to be chaste so as to serve God's purposes. This requirement of chaste possession means that even when inhabiting or controlling the land, it is only God's presence in the people's prayers and their conduct that makes it the true promised land. Conversely, even when away from the land or lacking control of it, prayer and obedience generate remembrance and hope; in effect, the people inhabit the promised land in their heart.[23]

Looked at another way, one can see a fundamental ambivalence in the attitude of the people of Israel toward the land, which of itself is not sufficient and, if loved passionately, is even a danger to their special mission. From the outset, in the Garden or with Abraham, the land is a somewhat abstract reality, a symbol and token of relationship to God, whereas with other peoples (the nations) land *was* sufficient. These others, with their nature gods and Mother Earth myths, might almost be thought to have grown out of their land. In contrast, Abram is brought from outside into a land that others have loved and nurtured—a land he did not know or choose. For him, as for his descendants, it has no intrinsic value; God could reassign a different land. God's main interest, moreover, is in the way Israel (a person and then a people, not a place) lives on the land in communal obedience, justice, and worship. He does not take much interest in

---

22. Mendenhall, *Ancient Israel's Faith and History*, 131, 133–35, 169.

23. As the sins of the people and their rulers catch up with them, and exile looms, Jeremiah spells out the conditions for their lawful residence in the land: "If you really change your ways and your actions and deal with each other justly, if you do not oppress the alien, the fatherless, or the widow, and do not shed innocent blood in this place, and if you do not follow other gods to your own harm, then I will let you live in this place, in the land I gave your forefathers for ever and ever" (Jer 7:5–7). Living in the land without accepting these precepts is to treat it as a refuge of one's own—"a den of robbers" (Jer 7:11).

the life of the land itself and its fruits, unlike the nature gods worshiped by the nations.[24]

All of this is consistent with the eventual genius of the Jews in living as "Israel," over many centuries almost completely cut off from the physical land, not to mention sovereignty over it. During the Babylonian Exile, therefore, the prophets remember Jerusalem and praise and worship God more deeply than ever.[25] God's universal nature is recognized amid hints that the entire world is the promised land in which humanity lives by God's grace as Abraham did when residing as a stranger in his own land, or as Moses did in the wilderness on the way to the land.[26]

Israel's worship of its God as the benevolent Creator is in stark contrast to the thinking of the nations. For example, according to Walter Wink, in the Babylonian *Enuma Elish*, the father and mother of the younger gods plan to kill their offspring for making too much of a frolicsome racket. One of the children kills the father first. Before the mother can exact her revenge, the children get their youngest sibling, Marduk, to kill her, in exchange for being made their undisputed ruler. After killing his mother with maximum brutality, "[h]e stretches out her corpse full length, and from it creates the cosmos. . . . Creation is an act of violence."[27] The corollary is that "[t]he whole cosmos is a state and the god rules through the king."[28]

---

24. See Brueggemann, *The Land*, 54, describing "the central temptation of the land" and its connection to gods who are "subject to manipulation, ready to serve human ends."

25. Brueggemann: "It is in the context of Exile that Israel told its best stories." Ibid., 136. Much of the book of Genesis, for example, is believed to have been formed in this period as part of the profound meditation of the "exiles" on their homeland and how they lost it, as well as an "argument" with the civilization and theology of Babylon. See Howard-Brook, *Come Out My People*, 13–21.

26. Brueggemann, xiii: "[I]t is entirely possible that Israel's land stands in for and epitomizes all land." The "already, but not yet" experience of a mysterious promise is captured by Buber: "[E]ven before Israel becomes a people, the family which is to become a people learns, in the land in which it has not yet settled but is merely a wandering guest, by a mysterious Promise that the land is preordained for it. . . ." *On Zion*, 148–49. The story of Abraham's purchase from Ephron the Hittite of the plot of land at Hebron with the cave of Machpelah in which to bury Sarah shows relations of deep cordiality between him and the Hittites who inhabited the area, as Abraham humbly declares, "I am an alien and a stranger among you," while they praise him as "a mighty prince among us" and offer to give him land and the best grave they have (Gen 23).

27. Wink, *Engaging the Powers*, 14.

28. Ibid., 16.

But Israel's God wants humanity to desire and enjoy creation as a creature. Rather than passively praising God, humanity's purpose is to be deeply in and of creation as God's servant and representative—and to offer itself back to God to be further shaped into a truer image of God. The relationship with the land is central to this process. Scripture returns continually to the importance of the promised land to the chosen people as the sign of God's benevolence. They must believe in God as acting in this world, caring about this world and about them and about how they act in this world. The world is not evil or illusory; it is real and good, but it means nothing without relation to God.[29]

The essence of this relationship to God through the land is brought out in Deut 11:10–14, where YHWH explains the difference between Egypt, with its human-controlled irrigation agriculture, and the hilly promised land, which "drinks rain from heaven," tended by God. "If you faithfully obey the commands I am giving you today—to love the LORD your God and to serve him with all your heart and with all your soul—then I will send rain on your land in its season, both autumn and spring rains, so that you may gather in your grain, new wine, and olive oil."[30]

And yet, all told, "exile" has been the overwhelming norm in the Jewish experience, including the sense of internal exile felt by the Jews in the post-exilic, Second Temple period (538 BCE to 70 CE).[31] Since the time of the Babylonian Exile (587 BCE), in fact, most Jews have not lived in

---

29. Of course, the Bible gives grounds to contest God's benevolence, especially to other nations. Michael Prior argued that it is possible to develop a Jewish theology of universal liberation with a strong dependence on the Hebrew prophets (as this paper does), but "it would be no more difficult to construct a theology of oppression on the basis of other Old Testament traditions, especially those dealing with (the mythologized) Israelite origins that demanded the destruction of other peoples." See Masalha, *The Bible and Zionism*, 271–77, discussing Prior's research and highlighting a number of "genocidal metanarratives" that Prior identified in the Old Testament. It may be that the most sensible and fruitful way to read the Bible is as a collection of conflicting texts torn between a loving God of creativity and brotherhood versus a God of domination and exclusion. This is the thesis of Wes Howard-Brook's densely researched volume, *Come Out, My People*; see note 15.

30. See Buber, *On Zion*, 24–25; also Brueggemann, *The Land*, 49: "Israel's involvement is always with land and with Yahweh, never only with Yahweh as though only to live in intense obedience, never only with the land, as though to simply possess and manage."

31. "Most first-century Jews did not believe the exile had ended. The Temple had not been rebuilt properly; the Messiah had not yet arrived; the general resurrection had not occurred; the Torah was not being observed perfectly; the Gentiles were not flocking to hear the word of the Lord on Mount Zion"; Wright, *What Saint Paul Really Said*, 33.

the land. They remained in Babylon or Alexandria and then settled in an ever-growing number of far-flung Diaspora communities. The few that began to trickle back in 538 BCE only briefly regained full political control of the land. They survived for six centuries by accommodating, as well as resisting, foreign political domination (Persian, Greek, and Roman).[32] Moreover, the time of the prophets was over. In its place came the time of the scribes and priests, who narrowed Israel's communal pursuit of holiness through obedience to purity codes that separated them from non-Jews. Apocalyptic and messianic visions emerged of future, dramatic deliverance by God, victory for Israel, and renewal of the world.[33] These aspirations far exceeded mere worldly dominion over the physical territory of Canaan, Judea, or Palestine.

Choices of the Chosen

In the final period of Jewish national history (the first century of the Common Era), the question of whether and how God would keep his promise to the people of Israel—and how the people should obey God's will—came to a climax in radically different movements that split on the issue of what the Promise meant.[34] The movements occurred under pressure from Rome, which was drawing innumerable nations into a universal empire. Both the Gentile nations and many Jews seemed to be learning to get along in the Pax Romana, while "Hellenized" (assimilated) Jews lived

---

32. Borg and Crossan, *The Last Week*, 12.

33. An important apocalyptic text, the book of Daniel, was written in the second century BCE in response to the persecution of the Hellenistic-Seleucid King Antiochus IV Epiphanes, who, among other outrages, forced his own image into the Temple sanctuary. "Some Jews (whom we know as the Maccabees) turned to arms and fought a successful military war on earth against *his empire,* while other Jews turned to visions and the hope for an absolute divine judgment against *all empires,* past, present, and future. The empires are associated with chaos, the sea, and bestial powers. The transcendental judgment of God involves a triumph of order over chaos, of sky over sea, and of the human over the bestial. Dan 7 records one such vision and interpretation in which God conducts a divine court case or heavenly trial against all major empires up to and including Antiochus IV." Ibid., 131.

34. "It is important to note that the Old Testament is the foundation of two religious movements: Christianity and Rabbinic Judaism.... The Old Testament does not stand on its own for Judaism or for Christianity. Jews have found its fulfillment in the Mishnah and the Talmud, and Christians have found its fulfillment in the New Testament. Incidentally, Christianity preceded the emergence of Rabbinic Judaism." Ateek, *A Palestinian Christian Cry,* 54.

prosperously in Roman cities around the Mediterranean Sea, and Jewish Temple authorities in Jerusalem collaborated actively with Rome.[35]

Others in Palestine rejected the status quo, such as the followers of Jesus, the Zealots, and the rabbis:

1. Jesus of Nazareth, a Jew, proclaimed a message of love, compassion, and service, which was adopted by his exclusively Jewish disciples and offered to all humankind, regardless of nationality and in defiance of the universal cosmic claims of the Roman Empire, which preached a competing cosmology of history.[36] National liberation of the Jews was not the point;[37] nor was mystical election and the ethnic particularism of Judaism by way of separation from the Gentiles. The arc of Jesus Christ's life story reprised the promise (the Annunciation and the Nativity) and travail (baptism recalls the exodus, the temptation in the wilderness recalls the wanderings in the wilderness) of Israel's story, but with full consciousness and intentionality. Christ was seen by some to embody and perfect the Jews' experience as a people, but he was rejected by the religious-political authorities who had substituted for God a religion in which they were the masters—and was put to death by their patron, Rome.

   In this story, the promised land is transformed into the kingdom of God, which consists of concretely loving God accessed through brotherly and sisterly love for the stranger, the "Other," the outcast, even the enemy, here in this world. The covenant with Israel now, through the gospel, becomes a blessing to all peoples. The deep truths of the Torah belong to all people.[38] The people of Israel become all who follow Christ, namely, the universal church.

---

35. Under Roman domination "the Temple became the central economic and political institution in the country." Borg and Crossan, *The Last Week*, 15.

36. The Romans from the time of Augustus preached their own "gospel" of salvation: "the good news about a divine child [Augustus] who will save the world from destruction by establishing permanent peace." It was preached that the Roman Emperor, a divine being, would bring peace and order through military victory and domination. Borg and Crossan, *The First Christmas*, 69, 75, 97, 159–65. See also Wink, *Engaging the Powers*, 89–90, 92, who describes how the peace that Rome imposed on its empire drew from deep mythological sources treating of chaos and order.

37. At the same time, it should not be overlooked that many of the teachings and actions recorded about Jesus condemn Rome's domination of Israel, tapping deep resentments and carrying on a long tradition of Jewish resistance to empire. See Horsley, *In the Shadow of Empire*, 83–96.

38. The New Testament presents Christ as the unifier for Jews and Gentiles: "For

Zionism and the Scriptures

The Jewish establishment persecuted Jesus' followers and, tragically, the Christians soon returned the favor, vilifying the Jews and perverting Christ's self-sacrifice into the *casus belli* of a profound enmity between Gentiles and Jews.[39] These Jews had played the universalist card, building a counter-community to Rome that was "not like the nations," but spanned all nations and all social classes. That counter-community was the foundation of Christianity, a product of Israel that is still under construction and whose adherents through the ages have often fallen into their own deadly infatuations with wealth, power, and spiritual pride—with being "like the nations."

2. Religious nationalists (called Zealots) reacted more directly against Roman domination and Jewish assimilation and collaboration. Violent and literal-minded, the Zealots aligned with the rigorist Shammaite branch of the Pharisees and led two massive popular uprisings in 66–70 CE and 132–135 CE, premised on the belief that God would restore Israel politically by giving it military victory against Rome.[40] The first rebellion, which began as a revolt against existing Jewish political authorities, led to the destruction by Rome of the Temple in Jerusalem. The second rebellion featured an apparent messiah, Simon Bar Kochba, and an attempt to rebuild the Temple, but resulted in the expulsion of all Jews from Jerusalem.

---

he himself is our peace, who has made the two one and has destroyed the barrier, the dividing wall of hostility" (Eph 2:14).

39. Kovel, *Overcoming Zionism*, 23: "Jesus was authentically Jewish and yet a breaking point in the history of Judaism, which becomes defined thereafter by those Jews who did not follow him." The importance and bitterness of the rivalry between the two offspring of the Old Testament faith is often overlooked. In post-Christian, post-Holocaust times, we are uncomfortable recognizing Jews' longstanding enmity toward Christians and Christianity; their horror at the phenomenon of Jewish conversion to Christianity as it steadily gained adherents. "The rabbis considered Jewish Christians worse than idolaters." Klinghoffer, *Why the Jews Rejected Jesus*, 116, 147. The Talmud and medieval Jewish sages took credit for the arrest and execution of Jesus and proclaimed his eternal punishment in the afterlife. Ibid., 73, 161. See also Shahak, *Jewish History, Jewish Religion*, 97–98: "All classical Jewish sources that mention [Jesus'] execution are quite happy to take responsibility for it; in the Talmudic account the Romans are not even mentioned."

40. Wright, *What Saint Paul Really Said*, 26–29: "[F]or the first-century Jew 'zeal' was something you did with a knife. Those first-century Jews who longed for revolution against Rome looked back to Phinehas and Elijah in the Old Testament, and to the Maccabean heroes two centuries before Paul, as their models. . . . If you want to see roughly what Shammaite Pharisaism was all about, look at the philosophy which inspired Yigal Amir to shoot Yitzhak Rabin in Tel Aviv on 4 November 1995."

3. Rabbinic Judaism also rejected universalism and assimilation, embracing a separation from the surrounding peoples, especially after the failure of the Bar Kochba insurrection in 135 CE, after which, with priests and secular rulers eliminated, the rabbis gained primacy and found a lasting political accommodation with Imperial Rome.[41] This movement drew on the tolerant, humane teachings of Rabbi Hillel (Rabbi Shammai's great rival), as well as on the pragmatic lessons of the Zealot disasters. The rabbis eschewed nation-state status to preserve the people of God in its new exile from Judea, passionately awaiting and preparing for God's action on their behalf sometime in the future.[42]

The Jewish Zealots had played the ultra-nationalist card against the Romans in violent rebellions and had lost. Having failed and been defeated by the Romans, the survivors accepted to become a non-territorial nation, a self-enclosed religious nation shorn of territorial status, but also transcending it, and renouncing any messianic activism. The Jews of Roman Palestine, whether or not they left Palestine, were absorbed into the pre-existing Diaspora (which already included the majority of Jews in the world).

Any return to power in the land, the rabbis taught, would be left entirely in God's hands. The people were not to take up the sword to reconquer the territory.[43] Attempts to hasten or even to predict the Messiah's

---

41. The history of the fifty years between the two uprisings was "glossed" to present the rabbis who assumed national leadership as "above all religious teachers, apolitical and opposed to dangerous nationalist delusions." But in fact Rabbi Yohanan ben Zakkai, who led the movement, "had supported the war against the Romans until its doomed outcome was obvious." Similarly, in the second revolt, "several leading rabbis of the time, including the illustrious Rabbi Akiva, had endorsed Bar Kochba, going so far as to call him the Messiah and encouraging their students to take up arms. Such fevered involvement in messianism does not suggest that the rabbinic party had entirely forsaken politics for the studious life." Goldberg, *The Divided Self*, 41–44.

42. "[A] measure of Jewish autonomy was speedily restored. . . . The *nasi* of the Sanhedrin was confirmed as patriarch of the Jews and given the right to collect taxes for Jewish institutions, to appoint judges for the Jewish courts," and other powers that constituted a quasi-autonomous local government within the empire. The reign of Emperor Constantine two centuries later began a hundred-year decline of that system, which ended in 425. Ibid., 44–46.

43. The Babylonian Talmud tells Jews "not to take the land of Israel by force," a powerful injunction considered to be one of the Three Strong Oaths. For differing rabbinical interpretations of this phrase from *Tractate Kesubos* (or *Ketuboth*) 111A, see Shahak and Mezvinsky, *Jewish Fundamentalism*, 18–19. Religious Zionists maintain that the three oaths do not apply to the "messianic times" that have begun with the

Zionism and the Scriptures

coming were strictly condemned. The price of ethnic-religious cohesion was to relinquish aspirations to sovereign power. Through good times and bad—although with periodic disastrous episodes where false messiahs led people astray—they stuck to their choice. But a sense of *national* identity persisted in the Jews' biblical memory.[44]

An Unresolved Tension

Cut off from hope of dominion over the land, the Jews were also cut off from any compelling need to understand God's ultimate plan in other than a passive light. Deprived of sovereign power, they tended to anticipate vaguely a triumphant retaking of the land someday as sovereign owners, rather than receiving it as stewards of God, commanded to make it bear the fruits of peace and justice for all humankind.[45]

In the meantime, always ultimately at the mercy of others, they navigated the currents of alien power and could console themselves with the conviction that their God ultimately held all power.[46] Thus they could offer their suffering and humiliation as a testament of faith in God. Doubtless, many Jews, especially in times of prosperity and relative security, harbored kindly feelings toward non-Jews and acted with compassion, but they received little encouragement from their rabbis, who generally inculcated

---

advent of Zionism. Non-Zionist Orthodox rabbis disagree. Masalha, *The Bible and Zionism*, 207.

44. Rabbinic Judaism, as it established itself over several generations, would decree that the interpretations of rabbis in the Mishnah and the Talmud embodied an "oral Torah" that, in effect, superseded the authority of the Jewish Bible. In the nineteenth century, Reform Judaism asserted the primacy of the Jewish Bible, thus incurring the condemnation of orthodox believers. In earlier times, the Karaites recognized only the Bible as authoritative, a "heresy" that brought implacable persecution from the rabbis with the cooperation of non-Jewish authorities. See Shahak, *Jewish History, Jewish Religion*, 36–41, 60. See also Klinghoffer, *Why the Jews Rejected Jesus*, 24–27 and 55: "Essential to rabbinic Judaism, this concept of an oral Torah recognizes the Pentateuch as a cryptic document, a coded text." This perspective concentrated great power in the hands of the rabbis.

45. Messianic dreams of world domination were on display in the episode of the false messiah Sabbatai Sevi in the mid-seventeenth century, who drew a huge following throughout the Jewish world. Sevi, among other extravagances before he was stopped and abjured to become a Muslim, handed out the kingdoms of the world to various of his followers. Rose, *The Question of Zion*, 1–5, citing Scholem, *Sabbatai Sevi*.

46. "The perfect philosophy of exile, messianism allows the Jews to view themselves, not as historical indigents and ciphers, but as a major force in history." Rose, 23.

suspicion of non-Jews and enforced rules of self-segregation such as not allowing Jews to share so much as a glass of water with non-Jews.[47]

Moreover, they were cut off from the experience of competing with others for power and administration of power—experiences that can humble and enlighten, as well as corrupt.[48] Rather, their corporate power was derived from privileges granted by non-Jewish rulers. The key was keeping a balance among competing rulers, including religious authorities.[49] In the Middle Ages, the Jews "inhabited an uneasy region close to the centers of power," and they "played political roles, even under the constraints of their inferior and alien status."[50]

Doubtless, not all Jews cultivated quietism, pacifism, or compassion for the "Other." Some harbored resentment and animus, dreaming of apocalyptic pay-back and looking uncritically to mythical figures such as Joshua as models of violent triumph over non-Jews. A current of visceral antipathy to non-Jews also took root among some.[51] The more insular, antagonistic members of the community in effect ignored the collective aspect of Rabbi Hillel's dictum that the Jews could not be *only* for themselves.[52] In response to charges that this was extreme xenophobia, such cantankerous individuals could cite prophecies that once God had brought about the triumph of the Jews over the nations, those nations would then

---

47. "According to Ephraim Urbach, 'the type of Gentile that they encountered . . . determined the reaction of the sages.' Against the view of Rz.[abbi] Eliezer, 'No Gentile has a share in the world to come,' R. Joshua argued: 'But there are righteous men among the nations who have a share in the world to come.' (*tSanh.* 13:2) Probably the dictum, 'Even a Gentile who studies Torah is like the High Priest' is only the outcome of a positive experience." (Poulin has quoted Urbach, *The Sages, their Concepts and Beliefs*, 543–44.) "But the same R. Yohanan held: 'A Gentile who studies Torah is deserving of death.'" Poulin, "Loving Kindness towards Gentiles," 97; see www.erudit.org/revue/theologi/2003/v11/n1-2/009526ar.pdf; accessed on Feb 20, 2012.

48. Hannah Arendt called this condition one of "worldlessness," which she said resulted in an inability to understand their history and the implications of their own actions and those of their opponents. Arendt, *The Jewish Writings*, xlvi–xlvii, l.

49. Biale, *Power and Powerlessness*, 61: "The Jews were successful in exploiting the fragmentation of power in Christian Europe by playing off secular against religious authorities."

50. Ibid., 59.

51. See Kovel, *Overcoming Zionism*, 27–31, discussing "certain counter-racisms" in Jewish history.

52. The centrality of the tension between the self (individual or tribal) and the "Other" echoes in Rabbi Hillel's best known saying: "If I am not for myself, then who is for me? If I am only for myself, then what am I?" See the Talmudic tractate *Pirkei Avot* 1:14, at http://www.jewishvirtuallibrary.org/jsource/Talmud/avot1.html; accessed on Feb 18, 2012.

understand and accept the singular holiness of the Jews and so find their own subservient beatitude.⁵³

The political status of Jews became unsettled as the medieval webs of privilege based on membership in a guild, town, order, feudal domain, family—or, in the case of Jews, the Jewish nation—was gradually replaced by a system where the state emerged as the "sole object" of political loyalty in Europe, ruling over individual citizens.⁵⁴ The Jews began to be regarded not just as a religiously suspect group but also as a "foreign body, to be either thoroughly absorbed or expelled."⁵⁵ The classic secular formulation of this two-sided view came in the 1789 French debate over emancipation of the Jews, when it was said, "The Jews should be denied everything as a nation, but granted everything as individuals."⁵⁶

After centuries of insular existence, the lid was lifted in Enlightenment-Revolutionary Europe and America. Over the next few generations, Jews found themselves confronted with a bewildering host of new options. Jewish identity was no longer enforced by the state, leaving the rabbis and the Jewish community with only internal social and religious sanctions to maintain cohesion. A sort of identity vacuum developed as Jewish identity became a matter of individual choice and definition. The old Gentile regimes had been harsh, but the lines were clear, in part because they had delegated to the rabbis great power within the Jewish community, power the rabbis exercised forcefully to maintain a fierce and passionate Jewish identity and cohesion based on fidelity to the Torah and obedience to the comprehensive Halachic legal codes.⁵⁷

---

53. See Shahak, *Jewish History, Jewish Religion*, 23–27. Shahak paints an unrelievedly dark and harsh picture of Jewish hostility toward non-Jews, but provides detailed information that documents the violent impulses that lay dormant in the community from 135 CE until the birth of Jewish terrorist groups in the 1920s and '30s that went on to spearhead the ethnic cleansing of Palestine in 1948. For a twentieth-century taste of this hostility, see Shahak and Mezvinsky, *Jewish Fundamentalism*, ix, quoting Rabbi Kook: "The difference between a Jewish soul and the souls of Non-Jews—all of them in all different levels—is greater and deeper than the difference between a human soul and the souls of cattle." Yet Kook also claimed that "all the civilizations of the world will be renewed by the renascence of our spirit." Quoted in Rose, *The Question of Zion*, 24.

54. Biale, *Power and Powerlessness*, 143.

55. Ibid., 90.

56. Ibid., 112.

57. "Once the modern state had come into existence, the Jewish community lost its power to punish or intimidate the individual Jew. The bonds of one of the most closed of 'closed societies,' one of the most totalitarian societies in the whole history of humankind, were snapped." Shahak, *Jewish History, Jewish Religion*, 15. "[F]or the first

Traditionalist rabbis fought to preserve a closed community. Against them, proponents of the Haskalah, or Jewish Enlightenment, and then the founders of Reform Judaism, supported deep engagement with non-Jewish society, abandoned the Halachic strictures, and modernized the faith, making it more philosophical and personal. As secularism spread in society, many Jews went further, turning away from belief in God, if not completely away from tradition and their Jewish identity. Among elites, significant numbers converted to Christianity for social reasons. The Jewish population of Europe and Russia exploded. Huge numbers of Jews emigrated to cities, some prospering, others struggling or working in factories.[58]

Ratcheting up the intensity of the choices and debates was the emergence during the nineteenth century of new forms of nationalist, ethnic anti-Semitism.[59] For Jews who had left the traditional community and were trying to make their way in the larger society, it could seem that whatever choice a Jew made he would be despised and hated by non-Jews.

Jewish and non-Jewish thinkers alike wrestled with "the Jewish Question," asking what it meant to be a Jew and what place the Jews should occupy in society. Faced with the lack of any organized, sanctioned way for Jews to exercise political power as a people, some Jews concluded that their Diaspora history was one of powerlessness and that the essence of Judaism was precisely to eschew power in favor of apolitical ethics and spirituality.[60] That stance evolved into a commitment by many Jews to radical social-political reform of the entire society.[61] Other Jews, who were secular, agreed that the Diaspora was a time of complete powerlessness, but turned away in scorn in order to win Jewish power through a variety of Jewish political parties.[62]

---

time since about AD 200, a Jew could be free to do what he liked, within the bounds of his country's civil law, without having to pay for this freedom by converting to another religion." Ibid., 16; see also 54.

58. Biale, *Power and Powerlessness*, 120–21.

59. Jews were hated by reactionaries across Europe as symbols and agents of the dissolution of traditional structures. Ibid., 66–69. Many non-Jews were simply ignorant and envious of Jewish achievements. Herzl sharply distinguished modern anti-Semitism from the religious persecution of earlier ages, attributing it to resentment of Jews' impressive economic gains after their emancipation. Theodor Herzl, *The Jewish State*, 89–90. See also Arendt, *The Jewish Writings*, 22: "[M]odern anti-Semitism . . . has always reproached Jews with being bearers of the Enlightenment."

60. Biale, *Power and Powerlessness*, 114–17.

61. Ibid., 108, 118–19.

62. Ibid., 123–27.

Zionism and the Scriptures

From this crisis of identity, Zionism emerged as an aggressive nationalist response to the perceived irrelevance of Judaism in the modern world.

THE PROMISE SECULARIZED

Since the second century, to be Jewish to some significant degree had meant to wait for the return to Jerusalem with eager longing ("next year in Jerusalem!") and infinite patience. For some Jews who rejected this age-old stance, but who also feared—or despaired of—assimilation, taking over the physical city of Jerusalem and the territory of Palestine was a brilliant solution to the "Jewish Question." The objective was quintessentially Jewish, while the modus operandi and lifestyle goals were in line with dominant nationalist ideologies of the time.[63]

Nor were Jews the only ones drawn to radical solutions. In general, the late nineteenth and early twentieth centuries were a deeply unsettled period of change that generated many transformative ideologies aimed at filling the vacuum left by the collapse of traditional authorities (for example, various types of Socialism, Anarchism, Fascism, Freudianism, and Fundamentalism). Nationalism was pervasive. Unlike most other fervent nationalisms, the Jewish variant (Zionism) necessarily had to emphasize ethnic, if not racial, bonds, because Jews were scattered across so many countries, languages, and cultures. Thus Jews who thought they were already nationalists—in their capacity as citizens of nations such as Germany, France, and Italy—had to learn to be Jewish nationalists in a personal conversion process somewhat like that of Socialist workers shedding "false consciousness" to embrace their true identity as "proletarians."

As the Orthodox rabbinic establishment continued to insist that it was necessary to wait in faithful obedience to the Torah and Halacha for God to act before being restored to Jerusalem, and Reform Jews eschewed even the dream of collective return to the promised land, Zionists rejected Judaism. They proclaimed that it was time for the Jews to be like the nations.[64] The choice, in effect, was framed as between two options: to take the land without God or to keep God without the land. Jews everywhere

---

63. Rabkin, *A Threat From Within*, 37, notes, as have others, that Zionism can be seen as a form of "collective assimilation." Rabkin's extensive documentation of the original and continuing rejection by Jews of Zionism and Israeli nationalism on religious, theological grounds complements and balances Shahak's tracing of aggressive traits of "classical Judaism" in Zionist thought. See note 53.

64. As the early Zionist Micah Berdichevsky put it: "We are the last Jews—or we

had to decide whether the Jews were a nation or a religious group, though neither category alone could capture the unique mix of religion, community, and history that binds together the Jewish people.[65]

Zionists saw themselves as charting a middle way, avoiding stultifying traditional orthodoxy, assimilationist extinction, and growing nationalist anti-Semitism: to be a Jewish nation as other nations were French, German, or Russian.[66] The Zionists both reacted to the intolerance of surging nationalisms in Europe and were attracted to the sense of communal fulfillment of ethnic nationalism.[67] At the time, nationalism was seen by many as normative for human societies, and thus Zionism was the way Jews could become normal.[68] They would be neither too Jewish nor too universal; they would just be the Jewish nation.[69]

But what of the complexities of the narrative told in the Bible? Zionism avoided the need to address the complex nature of God's intentions for the Jews by simply eliminating God as an actor in Jewish history. The ethical and poetical beauties of Judaism could be acknowledged, but God himself was dead. The biblical narratives were "historicized" and mined as a record of the early history of the Jewish people.[70]

---

are the first of a new nation." Berdichevsky, *Wrecking and Building* (1900), quoted in Goldberg, *The Divided Self*, 95, 106; see also Rose, *The Question of Zion*, 70–83.

65. Berdichevsky offered this thumbnail sketch of the Jewish dilemma: "Some leave the House of Israel to venture among foreign peoples, devoting to them the service of their hearts and offering their strength to strangers; while at the other extreme, the pious sit in their gloomy caverns." Quoted in Goldberg, *The Divided Self*, 94–95. The question of being a nation versus being a religion "reflects an eternal source of conflict in Jewish public discourse." Segev, *One Palestine*, 47. The debate could only occur in times when Jews had choices, such as after Emancipation.

66. Herzl particularly admired the Prussian Chancellor Bismarck's galvanizing of the German people into a potent military power. Piterberg, *The Returns of Zionism*, 32.

67. Kovel sees the ethnic nationalism of both anti-Semites and Zionists as expressions of "efforts to relocate a communal self" in a world of crumbling social structures. Kovel, *Overcoming Zionism*, 43.

68. "Since nationalism was then considered the cure-all for political ills, it was inevitable that somebody would propose it as the answer to the Jewish problem." Fromkin, *A Peace to End All Peace*, 272.

69. "The issue of normalcy most divides the Israeli right from the left. The left longs for normalcy and wants Jews to be a nation like all other nations. The entire Israeli right, on the other hand, is united in its resentment of the idea of normalcy and its belief, along the lines of the Jewish religion, that Jews are exceptional . . ." Shahak and Mezvinsky, *Jewish Fundamentalism*, 12.

70. Masalha, *The Bible and Zionism*, 16, 25–26. David Ben-Gurion is quoted as saying, "It is not important whether the [biblical] story is a true record of an event or not. What is important is that this is what the Jews believed as far back as the period of

Zionism and the Scriptures

For atheists like David Ben-Gurion, "God" was merely a concept that primitive people used to make claims on each other and to justify aggression against other peoples. This is completely contrary to the message of the Bible, which teaches "the praiseworthy deeds of the LORD," so that the people "would put their trust in God and would not forget his deeds but would keep his commands. They would not be like their forefathers—a stubborn and rebellious generation" (Ps 78:4, 7–8).[71] For Zionists, the exceptionalism of the Jewish people was located within their own nature as a culture, not as a matter of the grace and action of God in continually renewing his covenant with them.

Instead of bringing the Jewish people into right relationship with God, Zionism offered to make them masters of their own destiny. The Zionists in effect would rescue the Jews from their failed God (who, in the Zionists' dark view of the Diaspora, had left them scorned and oppressed)[72] as well as from Gentile political domination. The community of people that had formed around the old faith was to be liberated and remade as its own ultimate good, demanding the unbounded devotion once given to God and God's Law. As the frankly atheist Ben-Gurion put it, "The Jews can be considered a self-chosen people."[73] An abstract ideal of the people's "peoplehood" was enthroned in God's place. Implicit in this idea was rejection of the actual Jewish people in the Diaspora, which helps

---

the First Temple." So, even though the conquest narrative of Joshua may be completely mythical, it still served—and serves—as a warrant for ethnic cleansing. Ibid., 35. As Ben-Gurion wrote in his memoir, "Without a messianic, emotional, ideological impulse, without the vision of restoration and redemption, there is no earthly reason why even oppressed and underprivileged Jews . . . should wander off to Israel of all places." Quoted in Rose, *The Question of Zion*, 45, citing David Ben-Gurion, *Israel: A Personal History*, 25–26. It has been noted that Ben Gurion's and other Zionists' pseudo-literal reading of the book of Joshua and other Hebrew Bible texts more closely resembles certain Protestant approaches to the Old Testament than it does any Jewish traditions of exegesis. Piterberg, *The Returns of Zionism*, xvi, 273 (translating Anita Shapira from the Hebrew: "There is similarity between Protestantism and its attitude to the Scriptures, and the attitude to the biblical 'literalness' [*peshat*] of the [Zionist] Jews").

71. "[I]n contradistinction to all other histories of people and nations, in the Bible glorious deeds are not done by the people and or by heroes. The glorious deeds are God's work." Tarazi, *Land and Covenant*, 254–55. Moreover, the Bible is a spiritual teaching tool. The biblical authors were "clearly not interested in any historical events except to show that the kings of Israel and Judah were unfaithful to God's Law." Ibid., 252–53.

72. Gershom Scholem (formerly Gerhard Scholem) described the belief of some Jews in the Diaspora that they "had worshiped a powerless divinity." In Piterberg, *The Returns of Zionism*, 174.

73. Masalha, *The Bible and Zionism*, 17.

explain Zionists' frequent expressions of shame and repugnance regarding diasporic mores and attitudes.[74] New lines were drawn to define "peoplehood correctness," to coin a term. Failure to embrace the goal of national power exposed one as a "self-hating" Jew.

Also discounted were the harsh historical lessons of Jewish nationalism, which had always led to disaster in the past. Helping to dull the Zionists' historical consciousness was the Zeitgeist of the time in which Zionism took root, the frankly imperialist world of the nineteenth and early twentieth centuries, where carving out a secure territory from land occupied by "backward" natives seemed perfectly acceptable.[75] Indeed, Zionism should be seen as just one branch of the vast Romantic project of "Orientalist" appropriation of the culture, the history, and, ultimately, the geography of the East.[76] Ironically, when the Zionist carve-out of Palestine finally materialized in 1948, colonialism had just entered its twilight.

Like the Nations

Zionism, in effect, declared that the Jewish people were "like the nations" and that their greatness was self-made—defying two core precepts of Jewish Scripture. The God of the Bible had long ago anticipated just that attitude. In Deut 8:17–18, 20, God says to Israel about moving into the promised land, "You may say to yourself, 'My power and the strength of my hands have produced this wealth for me.' But remember the LORD your God, for it is he who gives you the ability to produce wealth, and so

---

74. "In their robust rejection of their Diaspora past, the early settlers expressed themselves in language that smacked of self-hatred. . . . An unparalleled historical example of a small, homeless, dispersed people managing to survive for two millennia by means of resilience and adaptability and religious faith wherever fate happened to land them was being dismissed as shameful, embarrassing and unworthy." Goldberg, *Divided Self*, 96. These feelings came out most sharply in response to the Holocaust. For one youth leader in Palestine, Moshe Tabenkin, "rejection of the Diaspora . . . now turned into personal hatred of the Diaspora. I hate it as a man hates a deformity he is ashamed of." Ibid., 135. "Human dust," a phrase coined in the 1930s by a Zionist writer about "the masses of east European Jewry blown hither and thither by the wind," became the "standard label of the *Yishuv* leadership for Holocaust survivors." Ibid., 136.

75. Moreover, an ambitious person like Herzl could believe that "having a successful colonial European-like venture in the East was the ultimate admission into the West," as Piterberg argues in *The Returns of Zionism*, 39.

76. Said, *Orientalism*, 306–7: "Orientalism governs Israeli policy towards the Arabs . . ." What made Zionism unique, however, was the need of its European founders to construct an "oriental" identity for themselves to legitimize not only conquest but complete displacement of the people living in Palestine.

confirms his covenant . . . ." Then he spells out the fatal consequences of such boastful forgetfulness: "Like the nations the LORD destroyed before you, so you will be destroyed for not obeying the LORD your God."[77]

Far from welling up from the mass of Jewish people, the Zionist cause initially attracted only limited interest and scant active support.[78] The vast majority of Jews looking to escape continuing oppression in Russia and Eastern Europe emigrated to the Americas and Western Europe rather than to Palestine. And the vast majority of those emigrants built strong relationships of friendship and solidarity with non-Jews in liberal, modern societies. Indeed, from the ranks of the Jews came secular prophets of universal betterment, such as Karl Marx, Sigmund Freud, Leon Trotsky, and Harold Laski—as well as other contributors to human progress such as Albert Einstein and many of the gifted individuals who made Hollywood. Although eschewing religion, they were a living testament to the profound sense of human solidarity that three thousand years of Jewish culture had generated, despite external hostility and internal clannishness.[79] Among those who did not embrace secularism, various modernizing, reformed understandings and practices of Judaism were elaborated to preserve the philosophical essence of Jewish tradition, seen as an ethic of peace and solidarity, to make it communicable to non-Jews, and to allow Jews to

---

77. Masalha, *The Bible and Zionism*, 28. Masalha refers to an article by Amos Oz describing the triumphalist mood of Zionists in 1967 as captured by a Shaul Tchernichovsky poem, "I Have a Tune," which urged readers to seize the land by their own power, a contradiction in terms of the Deuteronomic precept. Even more succinctly, the Hebrew term *bittahon*, "which originally referred to trust in God, now [in modern Hebrew] denotes military security." Rose, *The Question of Zion*, 42.

78. "The majority of the Jewish people opposed the creation of a Jewish state well into World War II . . . and feared the consequences of a national and political revival." Avraham Burg, *The Holocaust Is Over*, 37. See also Fromkin, *A Peace to End All Peace*, 294: "[O]pposition [to the Balfour Declaration] came from leading figures in the British Jewish community. Edwin Montagu, Secretary of State for India, led the opposition group within the Cabinet. . . . Judaism, he argued, was a religion, not a nationality, and to say otherwise was to say that he was less than 100 percent British. . . . The evidence suggests that in his non-Zionism, Montagu was speaking for a majority of Jews." Segev points out that many Jews living in Palestine, especially the "pre-Zionist population," did not support Zionism. Segev, *One Palestine*, 16–17. More generally, "[political] Zionism had very little appeal to the Jews of the Middle East." Shiblak, *Iraqi Jews*, 17.

79. It might be objected that they were motivated less by sympathy for others than by anxiety of being persecuted themselves, but this precisely proves that their actual experience as the chosen people fitted them beautifully to stand up for all oppressed groups. Scripture long ago made the point: "Do not oppress an alien; you yourselves know how it feels to be aliens, because you were aliens in Egypt" (Exod 23:9).

participate fully in society.[80] Until the Nazi horrors reached their peak, few Reform Jewish leaders supported Zionism.[81]

Still, Zionism proclaimed itself the active response to the twin threats of persecution and assimilation. And it centered upon an essential element of what it had always meant to be Jewish: to be the people to whom God promised the land, where they would flourish. By contrast, the Orthodox seemed to have given up on actually taking God up on his promise and had cut themselves off from fully engaging with the world; Reform Jews, in this view, had jumped to a vacuous sort of Judaism that seemed to ignore the intense particularity of God's promise and relationship to the Jews.[82]

Thus, despite their original atheism, the Zionists pumped new blood into the promise by which Jews lived. Where the rabbis seemed to have deferred the promise of the promised land into little more than a ritual invocation, and the reformed and secular Jews did not know what to do with it,[83] these new men and women put their faith into action to move into the land, radically actualizing the promise. Along with the trauma and profound disruption of the Holocaust (which converted even staunch

---

80. "The Reform movement sought to present Judaism as the religion most exclusively concerned with morality." Meyer, *The End of Judaism*, 67, 72. Burg quotes a leading American Reform voice, Rabbi Julian Morgenstern, writing in 1941: "The undeniable lesson of Jewish history . . . teaches that Israel's ability and destination are expressed only by religion and only by Israel's role as carrier of the religious spiritual legacy." Burg, *The Holocaust is Over*, 38, citing Schiff, *Assimilation in Pride*. Burg adds, 36, "In his early work, Morgenstern viewed Zionism as an ideology of identity by negation. The Zionist reaction to assimilation, including the retreat to the Middle East, seemed to him an admission of defeat and acceptance of anti-Semitic values. Zionism was escaping Judeophobia instead of repairing Judeophobic societies. . . . It was treason and dereliction of duty, in violation of the universal tenets of Jewish values of identity and inclusion." See also Goldberg, *Divided Self*, 82–89.

81. The bitter struggle of American Reform rabbis against the high-pressure campaign of Zionists to transform Jews into a political nation is chronicled by Kolsky in *Jews Against Zionism* and by Ross in *Rabbi Outcast*.

82. "When Reform rabbis took control of our national feasts a hundred years ago and let them vanish into a religion that no one believed in any longer, they did not in fact succeed in dissolving the Jewish people into a 'Mosaic confession.' But they did achieve one thing: they destroyed the legends of its founding." Arendt, 149 (writing in 1942). As for traditional rabbis, Arendt charged them with seeking "for generations to bury a living people under the monument of exact philology and dead history." *The Jewish Writings*, 32.

83. Some in the Reform movement "went so far as to systematically remove all references to the Holy Land and Jerusalem from their liturgy." *Zionism and the Creation of Israel*, www.mideastweb.org/Zionism.htm; accessed on Feb 23, 2012.

non-Zionists such as Morgenstern),[84] the gravitational pull of nostalgia for the promised land explains why, over time, so many Orthodox, Reform, and secular Jews succumbed to Zionism and the radical notion of a Jewish state.[85]

The seemingly modest Zionist goal of a land that Jews can call their own has lacked the spiritual connection to the "Other," that is, to the peoples and the nations in God's original promise to Abraham. Israel and its supporters, like the Zealots before them, have drastically reduced the promise, overlooking its universalist and spiritual aspects and giving importance only to the political destiny of one people in isolation. Thus the tragedy of Zionism: a utopian liberation movement that did not seek domination or war finds itself mired in an endless war of domination that is steadily taking on more overtones of a religious *Götterdämmerung*.[86]

Religious tribalism, meanwhile, has been called upon to compensate for Zionism's defects as a secular, humanist project. This is ironic, since the aim of the first Zionists was to free the Jewish people as much from the dominance of inward-looking Jewish religion as from the dominance of Gentiles. It did not turn out that way. As Piterberg points out, the typical path of "Central European nominal Jews" was "not from Judaism to Zionism but the other way around." They were "completely alienated from Judaism and knew very little about it."[87] Now, however, the secular Zionist movement, which at its inception was imbued with zeal and called forth extraordinary idealism, courage, sacrifice, and creativity—along with ruthless expulsion of the indigenous Palestinians—is allied to reactionary religion (settler fundamentalists and apocalyptic Christian Zionists) and dependent on reactionary non-Jews.[88]

---

84. Burg, *The Holocaust is Over*, 38. For Morgenstern, see note 80.

85. See Piterberg, *The Returns of Zionism*, 114, quoting the title of an essay by Amnon Raz-Krakotzkin: "There is No God But He Promised Us the Land."

86. The utopian aspect of Zionism is most apparent in Herzl's novel, *Altneuland*. Concluding in the near future, it shows a paradisical, just-established Jewish Zionist state in Palestine largely emptied of its indigenous population. Piterberg classifies the Zionist project as an example, among others, of "utopian colonialism"; *The Returns of Zionism*, 36–42.

87. Piterberg, *The Returns of Zionism*, 82.

88. Masalha, *The Bible and Zionism*, 135–64, describes the post-1967 transition from secularism to messianism among a growing number of Israelis. Just as secular Zionists made use of religious tradition, religious Jews found ways to make use of secular Zionism. One of the first rabbis to support Zionism was Rabbi Abraham Kook, who in 1920 became the first Ashkenazi chief rabbi of Palestine. He believed that even atheist Jews could be unwitting agents of the Jewish messianic "in-gathering" and redemption

A Wilderness of Hatred

Looking back, one sees that the Zionist path to the promised land has led the Jews not into a homeland in which their union with God will come into redemptive flower, but into a wilderness of hatred and violence. From the beginning, the difficulty of establishing the State of Israel amid the growing hostility of the Arabs bred cynicism and contradiction. Most glaring is the fact that this Jewish declaration of liberation and autonomy has from the beginning depended heavily on the support of Gentiles, from Lord Balfour to Harry Truman to George W. Bush. In making its case to these outsiders, moreover, it has offered its sponsors arguments based on Western imperialism, Western guilt, Western contempt and fear of Arab and Muslim cultures, and, most recently, Western (mostly American Christian) apocalyptic fantasies.

Zionism has even traded on anti-Semitism itself. A major reason for Gentile support in the early years was to eliminate or attenuate an imagined, pervasive, conspiratorial Jewish influence in the West—a motive that political Zionism's founder, Theodor Herzl, applauded.[89] From their earliest ventures into diplomacy in the 1890s, Zionists willingly received

---

when they promoted Jewish nationalism: "A Jewish nationalist, no matter how secularist his intention may be, is, despite himself, imbued with the divine spirit even against his own will," Kook wrote. He even implied that the dirty work of nation-building needed irreligious Jews, "when statehood requires bloody ruthlessness and demands a talent for evil." Quoted in Goldberg, *To the Promised Land,* 154–56. Kook died in the 1930s, before Jewish statism produced ethnic cleansing and militarism, and before the 1967 capture of the holy sites of East Jerusalem and the West Bank generated a wave of support for the religious Zionism of his son Zvi Yehuda Kook's National Religious Party.

89. In his diary, Herzl wrote, "The antisemites will become our most loyal friends, the antisemitic nations will become our allies." Quoted in Segev, *One Palestine,* 47. Herzl and his close collaborator, Max Nordau, openly argued that "the Jews constitute a foreign, destructive element for the countries in which they live" (quoted in Rabkin, *A Threat From Within,* 174, citing a leading Jewish anti-Zionist source, Ruth Blau, *Les gardiens de la cité: histoire d'une guerre sainte*). The idea was not new. In the early 1800s, the German philosopher Johann Gottlieb Fichte, a seminal theorist of nationalism, said, "To protect ourselves [Germans] from them [Jews], there is no other means but to conquer their promised land and banish all Jews there." Quoted in Elon, *The Pity of It All,* 99. "Historically, Zionism is both a reaction to antisemitism and a conservative alliance with it." Shahak, *Jewish History,* 69. Herzl allied himself with Tsar Nicholas II's notorious anti-Semitic minister, Count von Plehve, who organized pogroms. They both wanted to remove Jews from Russia and to oppose the Socialist movement. Dr. Joachim Prinz, a Zionist rabbi (and later chairman of the Conference of Presidents of Major Jewish Organizations), published a book, *We Jews,* warmly welcoming the Nazis' ascent to power. Ibid., 71; Ross, *Rabbi Outcast,* 141.

support from leaders who saw Zionism as a way to placate powerful Jewish forces and export "the Jewish problem."[90]

Totally focused on its own immediate survival in a sea of despised and hostile Arabs, the State of Israel has embraced geopolitical cynicism, allying itself with despots such as the Shah of Iran and Idi Amin Dada, and despotic countries such as Apartheid South Africa, and Argentina under the Junta. The policy of "cruel Zionism," in Ben Gurion's phrase, which included provocateur bomb attacks against Jewish lives and properties, forced Arab Jews to cast their lot with Israel.[91] Shrinking from no policy that might undermine Palestinian resistance, it even helped to promote the rise of Hamas in the 1970s and '80s as a counter to Yassir Arafat's then-dominant Fatah Party.[92] Moreover, in working with "dispensationalist" Christian Zionists, who wish to help Israel to triumph so as to hasten the advent of an apocalypse that would feature the destruction or conversion to Christianity of the Jewish people, Israel has shown how desperate it is for allies.[93]

Israel's brittle defense against criticism is to flaunt the world's anger against it, label it irrational, unconscious, incurable anti-Semitism, and put its critics on the defensive. Rather than ponder why so many people are angry with it, Israel has come to justify its own brutal policies by dwelling on the darkness of others: the cruelty and brutality of medieval Christians, the Nazi regime, and the most violent Islamist extremists. Israel is thus

90. For example, Arthur James Balfour, the British foreign secretary who authored the 1917 declaration of support for a "Jewish national home," also sponsored legislation to curb Jewish immigration into Britain. Segev, *One Palestine*, 38–41. The British leaders who supported Balfour's declaration were "in many ways anti-Semitic. They believed the Jews controlled the world." Ibid., 33. See also Fromkin, *A Peace to End All Peace*, 42–43, 197, 466.

91. Shiblak, *Iraqi Jews*, 24–25, 151–52, 159. These events, which in Iraq, for example, fostered a mass exodus of Iraqi Jews to an Israel eager to boost its Jewish population, were the culmination of a ten-year process of growing antagonism between Iraqi Jews and non-Jewish Iraqis that fed on resentment against the British colonial power that also sponsored Zionism in Palestine (ibid., 73–74) *and* against communism in the wake of the sudden Soviet endorsement of the State of Israel in 1948 (even though Jewish communists were staunch anti-Zionists); ibid., 84–85. In 1949–51, extremist nationalists vying for power scapegoated indigenous Jews to justify the Iraqi military defeat by Zionist forces, to polarize their people, and to despoil wealthy Jews. For the Israelis, the spectacle of Arab-Jewish refugees helped to whip up anti-Arab feeling in the West and undercut sympathy for Palestinian refugees; ibid., 99–102.

92. Masalha, *The Bible and Zionism*, 219; Ateek, *A Palestinian Christian Cry*, 7–8.

93. See Stephen Sizer, *Christian Zionism*. See also Mark Braverman, *Fatal Embrace*, which describes how post-Holocaust guilt has caused mainline Christian churches to fail to challenge Israel's oppressive treatment of the Palestinians.

invested in the evil-doing of non-Jews, morally enthralled by the terrorist violence and injustice of its enemies, past, present, and future.[94]

SHARING THE PROMISE

Thus the hope of freedom and renewal that gave birth to Israel has darkened into fanaticism and cynicism that are not tenable.[95] The situation is moving steadily closer to the kind of scene of judgment that the great prophets of Ancient Israel described. As Walter Brueggemann has written concerning the iniquities and arrogance that brought low the kingdoms of Israel and Judah, "The very promised land that promised to create a space for human joy and freedom became the very source of dehumanizing exploitation and oppression.... Time after time, Israel saw the land of promise become the land of problem."[96]

Yet the problem holds paradoxical promise. Brueggemann notes that it was against the backdrop of the exile to Babylon, Israel's lowest point, "without land or even prospect of land," that Israel's "most remarkable expression of faith" emerged—including, for example, the creation account of Genesis 1, many of the Psalms, the tender lyricism of Second Isaiah, and Ezekiel's vision of a restored Israel. The crisis of losing the land was liberating on the moral and spiritual planes. In raising their eyes away from their

---

94. Herzl famously said, "The enemy forces us, without any willful act from our side, to become one people." Quoted in Meyer, *The End of Judaism*, 72; Goldberg, *Divided Self*, 86. Arendt, writing in 1935, remarks, "When, almost two years ago, the German Jewish community, in its entirety, had to respond to the isolation imposed by the [Nazi] laws of exception, and the material and moral ruin of its collective existence, all Jews, whether they liked or not, had to become aware of themselves *as Jews*." Arendt, *The Jewish Writings*, 31. She was, however, always alert to the historical temptation of Jewish leaders to trade on the enmity of others so as to reinforce a merely negative Jewish unity. Thus, in 1944, she excoriates Herzl's dictum that "a nation is a group of people . . . held together by a common enemy." Such thinking created "an utter confusion in which nobody could distinguish between friend and foe, in which the foe became the friend, and the friend the hidden, and therefore all the more dangerous, enemy." Ibid., 359.

95. Copious documentation is available on Israel's long and ongoing history of systematic brutality toward the Palestinians. See, e.g., Kovel, *Overcoming Zionism*; Ilan Pappé, *The Ethnic Cleansing of Palestine*.

96. Brueggemann, *The Land*, 10. Rabbi David J. Goldberg has quipped, "It could be said that 'the Israeli problem' has replaced 'the Jewish problem' as a neurosis in search of a cure." Goldberg, *Divided Self*, 197.

wrecked former dominion and toward God, these prophets saw God's plan for Israel in the light of peace and fulfillment for all humankind.[97]

In contrast, many Jews today in their concern for Israel have shelved that vision and put themselves on a slippery slope to moral degradation and political disaster. Those who still proclaim a universal mission for the Jews are hardliners who pursue brutal external and internal policies that bring darkness to the world, not light. Privileged agents of a wrathful God, they are plunged in spiritual darkness that obscures the humanity of the Palestinians, and their own humanity as well. Yet the great majority of Jews are not bloody-minded fanatics or heartless cynics. If they would heed their forebears, who fought against zealots themselves, they would recognize their opportunity to carry affirmatively the light of the prophets into our world, not just in words and private actions, but via the medium of the promised land.

In the history of great injustices, none may have ever emerged from a more heart-rending historical predicament or involved so many self-sacrificing, idealistic individuals, as they wrestled with prejudice, persecution, and identity issues.[98] Nonetheless, the very effort of Zionists to make the Jews like the nations is proving that they never have been, nor can they ever be, like the nations. With its militaristic oppression of the Palestinians, the State of Israel is threatening to harden the heart of the Jewish people. By the same token, however, it is challenging Jews to rethink their situation and reconnect with their history. The very magnitude of the spiritual danger may generate a correspondingly profound change of

---

97. Brueggemann, *The Land*, 8.

98. The late nineteenth-century recrudescence of anti-Jewish prejudice was a wake-up call to many Jews who had assumed their integration into the larger society but came to feel that some sort of Jewish national movement was called for. An early example was Leo Pinsker, who responded to the return of pogroms in Russia after the 1881 assassination of Czar Alexander II by authoring *Auto-Emancipation: A Warning to His People by a Russian Jew*. Goldberg, *To the Promised Land*, 20–29. Even before Herzl recognized the significance of the Dreyfus Affair in France, Bernard Lazare, a socialist, flagged the case and the larger phenomenon of a new, invisible "ghetto" forming in the minds of many non-Jewish Europeans, and he explored the idea of a Jewish return to Palestine. Piterberg, *The Returns of Zionism*, 6–7, 9–10. Hannah Arendt credited Zionism with helping her to understand her own political identity as a Jew, and she worked for Zionism in the 1930s, although, like Lazare, she turned against mainstream, Herzlian Zionism. Arendt, *The Jewish Writings*, lii–lv, 383. Justice Louis Brandeis and Albert Einstein were two more early supporters of Zionism, although Brandeis broke with Ben-Gurion, and Einstein became a severe critic as its harsh ethnocentricity was manifested.

heart, opening the Jewish people to hear with fresh ears God's command that they be "a kingdom of priests and a holy nation" (Exod 19:6).

When Prime Minister Golda Meir told the philosopher Hannah Arendt that she believed not in God but in the Jewish people, Arendt, although herself an atheist, responded that the greatness of the Jewish people was that it believed in God.[99] Arendt thus prophesied the necessity of recourse to faith in God in order to preserve her people.

The distortion of God's promise of land into a mere title deed to a physical territory is replicated in a parallel distortion that turns a faith community with a highly diverse political, cultural, and geographic history into a mere genealogical group untethered from the beliefs, traditions, and history of the forebears, which become little more than artifacts of a shared past.[100] The primacy given to genealogical identity produces a mirror image of racial anti-Semitism, which does not concern itself with the values, beliefs, or actions of its targets, but only seeks to identify physical human beings for persecution. Likewise, Zionism privileges some individuals merely for their genealogical origins as Jews to command their allegiance and to dispossess others of property and basic rights.

---

99. Segev, *The Seventh Million*, 358, citing Elisabeth Young-Bruehl, *Hannah Arendt*, 332. More precisely, Israel was the people that followed God's Law. Tarazi observes, "[I]t was the law granted it in the wilderness of Sinai that brought Israel into existence and maintained it . . ." Tarazi, *Land and Covenant*, 256. Ancient Israel, like a flock of sheep, only came into existence as a people by virtue of its relationship to its "shepherd," YHWH. "Then they will know that I, the LORD their God, am with them and that they, the house of Israel, are my people, declares the Sovereign LORD. You [are] my sheep, the sheep of my pasture . . . and I am your God, declares the Sovereign LORD" (Ezek 34:30–31). The image is exact: "[W]hoever has witnessed the activity of shepherds in the Near East will have noticed . . . the flock is not an agglomeration of sheep, but rather the creation of the shepherd. Without him the sheep would scatter and ultimately perish. . . . there is a flock only where there is a shepherd who walks ahead of the sheep that recognize the sounds emitted by him and thus follow his voice." Tarazi, 257.

100. Thus Arendt charges that the Zionist understanding of Jewish identity "is nothing less than the uncritical acceptance of German-inspired nationalism. This holds a nation to be an eternal organic body, the product of inevitable natural growth of inherent qualities; and it explains peoples, not in terms of political organizations, but in terms of biological superhuman personalities." Arendt, *The Jewish Writings*, 366–67. See also Masalha, *The Bible and Zionism*, 25–27.

Zionism and the Scriptures

Back to the Garden

Only a vision that draws on the profound spiritual resources of the Jewish faith, tradition, and history can summon the energy necessary to undo decades of violence to others and to self and to shift the energy of Zionism in a positive direction. Jews have always had the mission to "seek peace and pursue it" (Ps 34:14). Judaism is the original religion of peace. "The law will go out from Zion.... Nation will not take up sword against nation, nor will they train for war anymore" (Isa 2:3–4). The people of Israel were the first to understand their God as putting justice, compassion, forgiveness, and neighborliness at the heart of religious obligation, and faith in God at the heart of their life.

So the true existential challenge is a matter of the heart. The most basic test that Jews have faced through the ages has been to remain faithful to the Jewish ethos, even at the risk of hardship and violence. The danger today is not external persecution but internal abasement. The test is to remain loyal to the Jewish way of peace in the face of powerful pressures to dehumanize and crush the Palestinians. Moving to a posture of peace and mutual forgiveness with the Palestinians is to become vulnerable to hardship, betrayal, and potential violence. But this is the cost of fidelity to the Jewish way—and the alternative looks at least as dangerous.[101] Zionism has *de facto* returned the Jews to their primordial existential situation, where they are masters of their garden, but to live in it they must submit to God's law of love. The extraordinary fact is that only because of the passionate mistakes of Zionism are the Jews in a position to fulfill God's promise, to take an unprecedented step toward peace on earth: they again occupy the land of Israel and thus have the power to possess it in the generous, compassionate way that God has always wanted—to make it the promised land. The alternative is to possess a cursed land.

The reverse alchemy of Zionism's attempt to debase the gold of Judaism into just another leaden ethnic nationalism has revealed the radiance of God's original plan for his people and has put the true promised land within reach. In finding a path beyond Zionism, Jews would be blazing a trail away from nationalism and war that all humankind could follow. Acting as healers and intercessors for the whole family of those made in the image of God, the Jews would really be a "kingdom of priests" (Exod 19:6), Israel a "holy nation" (Exod 19:6), and Abraham's name "a blessing" to "all peoples" (Gen 12:2–3).

101. There are many Israelis and Palestinians who have overcome deep wounds of grief and have joined together in deep, life-giving communion. See note 13.

The situation in Israel-Palestine today is apocalyptic in the etymological sense of being revelation-forcing—and thus choice-forcing. It offers Jews and their friends a stark choice—"a blessing" or "a curse" (Deut 11:26–28)—with no split-the-difference middle way. They must decide if their destiny is to follow the light of brotherhood and sisterhood or to dwell in the darkness of alienation and war. In ages past, when Jews wielded little direct power, there were few external consequences to avoiding that fundamental choice. A Jew could have leanings one way or the other but accept that both interpretations of God's will were woven deeply into Scripture and the tradition. Now, with Israel a sovereign state facing urgent, existential crises, the choice is inescapable. To paraphrase Ben-Gurion, there is "no earthly reason" for Jews simply to hang on in Israel; those who remain will have to choose either endless holy war, or holy, transformative peace.[102]

Saving the Nations

It is time for something new from the chosen people, something beyond Zionism, something bigger that transforms Zionism and that is a return to God. As the Psalmist sang, "Too long have I lived among those who hate peace. I am a man of peace; but when I speak, they are for war" (Ps 120:6–7).

The three fundamental impulses underlying Zionism are "the negation of exile, the return to the land of Israel, and the return to history."[103] But the prescription was too simplistic. Exile is in a sense the beginning of the Jewish story (recall the expulsion from Eden and the call to Abram), the beginning of their history (recall Egyptian slavery, the exodus, and the wilderness wandering), and the historical condition in which they have worked out their resilient identity. Exile "is not *one* of the foundations of Jewish existence—it is the central foundation of its definition."[104] The age-old "yearning for the promised land of Israel . . . was neither expressed in colonial terms of ownership, nor was it accompanied by a nostalgic evocation of an ancient past."[105] If that is the case, then the emancipation of the Jews in the eighteenth and nineteenth centuries presented an existential threat to the Jewish people. It undercut the legal manifestation

---

102. See note 70, above.
103. Piterberg, *The Returns of Zionism*, xiii.
104. Ibid., 117, quoting Amnon Raz-Krakotzkin, *Exile within Sovereignty*.
105. Ibid.; see also 107: "Judaism is an exilic phenomenon."

Zionism and the Scriptures

of the exile. In the new environment, traditionalist Orthodoxy, Reform Judaism, and individual assimilation all failed to embody the full reality of the Jewish experience. Zionism attempted to fill that emptiness, but its gross simplification of Jewish identity—chasing after the idol of nationalism, engendering a violent conflict with the Arab people, and flouting international law—has inflamed the Jewish identity crisis.

What is needed is a way to reconnect with the spirituality of exile, which expressed devotion to a higher purpose than mere prosperity, power, and pleasure. A line of Jewish thinkers has probed in this direction under the concept of "the conscious pariah," the individual or group that purposely identifies with the pariahs (the outcasts and downtrodden) of society.[106] Karl Marx, Sigmund Freud, Franz Kafka, to name a few, might be seen as having pursued forms of this spiritual path, which also has clear affinities with core aspects of Christian thinking, manifested in such schools of thought as the Social Gospel, Liberation Theology, or the concept of the Christian as merely a sojourner in this world. For Israelis and their supporters, however, there is a very down-to-earth opening to such a path: that is, to connect with the exilic, pariah reality of the Palestinians.

If this "kingdom of priests" (Exod 19:6) is to find wholeness and bring blessings to all humankind, it must begin by seeking God's blessing. It must, as God instructs, love the "peoples," starting with the Palestinians. God "defends the cause of the fatherless and the widow, and loves the alien, giving him food and clothing. And you are to love those who are aliens, for you yourselves were aliens in Egypt" (Deut 10:18–19).

How far might God go in leading Israel to truly reconnect with its history as a God-driven people by showing love to the alien? Listen to Ezekiel (47:22–23) giving instructions regarding the land:

> "You are to allot it as an inheritance for yourselves and for the aliens who have settled among you and who have children. You are to consider them as native-born Israelites; along with you they are to be allotted an inheritance among the tribes of Israel.

---

106. Piterberg sets up a dichotomy: "The Sovereign Settler versus the Conscious Pariah: Theodor Herzl and Bernard Lazare"; *The Returns of Zionism*, 1–51. Following Lazare, Kurt Blumenfeld and Hannah Arendt developed the conscious-pariah concept further. See Arendt, *The Jew as Pariah*, ed. Feldman. Yet all three thinkers had been drawn to aspects of Zionism; all three believed the Jewish people possessed a collective political identity that should be exercised for the betterment of humankind. See also Kovel, *Overcoming Zionism*, 42, noting many distinguished Jews "who variously contributed to civilization by accepting Jewish marginality as a creative challenge rather than trying to abolish it through nation-building."

In whatever tribe the alien settles, there you are to give him his inheritance," declares the Sovereign LORD.

This is a prophecy of full equality and fraternity with Palestinians, seen not as compromise or condescension by the Jews, but as God's will, God's program for bringing his people to fulfillment—and thus to becoming a blessing to the peoples.[107]

Ezekiel's God explains the Promise in words that demand that his people seek peace:

> I will show the holiness of my great name, which has been profaned among the nations, the name you have profaned among them. Then the nations will know that I am the LORD, declares the Sovereign LORD, when I show myself holy through you before their eyes. For I will take you out of the nations; I will gather you from all the countries and bring you back into your own land. . . . I will cleanse you from all your impurities and from all your idols. I will give you a new heart and put a new spirit in you; I will remove from you your heart of stone and give you a heart of flesh. (Ezek 36:23–26)

The Israelis and their brother and sister Jews around the world are living out the story of their holy book. The whole world is in a sense reading it with them. The themes and values, hopes and pathos of ancient Israel permeate humankind's consciousness through the humanism born of Judeo-Christian ethics and spirituality. In a multicultural, deracinated world, all humankind is focused on the drama of identity and otherness, belonging and exile, that is the very core of the story of God's chosen people. Intently watching the drama of Israel and Palestine, the world wonders what it has to do with God.

The Jews' land story acknowledges that people need "land" in the sense of a special place, a connection to creation, an identity. Beyond that, however, their tradition and history show that "land" must be received and experienced and shared—like life itself—as God's gift, or it becomes God's curse.[108] The constant temptation of any person or group that has come to believe that God cares about them and desires to guide them is to fall

---

107. See also Lev 19:34: "The alien living with you must be treated as one of your native-born. Love him as yourself, for you were aliens in Egypt." Throughout the Old Testament there is a repeated refrain that the proud rulers of Israel and Judah should see themselves as like the people in their midst who are strangers and foreigners; they should identify with them. The strangers are brothers. The foreigners must be made to feel at home.

108. As Brueggemann says, *The Land*, 54: "Yahweh is the Lord of *gifted existence*,

into perfectionism and/or triumphalism, the two sides of the same coin of doubting or trying to manipulate God's love. They are the two aspects of age-old human attempts to usurp God's authority on the vertical axis of holiness and the horizontal axis of community. The genius of Moses and the prophets—the tradition that fostered the stories of Job and of Isaiah's "suffering servant"—has been to understand that it is loving kindness that causes God to stoop to care about the hearts of men and women (by giving them intelligence and free will) and that loving God means mirroring his humility and his giving without recompense.

Put another way, as long as there is not justice in the land, the people of Israel have not actually taken possession of the promised land. There exists a spiritual barrier to true possession of the land that is just as effective as were the cherubim and the "flaming . . . flashing" sword that kept Adam out of the Garden of Eden after the Fall (Gen 3:24), or the vast wilderness of Sinai, or the swords of Babylon and Rome, that kept Israel out of the promised land. The barrier today is the human reality of the people of Palestine. As long as Palestinians are oppressed, the people of Israel do not truly possess the land (see Deut 16:20); they merely cling to a soul-destroying idol that turns the Zionist impulse toward liberation into a new form of tribal ghettoization.[109]

In some fashion, then, it must be Israel's mission to possess the promised land to the benefit of all humankind, by sharing it with the Palestinians. In doing so, they can invoke King David himself, who said to God: "But who am I, and who are my people, that we should be able to give as generously as this? Everything comes from you, and we have given you only what comes from your hand. We are aliens and strangers in your sight, as were all our forefathers" (1 Chr 29:14–15).

---

taken freely and without merit. And the way to sustain gifted existence is to stay singularly with the gift-giver."

109. See Buber, *On Zion*, 49: "Only in the realm of perfect faith is it the land of these people." The concept of possession is itself perhaps problematic: "In ruling in a dispute between two people who claimed ownership of a tract of land, Rabbi Ezekiel Landau [of Prague, 1713–1793] is reputed to have put his ear to the ground and then to have announced, 'The earth has rendered its decision: I belong to neither of you, but both of you belong to me.'" Quoted in Philadelphia Jews for a Just Peace, *Thou Shalt Not Stand Idly By*, 12. In the same vein, Abuna Elias Chacour, now the Melkite Archbishop of Galilee, titled a book about the people of Palestine, *We Belong to the Land*. The same dichotomy may be said to pertain to God, whom some perceive as belonging to them, while others feel they belong to God. This shows, yet once more, how the promised land functions to test and search out the hearts of the followers of the God of Israel.

This language is in tune with Lazare's and Arendt's secular concept of a collective "conscious pariah" that identifies with the "Other."[110] In stark contrast to the autonomous, self-absorbed attitude of Romantic nationalism that has imbued the mainstream of Zionist thinking,[111] the exilic pariah attitude conveys the idea that godly identity is a product of relationship and mutual discovery within an environment in which each person and each people is accorded respect.

The Jews of Israel and the world need to embrace the whole package: really to believe that they are chosen and really to believe that they are chosen to help God restore the brotherhood and sisterhood of humanity, "chosen to overcome chosen-ness," as Kovel puts it;[112] or, to quote Buber, to create "a particular Jewish type of society which has a special importance for the development of a real humanity."[113] Then, God's vision for Israel and humanity shall be made manifest in our time:

> It is too small a thing for you to be my servant to restore the tribes of Jacob and bring back those of Israel I have kept. I will also make you a light for the Gentiles, that you may bring my salvation to the ends of the earth (Isa 49:6).

BIBLIOGRAPHY

All quotations from the Bible are drawn from the New International Version.

Literature

Arendt, Hannah. *The Jew as Pariah: Jewish Identity and Politics in the Modern Age.* Edited by Ron H. Feldman. New York: Grove/Atlantic, 1978.

---

110. See note 106.
111. See Piterberg, *The Returns of Zionism*, 139, 143.
112. Kovel, *Overcoming Zionism*, 22.
113. Buber, *On Zion*, 137. The modern Jewish community does not lack for thinkers and leaders who, while speaking in a more universal idiom of human rights, have picked up the anti-nationalist mantle of Buber, for example, Uri Avnery, Anna Baltzer, Mark Braverman, Avraham Burg, Noam Chomsky, Marc Ellis, Norman Finkelstein, Jeff Halper, Amira Hass, Adina Hoffman, Michael Lerner, Sara Roy, Alice Rothschild, and Brian Walt. Working within the Palestinian community are many equally enlightened individuals, such as Ali Abunimah, Naim Ateek, Mubarak Awad, Omar Barghouti, Elias Chacour, Mitri Raheb, Michel Sabbah.

———. *The Jewish Writings*. Edited by Jerome Kohn and Ron H. Feldman. New York: Schocken, 2007.
Ateek, Naim Stifan. *A Palestinian Christian Cry for Reconciliation*. Foreword by Archbishop Desmond Tutu. Maryknoll, NY: Orbis, 2008.
Benamozegh, Elijah. *Israel and Humanity*. New York: Paulist, 1995.
Ben-Gurion, David. *Israel: A Personal History*. London: New English Library, 1972.
Bensoussan, Georges. *Une histoire intellectuelle et politique du sionisme*. Paris: Fayard, 2002.
Biale, David. *Power and Powerlessness in Jewish History*. New York: Schocken, 1986.
Borg, Marcus J., and John Dominic Crossan. *The First Christmas: What the Gospels Really Teach About Jesus's Birth*. New York: Harper Collins, 2007.
———. *The Last Week: What the Gospels Really Teach About Jesus's Final Days in Jerusalem*. New York: Harper Collins, 2006.
Braverman, Mark. *Fatal Embrace: Christians, Jews, and the Search for Peace in the Holy Land*. Austin, TX: Synergy, 2010.
Brueggemann, Walter. *The Land: Place as Gift, Promise, and Challenge in Biblical Faith*. Minneapolis: Fortress, 2002.
Buber, Martin. *On Zion*. Syracuse, NY: Syracuse University Press, 1973.
Burg, Avraham. *The Holocaust Is Over: We Must Rise From Its Ashes*. New York: Palgrave Macmillan, 2008.
Chacour, Elias. *We Belong to the Land*. Notre Dame, IN: University of Notre Dame Press, 2001.
The Declaration of the Establishment of the State of Israel. At http://www.jewishvirtuallibrary.org/jsource/History/Dec_of_Indep.html. Accessed on Mar 13, 2012.
Elon, Amos. *The Pity of It All: A Portrait of the German-Jewish Epoch, 1743–1933*. New York: Holt, 2002.
Fromkin, David. *A Peace to End All Peace: The Fall of the Ottoman Empire and the Creation of the Modern Middle East*. New York: Holt, 2001.
Goldberg, David J. *The Divided Self: Israel and the Jewish Psyche Today*. London: Tauris, 2006.
———. *To the Promised Land: A History of Zionist Thought*. London: Penguin, 1996.
Herzl, Theodor. *The Jewish State*. New York: Dover, 1988.
Holy Bible. New International Version. Grand Rapids: Zondervan, 1989.
Horsley, Richard. *In the Shadow of Empire: Reclaiming the Bible as a History of Faithful Resistance*. Louisville and London: Westminster John Knox, 2008.
Howard-Brook, Wes. *Come Out My People*. Maryknoll, NY: Orbis, 2010.
Klinghoffer, David. *Why the Jews Rejected Jesus*. New York: Doubleday, 2005.
Kolsky, Thomas A. *Jews Against Zionism: The American Council for Judaism, 1942–1948*. Philadelphia: Temple University Press, 1990.
Kopelowitz, Ezra, editor. *Jewish Peoplehood: Change and Challenge*. Brighton, MA: Academic Studies Press, 2008.
Kovel, Joel. *Overcoming Zionism*. Ann Arbor, MI: Pluto, 2007.
Landau, Susan J. *Thou Shalt Not Stand Idly By: Reclaiming Jewish Voices of Conscience on Israel-Palestine*. Philadelphia: Philadelphia Jews for a Just Peace, 2008.
Masalha, Nur. *The Bible and Zionism*. New York: Zed, 2007.
Mendenhall, George E. *Ancient Israel's Faith and History: An Introduction to the Bible in Context*. Edited by Gary A. Herion. Louisville: Westminster John Knox, 2001.

Mendes Flohr, Paul, editor. *A Land of Two Peoples: Martin Buber on Jews and Arabs.* Chicago: University of Chicago Press, 1983.
Meyer, Hajo G. *The End of Judaism: An Ethical Tradition Betrayed.* n/l.: G. Meyer Books, 2007. http://wwwgmeyerbooks.com.
Nusseibeh, Sari. *Once Upon a Country: A Palestinian Life.* New York: Farrar, Straus and Giroux, 2007.
Pappé, Ilan. *The Ethnic Cleansing of Palestine.* London: Oneworld, 2006.
Piterberg, Gabriel. *The Returns of Zionism: Myths, Politics and Scholarship in Israel.* London: Verso, 2008.
Poulin, Joan. "Loving Kindness towards Gentiles according to the Early Jewish Sages." *Revue Théologique* 11.1-2 (2003) 89-112. At http://www.erudit.org/revue/theologi/2003/v11/n1-2/009526ar.pdf. Accessed on Feb 20, 2012.
Rabkin, Yakov. *A Threat from Within: A Century of Jewish Opposition to Zionism.* Translated by Fred A. Reed. New York: Zed, 2006.
Rose, Jacqueline. *The Question of Zion.* Princeton, NJ: Princeton University Press, 2005.
Ross, Jack. *Rabbi Outcast, Elmer Berger and American Jewish Anti-Zionism.* Washington, DC: Potomac, 2011.
Said, Edward W. *Orientalism.* New York: Vintage, 1979.
Schiff, Ofer. *Assimilation in Pride: Anti-Semitism, Holocaust and Zionism as a Challenge to American Jewish Reform Ideology.* Tel Aviv: Am-Oved, 2001.
Scholem, Gershom. *Sabbatai Sevi: The Mystical Messiah 1626-1676.* Princeton, NJ: Princeton University Press, 1975.
Segev, Tom. *One Palestine Complete: Jews and Arabs Under the British Mandate.* 1999. Reprint. New York: Owl, 2001.
———. *The Seventh Million: The Israelis and the Holocaust.* New York: Holt, 2000.
Shahak, Israel. *Jewish History, Jewish Religion: The Weight of Three Thousand Years.* London: Pluto, 1994.
Shahak, Israel, and Norton Mezvinsky. *Jewish Fundamentalism in Israel.* London: Pluto, 1999.
Shiblak, Abbas. *Iraqi Jews: A History of Mass Exodus.* 1986. Reprint. London: SAQI, 2005.
Sizer, Stephen. *Christian Zionism: Road-map to Armageddon?* Nottingham, UK: InterVarsity, 2004.
Tarazi, Paul Nadim. *Land and Covenant.* St. Paul, MN: Orthodox Center for the Advancement of Biblical Studies, 2009.
Urbach, E. E. *The Sages, their Concepts and Beliefs.* Jerusalem: Magnes, 1987.
Wink, Walter. *Engaging the Powers: Discernment and Resistance in a World of Domination.* Minneapolis: Fortress, 1992.
Wright, N. T. *What Saint Paul Really Said.* Grand Rapids: Eerdmans, 1997.
Young-Bruehl, Elisabeth. *Hannah Arendt: For Love of the World.* New Haven: Yale University Press, 1982.

Websites

http://www.combatantsforpeace.org/. Accessed on Feb 20, 2012.
www.erudit.org/revue/theologi/2003/v11/n1-2/009526ar.pdf. Accessed on Feb 20, 2012.

Zionism and the Scriptures

http://www.jewishvirtuallibrary.org/jsource/History/Dec_of_Indep.html. Accessed on Mar 13, 2012.

http://www.jewishvirtuallibrary.org/jsource/Talmud/avot1.html. Accessed on Feb 18, 2012.

www.mideastweb.org/Zionism.htm. "Zionism and the Creation of Israel." Accessed on Feb 23, 2012.

http://www.theparentscircle.com/. Accessed on Feb 20, 2012.

Zionism and Ancient Christianity

3

Early Christians
Belonging Everywhere and Nowhere

Carole Monica Burnett

THE FOLLOWING WORDS WERE written by Sir Walter Scott, a patriotic Scottish Christian, in the early nineteenth century:

> Breathes there the man with soul so dead
> Who never to himself hath said:
> "This is my own, my native land"?
> Whose heart hath ne'er within him burned
> As home his footsteps he hath turned,
> From wandering on a foreign strand?[1]

Contrast those lines of poetry with a well known piece of anonymous Christian apologetics (verbal self-defense) probably from the turn of the third century:

> For Christians cannot be distinguished from the rest of the human race by country or language or customs. They do not live in cities of their own. . . . They live in their own countries,

---

1. From "The Lay of the Last Minstrel," Sir Walter Scott (1771–1832), public domain. This excerpt is printed in, among other places, the anthology *One Hundred and One Famous Poems*, 110.

but only as aliens. They have a share in everything as citizens, and endure everything as foreigners. Every foreign land is their fatherland, and yet for them every fatherland is a foreign land.[2]

These two pieces of writing were composed in entirely different contexts. The first was spawned in Georgian Britain, a milieu similar to our own in the United States today; that is, a society that adhered to at least nominally Christian customs while regarding patriotism as a sublime quality. The second excerpt, however, reflects the need of Christians under persecution in the pre-Constantinian Roman Empire to exonerate themselves as law-abiding citizens while maintaining their distinctive religious identity. The anonymous ancient Christian writer explicitly states that although Greco-Roman Christians were born and lived in particular locations within an empire ("they live in Greek and barbarian cities alike, as each man's lot has been cast"),[3] the Christian life was independent of particular cultures and locations.

This essay will undertake two tasks: (1) to investigate the relationship between ancient Christian belief and the concept of personal attachment, emotional or spiritual, to a particular land or city, and (2) to examine patristic interpretations of the Old Testament promise of land to the Hebrew people—not just any land, but a particular area in a specified part of the world. Did early Christians believe that a heart burning with patriotic fervor was conducive to spiritual growth? Did they perceive the divine promise of land to the Hebrews as still valid even after the old covenant had found its fulfillment in the new? The answers to these questions bear momentous ramifications for the Christian Zionist movement today.

The implications of early Christian thought for Zionism today of course depend on the definition assigned to the term "Zionism." For the purposes of this essay, Zionism, whether Christian or Jewish, will be defined as the movement to create a "Greater Israel" by expanding the borders of the modern State of Israel beyond the "Green Line" in order to judaize and to annex the lands that were allotted for Palestinian habitation by the United Nations in 1948. This expansionism is the activity to be evaluated in terms of ancient Christian theology. By contrast, the sixty-four-year-old existence of the State of Israel, within the boundaries

2. *Epistle to Diognetus* 5, ed. and trans. Fairweather, 216–17. The Greek word corresponding to "fatherland" in this excerpt is *patris*, a cognate of the Greek word for "father"; the translator, therefore, is merely reflecting the male-oriented linguistic and cultural milieu of the ancient author. For the Greek text see *A Diognète*, ed. Marrou, 62.

3. *Epistle to Diognetus* 5, ed. and trans. Fairweather, 217.

established by the internationally recognized authority of the United Nations, is not to be questioned in any way.

CONSULTING THE EARLY CHURCH: RATIONALE AND PRECAUTIONS

Some readers may be tempted to minimize, or even to deny, the significance of post-biblical but time-tested Christian literature for today's believers. It is important to remember, however, that it is not only Roman Catholic and Eastern Orthodox Christians who revere the centuries-old traditions of their churches: Anglicans rely on their "three-legged stool," namely, Scripture, tradition, and reason; and Methodists employ the "Wesleyan Quadrilateral," which consists of Scripture, tradition, reason, and experience. The Protestant Reformers, including Martin Luther and John Calvin, made abundant use of patristic literature. For Christians who do not specifically identify "tradition" as a source of authority, it will be helpful to consider the fact that the writings of the ancient church reflect the thought of biblical interpreters living in the same political and cultural milieu, under the same Roman Empire, as the New Testament writers did; moreover, the Greek patristic writers even expressed themselves in the same language as that of the New Testament and the Septuagint.[4] Therefore, it is reasonable to accord a special status to the leaders and thinkers of the ancient church—the same church that, during its first few centuries, determined the list of canonical books belonging to the Bible that we cherish today. The early church defined the Bible even as the Bible shaped the church. The interaction between Scripture and ancient tradition is too significant to be ignored by any serious Christian.

Nevertheless, to consult the patristic tradition on any question pertaining to Judaism and Jews is to navigate through perilous seas. The Christian church has damaged its own reputation and almost killed its credibility in regard to this area of inquiry by its anti-Semitic words and deeds throughout the centuries of the Common Era. The genesis and nature of ancient Christian vitriol against the Jews has been the focus of intensive scholarship since the Holocaust and World War II, beginning with Marcel Simon's seminal work, *Verus Israel*. The accumulation of Christian diatribes against the Jews, ancient and medieval, commonly referred to

---

4. The Septuagint is the Greek translation of the Old Testament, dating from the middle of the third century BCE, that was treated as canonical by the New Testament writers and the early church.

as the *Adversus Judaeos,* or *Contra Judaeos,* tradition, is a tragedy to be reckoned with. Thus, in examining the significance to early Christians of the land claimed for the Hebrews of the Old Testament, and in applying our findings to the current situation, there are important precautions to be observed. It is necessary that we find our way through the expressions of interreligious animosity, by no means denying their malicious nature, but also setting our sights on the constructive theological and moral teachings aimed at the edification of the faithful. Moreover, since the specific issues and dilemmas addressed by each ancient writer are crucial to understanding the genesis of each patristic work, the historical context must not be ignored.

Ancient Christian anti-Semitism, more aptly termed anti-Judaism, was based on religious differences, not on genealogical factors; in other words, the Nazi notions of Jewish blood versus Aryan blood played no part.[5] Religion—and here must be included both theology and ritual celebrations—was the issue, and triumphalism was the norm at that time. It was not unusual—as it is not even today—for any religious leader to guard zealously the identity of his or her faith community by drawing boundaries and discouraging followers from straying outside of them; ancient Christian preachers were no exception. For example, John Chrysostom's *Adversus Judaeos* ("Against the Jews") homilies,[6] preached at Antioch probably in 386–387, were aimed at "judaizing Christians"; that is, Christians who were participating in Jewish festivities and rituals.[7] In the late fourth century there was apparently some seepage out of Antioch's churches and into the city's large, well furnished synagogues. John Chrysostom, in addressing this situation, excoriated and even demonized (literally, with accusations of demonic possession)[8] the Jewish community. Other instances of early anti-Jewish rhetoric include *On Easter* by Melito of Sardis, the pseudonymous *Epistle of Barnabas,* and Justin Martyr's *Dialogue with Trypho the Jew,* all dating from the second century. Such harsh rhetoric, not uncommon among professional orators of the patristic age,[9] set the stage for a lamentable subsequent history of Christian persecution of Jews.

5. Simon, *Verus Israel,* 202–3.

6. John Chrysostom, *Homilies against Judaizing Christians,* trans. Harkins.

7. Robert L. Wilken, *John Chrysostom and the Jews;* Christine Shepardson, "Paschal Politics," 247–50; see also Shepardson, "Controlling Contested Places."

8. Shepardson, "Paschal Politics," 250.

9. Wilken, *John Chrysostom and the Jews,* 95–127, has described rhetorical conventions in the age of John Chrysostom.

While not excusing such abuse, it is possible to discern the theological concerns behind the rhetorical excesses.

Boyarin has argued that the use of the term "Judaism" to designate a religion, as we think of religion today, did not exist before the advent of Christianity, and was not a fixed linguistic convention until late antiquity.[10] The two terms "Christianity" and "Judaism," he demonstrates, took shape in contradistinction to each other. A logical conclusion from his findings is that our modern impulse to find common ground and to promote tolerance was simply not part of the patristic mindset, which emphasized the differences between the two religions. Whereas in the twenty-first century it is considered appropriate to minimize theological disagreement and, when it exists, to express it gently and courteously, this was not the custom in the ancient world. We cannot impose our modern standards upon a bygone society for whom diversity and tolerance were not cultural values.

In addition to being characterized, at times rightly, as belligerent toward Jews, some of the church fathers have been labeled as "supersessionist," that is, as stating that the special, unique relationship between the Jewish people and God had been terminated and replaced by Christianity and the church. "Supersessionist" has been seen as a damning epithet as hideous as the terms "racist" and "anti-Semitic." But is such an equivalency valid? One must keep in mind the fact that the church included, and still includes, believers of Jewish ethnicity. Moreover, when any given religion claims to possess the broadest and highest level of truth, does such a claim constitute hate speech? To adhere to the Christian faith is to attribute to Christ's sojourn on earth as well as his crucifixion and resurrection the most complete revelation that God has yet granted to humankind. If the corollary is that the Old Testament acquires its ultimate meaning through this revelation in Christ, as the church fathers believed, is such a perspective necessarily anti-Semitic or supersessionist? No, but certainly it is Christocentric. As will be shown, Christocentrism is a conspicuous feature of early Christian thought, whether or not any given piece of writing may be anti-Jewish or supersessionist. It is therefore essential to focus on Christocentrism as the operative factor in interpreting patristic attitudes toward the promised land of the Old Testament.

One more aspect of early Christianity to note here is that the ownership of Judea, Galilee, and Samaria was not at issue because the Roman imperial government was a fact of life. There was no nationalistic tug-of-war over land possession, as there is today. During the New Testament

---

10. Daniel Boyarin, "Semantic Differences," 65–85.

and patristic eras, the Holy Land was at first in pagan hands, and later, when the Empire had become officially Christian, the land was under Christian rule until the beginning of the Islamic period in the seventh century. Therefore, we obviously cannot uncover any pronouncements of the church fathers on the topic of modern Zionism. All that we can do is to identify patristic attitudes toward geographic loyalties and patristic understandings of the divine bestowal of land as recorded in the Old Testament.

With the preceding caveats in mind, let us now examine those ancient traditions that express a distinctively Christian outlook on the human love of homeland, as well as some samples of early Christian exegesis that are relevant to biblically based claims on the land in the vicinity of the Jordan River. Conclusions will be drawn from this examination in assessing the compatibility (or lack thereof) of Zionist expansionism with patristic thought. The early centuries—the centuries during which the church established its identity as a religious institution and defined the basic Trinitarian and Christological doctrines for succeeding generations of believers—provide ample resources for formulating a position on the current situation in the Holy Land from an authentically Christocentric perspective.

NEW TESTAMENT FOUNDATIONS

A tradition is not authentic unless it exhibits a continuous trajectory emanating from, and firmly rooted in, Holy Scripture.[11] Moreover, since the New Testament includes the earliest Christian literature, it therefore must serve as the starting point for any investigation of ancient Christian thought. The following paragraphs constitute nothing more than a brief outline of New Testament perspectives on homeland and on the promised land,[12] but hopefully provide a launching pad for the patristic study to follow.

---

11. One of the renowned patristic writers, Cyprian (Bishop of Carthage, mid-third century), expressed this imperative to test each tradition by applying the criterion of fidelity to Scripture, remarking, "For if we go back to the source and fountainhead of divine tradition, human error ceases"; see his *Epistle* 74.10, trans. Clarke, 76.

12. Insightful studies of biblical views on the promised land include the following: Church, Walker, Bulkeley, and Meadowcroft, eds., *The Gospel and the Land of Promise*; Ateek, *Justice and Only Justice*; Burge, *Jesus and the Land*; Burge, *Whose Land? Whose Promise?* Sizer, *Zion's Christian Soldiers?* Tarazi, *Land and Covenant*; Chapman, *Whose Promised Land?*

In the process of establishing the scriptural origin of patristic thinking about homelands, certain passages in the New Testament leap out as unequivocal exhortations to embrace an itinerant way of life. Not only are there the post-resurrection commands of Jesus to his apostles (Matt 28:19–20, "Go therefore and make disciples of all nations . . . ," and Acts 1:8, "you shall be my witnesses . . . to the end of the earth"),[13] but in his earthly ministry Jesus clearly advises followers to detach themselves from their homes. Here are three unambiguous passages from the synoptic Gospels:

1. Matt 19:29: Jesus says, "And everyone who has left houses or brothers or sisters or father or mother or children or lands, for my name's sake, will receive a hundredfold, and inherit eternal life."[14]

2. Luke 9:57–62: "Foxes have holes," says Jesus to a prospective follower, "and birds of the air have nests; but the Son of man has nowhere to lay his head." Then, after advising a reluctant inquirer to ignore his obligation to provide burial for his father, Jesus tells another, "No one who puts his hand to the plow and looks back is fit for the kingdom of God."[15]

3. Mark 1:16–20: When Jesus calls Simon and Andrew to be his disciples, they drop their work "immediately" to follow him; similarly, when he approaches James and John, who are mending nets with their father, they abandon their father and their livelihood without hesitation.[16]

The Gospel of John, though not prescribing physical dislocation from home and family, devotes three chapters (14–16) to Jesus' final discourse to his disciples, in which he exhorts them to expect hatred and persecution from the adversarial forces of "the world" (John 15:18–20). The disciples are "not of the world." The meaning of "the world" (Greek, *kosmos*) may be

---

13. All biblical quotations in this essay are taken from the RSV unless they occur in an excerpt from a patristic writing. The edition used here is *The Oxford Annotated Bible*, ed. May and Metzger. The version of the Greek New Testament used here is *The Greek New Testament*, ed. Aland, Black, Martini, Metzger, and Wikgren.

14. The Lucan parallel, at 18:29, reads, "for the sake of the kingdom of God."

15. The parallel passage, Matt 8:19–22, lacks the words about putting one's hand to the plow and looking back.

16. The Matthean parallel has retained Mark's two (characteristic) uses of "immediately," whereas the Lucan version includes variations on the narrative; see Matt 4:18–22 and Luke 5:1–11.

open to interpretation, but it is clear that spiritual, emotional, and physical gratification are not to be sought from earthly resources.

Having identified key passages from the Gospels pertaining to earthly homelands, let us turn to the matter of the promised land. Here the Epistles come into play. Paul, himself a Jew and therefore an heir to the old covenant, grapples with the demands of the Law and cites the history of ancient Israel, but does not mention the promised land.[17] As Sizer points out, Paul preaches salvation through faith, not through the land: "The kingdom which Jesus heralded is therefore now internal not territorial."[18] Itinerancy, however, is not encouraged. Although the lives of Paul and his fellow missionaries were itinerant and beset by physical hardships, the authors of the Epistles (Pauline, deutero-Pauline, and non-Pauline) do not urge average believers to follow their examples by uprooting themselves from their homes; rather, they expect the Christian community within a particular location to maintain its own identity and standards of behavior *in situ*. For example, Rom 12:2 instructs, "Do not be conformed to this world," and 2 Cor 6:14–18 asks, in regard to interfaith marriages, "What has a believer in common with an unbeliever?" and then proceeds to quote Isa 52:11, "Therefore come out from them, and be separate from them, says the Lord." In these passages the separation from one's native city is spiritual and psychological rather than geographical. The complete and ultimate separation, of course, will occur at the time of the believer's transition from the transitory, earthly dwelling to the eternal, heavenly home, as 2 Cor 4:16—5:6 makes clear: "Here indeed we groan, and long to put on our heavenly dwelling . . . while we are at home in the body we are away from the Lord. . . . [W]e would rather be away from the body and at home with the Lord." The Christian has yet to occupy his or her true home.

The Epistle to the Hebrews offers homiletic-style remarks both about home in general and about the specific area of land promised to Abraham. The question of its authorship and context is an intriguing area of investigation, especially in regard to its alleged supersessionism, which appears to manifest itself in its description of a replacement of the Jewish priesthood and tabernacle (or temple) by the high priesthood of Christ and his heavenly abode. The pejorative charge of supersessionism has been applied to the Epistle to the Hebrews in the past, but the most recent scholarly work

17. Church, "'Here We Have No Lasting City' (Heb 13:14)," 49, observes, "There is not one reference to the land of Israel in the writings of Paul, James, Peter, or Jude, or in the Book of Revelation."

18. Sizer, *Zion's Christian Soldiers?* 96.

renders an acquittal. One piece of evidence, according to Heen and Krey, is the author's use of *synkrisis,* a rhetorical device by which one good entity (here, Jewish ritual practice) is compared to an even better one (Christ's priesthood and sacrifice in the heavenly tabernacle).[19] Another argument is that the epistle's language of replacement is directed only to expiatory animal sacrifices, not to the Law and prophets or to Israel's sacred history, whether the epistle was addressed to Jewish Christians needing guidance and consolation in the wake of the destruction of the Jerusalem temple in 70 CE, or whether it pre-dates this event and is designed to exhort disheartened Jewish-Christians needing encouragement in the face of persecution. It is in light of recent literary analysis and historical-critical research that the epistle's perspective on Abraham and the promised land must be regarded.[20]

The stirring reminders in Heb 11 of the primacy of faith in salvation history, as exemplified by Old Testament heroes, include a startling depiction of Abraham as a stranger and sojourner in the land which God had given him (Heb 11:8–10). Why would Abraham have "sojourned in the land of promise, as in a foreign land," when his ownership of that land was divinely decreed and therefore beyond doubt, especially for this patriarch whose faith was solid? Why, one might ask, is Abraham not depicted here as having established a permanent home in the land? The author of the epistle provides an immediate answer: Abraham "looked forward to the city which has foundations, whose builder and maker is God." He and the other patriarchs and Sarah "all died in faith, not having received what was promised, but having seen it and greeted it from afar, and having acknowledged that they were strangers and exiles on the earth" (Heb 11:13).[21] The real content of God's promise, therefore, is a home in heaven, not the land of Canaan.[22]

19. Heen and Krey, "Introduction to Hebrews," xxi.

20. For historical-critical analyses, see Church, "'Here We Have No Lasting City' (Heb 13:14)," as well as a collection of relevant essays found in *The Epistle to the Hebrews and Christian Theology,* ed. Bauckham, Driver, Hart, and MacDonald.

21. The characterization of Abraham living as a foreigner in the promised land, sustained only by his faith in God—a characterization that appears in Heb 11:8–10 and in Irenaeus (quoted below in this essay)—is not unique to Christian literature. The Hellenistic-Jewish philosopher Philo, writing at Alexandria in the first half of the first century of the Common Era, had previously presented a similar depiction of Abraham. For Philo, Abraham was a paragon of faith in God and Stoic-like detachment from earthly loves. See Philo, *On Abraham* 14.63–66, trans. Colson.

22. In Heb 11:14 ("For people who speak thus make it clear that they are seeking a homeland," referring to the patriarchs' quest) the Greek noun translated in the RSV as

Earlier, in Heb 3 and 4, an exegesis of Ps 95:7–11 identifies God's "rest" (Ps 95:11) as a blessing yet to come, rather than as the entry into the promised land. Joshua had not led people to this "rest" (Heb 4:8). This "rest" is for those who, unlike the first generation of Hebrew refugees from Egypt, do not lapse from their faith. Christians are currently burdened by toil and hardship, but the epistle offers this assurance: "So then, there remains a sabbath rest for the people of God; for whoever enters God's rest also ceases from his labors as God did from his. Let us therefore strive to enter that rest, that no one fall by the same sort of disobedience" (Heb 4:9–11). The land between the Jordan River and the Mediterranean Sea is not the ultimate goal for the people of God, either before or after the advent of Christ.

Richard B. Hays provides a persuasive array of evidence to support his thesis that the Epistle to the Hebrews, addressed to Jewish-Christian readers, presents a new covenant that, while replacing the old covenant, is solidly grounded in the Torah and the history of Israel, and mandates a transformation, not any rejection or usurpation, of Israel's special status and relationship with God. The epistle's figural interpretation of the Old Testament "embraces and confirms Israel's story as truly revelatory, though incomplete"; according to the New Testament author, the promised land, the priesthood, the tabernacle, and the cultic sacrifices were intended to be provisional and to point forward to eschatological repose in Christ. Thus the Epistle to the Hebrews, in expounding distinctively Jewish truths and embracing "both continuity and discontinuity," is "no more supersessionist than Jeremiah."[23]

Rather than teaching supersessionism, the Epistle to the Hebrews identifies the goal shared in common by the people of the Old Testament and the believers in the New: it is the "lasting city" that is "to come" in the next life (Heb 13:14). God's promise has not been discontinued or invalidated, but now, in light of the peace to be found in Jesus Christ, believers can discern what the patriarchs saw and "greeted . . . from afar" (Heb 11:13). The eternal homeland of God's people is the same in both testaments.[24] This Platonic vision, in which the homeland, the priesthood, and the tabernacle on earth are imperfect copies of the true realities in heaven,

---

"homeland" is *patris*, the same word rendered as "fatherland" in the translated excerpt from the *Epistle to Diognetus*, quoted above. See n. 2. This same word, *patris*, is used by Philo in praising Abraham for detaching himself from his home country; *On Abraham* 14.63, trans. Colson, 36–37.

23. Hays, "'Here We Have No Lasting City': New Covenantalism," 155, 165, 167.

24. Bockmuehl, "Abraham's Faith," 369, observes, "The heavenly city and homeland

was likely a comforting message for Jewish Christians under Roman occupation, and perhaps also suffering persecution from fellow Jews, and of course it bears implications for Christians pondering Zionism today.

PERSECUTED CHRISTIANS AND THEIR HOMELAND

The early Christian martyrs were regarded by their admirers as embodying the pinnacle of faith and devotion, and, in fact, as following literally in the footsteps of Christ. In the present discussion of Christian martyrdom, the focus will be the renunciation of home and hearth rather than opposition to the state. Of course, as Christians maintained their grip on their religious identity, they publicly defied the might of the empire that controlled their world, the world that was known to them. At the same time, they were often compelled to withdraw from their families and from a clan-based culture that identified individuals in reference to their ancestry and living relatives; it is this form of detachment that concerns us here. The question is this: During the centuries of Roman persecution, did early Christian ideals allow room in the hearts of believers for emotional attachment to a place regarded as home, and, if so, was such an attachment regarded as a virtue? Most Christians today know intuitively the negative answer to this question, but here we will look at the explicit evidence.

The courtroom records (*acta*) and ancient narratives (*passiones*) of martyrdoms are peppered with martyrs' statements identifying their true monarch as God or Christ.[25] These are political declarations as well as confessions of faith. What is of interest, however, is the implicit attitude of detachment displayed by those who with no qualms departed from this earthly life with its bonds of home and family. In the martyrdom of Perpetua and Felicitas, for example, both young mothers relinquish their infants to the care of others, and Perpetua also turns her heartbroken father away, rejecting her filial role with its benefit of paternal protection.[26] Though illustrative of the martyrs' emotional detachment from human relationships in the face of death, this example still does not answer our question, and we must look still further to see the attitude toward homeland.

---

which Abraham sees and greets from afar is clearly not just *analogous* but *identical* with the city of the living God, the heavenly Jerusalem in 12:22."

25. See Ferguson, "Early Christian Martyrdom and Civil Disobedience," 79–80.

26. *The Martyrdom of Perpetua and Felicitas* 3, 5, 6, 15, in *Acts of the Christian Martyrs*, ed. and trans. Musurillo, 108–15, 122–25.

Not all of the defiant Christians were sentenced to death; instead, some were banished, sometimes to toil in the mines or, in the case of women, to staff the brothels.[27] An aspiring martyr therefore had to take into account the possibility of a miserable life far from home that could conceivably be even more dreadful than death. Also those who fled arrest and persecution in order to avoid the apostasy of pagan cult sacrifice were willing to suffer permanent displacement in an undetermined location; some did not survive the journey.[28] Later, after the reign of the first Christian emperor, Constantine, a different sort of dislocation occurred when Arian Christian emperors condemned to exile certain dissenting bishops, such as Athanasius of Alexandria, Hilary of Poitiers, and other pro-Nicene bishops; a few decades afterward, John (Chrysostom) of Constantinople died in exile after refusing to compromise his views. Thus the geographical displacement urged upon disciples in the synoptic Gospels became one of the sacrifices required of persecuted Christians.

Narratives, however, are far from the only genre of Christian literature produced during the era of persecution. Another was that of the moral treatise, in which renunciation of worldliness was frequently prescribed. Tertullian, a third-century theologian of Carthage, applied Jesus' statement about having "nowhere to lay his head" to the issue of how Christians should dress: the garb of Roman dignitaries, tainted by the idolatrous practices entailed in civil ceremonies, should be abhorrent to Christians, since, says Tertullian, the example of Christ, who had "nowhere to lay his head," indicates that he was clothed in simple garments.[29] In this instance Tertullian has chosen a synoptic passage referring to geographical itiner-

---

27. Forced labor in the mines of Sardinia was the notorious destination of many alleged miscreants, including Christians. Also the fourth-century historian Eusebius of Caesarea mentions banishment to the mines of Pontus in his *Historia ecclesiastica* 8.12; see translation by Williamson, *The History of the Church*, 344. The martyr Irene was initially sentenced to be imprisoned, naked, inside a brothel, during the reign of Emperor Diocletian; see *The Martyrdom of Saints Agapē, Irenē, and Chionē at Saloniki* 5–6, ed. and trans. Musurillo, 290–91. Sexual slavery as a punishment for Christian women is also mentioned by Eusebius, *The History of the Church* 8.12, 14, trans. Williamson, 342, 350–51.

28. Irene and her companions hid in the mountains while preserving the holy Scriptures from destruction by the imperial authorities. See Musurillo, 288–89. Another example appears in a letter of Bishop Dionysius of Alexandria, quoted at length in Eusebius, *The History of the Church* 6.41–42, trans. Williamson, 279; Dionysius asks, "Need I speak of the vast number who wandered over deserts and mountains till hunger, thirst, cold, sickness, bandits, or wild beasts destroyed them?"

29. Tertullian, *On Idolatry* 18, *Ante-Nicene Fathers* 3:72–73. Scripture text is Matt 8:20 or Luke 9:58, quoted from the RSV.

ancy[30] and has applied it to the obligation of Christians to maintain their own distinctive mores while avoiding complete assimilation into secular society, a moral obligation that the Pauline Epistles teach (as mentioned above), and to which the *Epistle of Diognetus* (quoted earlier) refers in describing Christians as being "aliens" in their native countries.

Another of Tertullian's moral treatises exhorts Christians to exercise the fortitude required for martyrdom. Although the general belief was that martyrdom was a divinely bestowed vocation, not a self-appointed task,[31] and thus was a sacred status, words of encouragement to endangered believers were evidently perceived as helpful. In his *To the Martyrs* Tertullian, influenced by Stoic philosophy, emphasizes detachment from the world, explaining that a Christian's place of residence is a matter of indifference: "It does not matter what part of the world you are in, you who are apart from the world."[32] Further on, citing Matt 6:21 (the verse immediately following Jesus' instruction in 6:20 to amass treasure in heaven), Tertullian states: "The leg does not feel the fetter when the spirit is in heaven. The spirit carries about the whole man and brings him wherever he wishes. And where your heart is, there will your treasure be also. There, then, let our heart be where we would have our treasure."[33]

Another third-century theologian, Origen, advises persecuted Christians that the way to achieve union with Christ is to "separate and cut off their soul not only from the earthly body but from every kind of body," imitating Abraham's example by departing from their countries, leaving their homes and lands behind. Total devotion to Christ requires calm detachment. The reward is the unimaginable treasures of God in heaven.[34] Origen's emphasis is not on Abraham's adopted land, but on his ready departure from his native land.

Thus both the narratives of martyrdom and the moral discourse addressed to Christians under persecution called for emotional disengagement from any particular earthly abode. Human ties had to be replaced by a consuming desire for Christ, and the state of being "double-minded" was to be avoided.[35] Christ was to be the Christians' sole attachment, and

30. See the section "New Testament Foundations," above.

31. Ferguson, 75.

32. Tertullian, *To the Martyrs* 2.5, trans. Arbesmann, 20.

33. Ibid. 2.10, trans. Arbesmann, 21.

34. Origen, *Exhortation to Martyrdom* 1.3, 1.5, 3.13–15, trans. O'Meara, 142, 144, 154–56.

35. In the *Didache* and in the portion of the *Epistle of Barnabas* that either is borrowed from the *Didache* or shares a common source, the Christian is exhorted to avoid

heaven the true homeland. There is no basis whatsoever in these early Christian traditions for any attempt to inculcate in fellow human beings (as Christian Zionism does) an emotional or spiritual attachment to any particular geographical homeland.

PRE-CONSTANTINIAN PERSPECTIVES ON THE PROMISED LAND

During the era of anti-Christian persecution, the Jews of Judea suffered disasters and hardships of their own. An obvious influence on early Christian exegesis of God's promise of land to Abraham was the state of affairs in the city of Jerusalem, namely, the situation resulting from the destruction of the Jewish temple in 70 CE and the deportation in 135 CE of all Jews from the city, which was renamed Aelia Capitolina. Christians saw these events as divine pronouncements that the formal worship and religious hierarchy of the Jews had been terminated.

Although this elimination of the Jerusalem temple, the focal point of Jewish piety, gave rise to triumphalist expressions of Christian supersessionism, there was a compelling need to uphold the continuing validity of the Hebrew Scriptures—the very Scriptures that had prescribed the temple cult—in the polemical debate with various Gnostic schools of thought. Gnostics sought to discredit the Old Testament with its positive depiction of the Creator and the creation. The orthodox leadership of the church strove to retain the Old Testament as holy canonical Scripture, yet claimed that certain legal traditions promulgated in it had become null and void. How could this paradox be convincingly sustained?

The *Epistle of Barnabas*

A tidy solution was to assert that the Jews had not correctly understood their own Scriptures and that the narratives and cultic practices presented in them were, unbeknownst to the Jews, symbols of Christ and the church. This reasoning appears in the pseudonymous *Epistle of Barnabas,* possibly written in Palestine or Alexandria, perhaps during

---

an ambivalent, wavering state of mind, designated by the Greek verb *dipsychein* and the adjective *dignōmōn*. See *Didache* 2.4 and 4.4, ed. and trans. Ehrman, 420–23, and *Barnabas* 19.5, 7, ed. and trans. Ehrman, 76–77. See also Kleist translation, 16, 17, 62, and 63.

the reign of the emperor Hadrian (117–138 CE),[36] or perhaps, according to another theory, during the reign of Nerva (96–98 CE).[37] The *Epistle of Barnabas*, though vehemently supersessionist,[38] anti-Jewish, and far from congenial to interfaith harmony, serves as an example of the redefinition and recasting of events, people, and places by ancient Christian writers utilizing typological exegesis to validate the Old Testament's continuing status as canonical Scripture[39] and to appropriate its venerable antiquity as an attribute of the church.[40]

Utilizing two Genesis passages, each describing the selection of the younger member of a pair of brothers for a special blessing (Jacob in preference to Esau, and Ephraim over Manasseh),[41] the author identifies the younger brother in each case as symbolizing the church and asserts that the people of Israel, unworthy of the covenant, were not the true recipients of it.[42] That the Jews themselves were responsible for the recent destruction of their temple is shown by Old Testament reproaches (in the prophets and elsewhere) against the behavior of the Israelites; their underlying fault, says pseudo-Barnabas, was that, "instead of putting their trust in their God who had made them, they put it in the building."[43] Thus this

---

36. Introduction to the *Epistle of Barnabas*, Kleist, 31–33. Kleist believes that Alexandria is a likely location because of the author's prodigious use of allegorical exegesis.

37. Parmentier, "No Stone Upon Another?" 143.

38. Skarsaune remarks that *Barnabas* is *sui generis* among supersessionist writings because it depicts Israel not as having been replaced by the church, but as never having been the people of God in the first place; see his "Supersessionist Theology?" 179. As Skarsaune notes here, the author of *Barnabas* dates the estrangement between God and the Jews as beginning from the fracturing of the stone tablets in Exod 32:19; see also *Barnabas* 4.7–8, trans. Kleist, 41.

39. Simonetti observes, "[T]he interpretive style of Ps.-Barnabas became ever more established as the specifically Christian method of reading the Old Testament. Radical reinterpretation in a typological vein secured the authority of the Old Testament for the Church which was now under attack from the Gnostics." See his *Biblical Interpretation in the Early Church*, 14.

40. Novelty was a serious drawback in establishing credibility in Greco-Roman culture, which respected ancient, time-honored tradition. Christians could ward off the accusation of novelty by reminding their detractors that Moses was more ancient than Plato, and that the Old Testament was the root of Christianity. See note 81 below.

41. Gen 25:19–26 and 48:9–19.

42. *Barnabas* 13–14, trans. Kleist, 56–58.

43. *Barnabas* 16, trans. Kleist, 60. Here there is a reference to the existence of a plan to rebuild the temple: "and now the subjects of the enemies are about to build it up again." Kleist connects this to Hadrian's leniency toward Jews; see 180 n. 166. A rebuilt temple would remove a crucial underpinning of supersessionist theology.

piece of writing clearly belongs to the inception of the *Adversus Judaeos* motif in Christian literature.

The Old Testament, according to this author, derives its value only retroactively, that is, in light of Christian interpretation. The actions and actors in the history of ancient Israel were mere images, or types, of the salvation that was to come in Jesus Christ. To name just a few examples, the temple symbolizes the human heart in which Christ dwells; the sacrifice of Isaac and the ritual of the scapegoat on Yom Kippur both prefigure the crucifixion of Christ; and when numerological analysis is employed, the number 318, referring to the 318 servants of Abraham who were circumcised, spells out the name "Jesus"; the name itself is identical to that of Joshua in the Old Testament (both names being *Iēsous* in Greek).[44] And the promised land? It is a prefiguration of the new creation in Christ:

> And what does *into the fertile land, a land flowing with milk and honey* [cf. Exod 33:3, Lev 20:24] mean? Blessed be Our Lord, brethren, who has endowed us with wisdom and understanding of His secrets; for the Prophet speaks of the Lord in figurative language. . . . In these latter days He made a second creation. The Lord says: *Behold, I make the last things like the first* [similar to Matt 19:30 and 20:16; also see Eph 1:10]. This, then, is what the Prophet announced when he said: *Enter into the land flowing with milk and honey, and rule over it.* Observe, therefore: we have been formed anew. . . . We, then, are the ones whom He has led into the fertile land.[45]

Obviously this author has transposed and reapplied the promise of land in such a way as to unite the Old and New Testaments.

While it is tempting to omit the *Epistle of Barnabas* from the present essay because of its anti-Jewish polemic, it serves as a very early example of the use of typology in a purely Christocentric exegesis of the Old Testament. The author of *Barnabas* unambiguously claims the Old Testament as foundational to the Christian faith and regards the promised land, with its center of religious worship now in ruins,[46] as Jewish property no longer. This line of argumentation apparently provided polemical tools for use in debates with Jews and judaizing Christians. Such a debate, using similar

44. *Barnabas* 16.6–10, 7.1–7, 9.8, and 12.8, trans. Kleist, 60–61, 46–48, 50, 55.

45. *Barnabas* 6, trans. Kleist, 45–46. Bracketed material represents the translator's notes.

46. It is not certain that Jerusalem had already been emptied of Jewish inhabitants and renamed at the time when *Barnabas* was composed, although the temple had been demolished.

tools, is highlighted in Justin Martyr's *Dialogue with the Jew Trypho*,[47] composed at the same time as, or perhaps a decade or two later than, *Barnabas*.

Justin Martyr

The Christian philosopher Justin, a Gentile native of Flavia Neapolis (biblical Shechem and modern-day Nablus in the West Bank) who was martyred around 160, is known as an apologist for the Christian faith in dialogue with pagans and Jews. In his *Dialogue with the Jew Trypho* he does not exhibit the same degree of anti-Jewish animus that is evident in the *Epistle of Barnabas*. Instead, Justin allows that Jewish practices such as circumcision and Sabbath observance are acceptable for Jewish believers in Christ, as long as they do not impose these practices on Gentile Christians.[48] Such latitude is rare in patristic literature even though it is legislated in Acts 15. Nevertheless, Justin presents the destruction of the Jerusalem temple and its animal sacrifices as the will of God for terminating the old covenant.[49] Thus his attitude toward private Jewish practices among Jewish-Christian believers differs from his perspective on the Jerusalem temple cult; the former is acceptable while the latter is no longer intrinsic to God's plan for salvation.

Justin embraced chiliasm, the belief in an eschatological reign of Christ on earth, and the New Jerusalem was for him the future abode of Christ. An important source on the relationship between chiliasm and Christian perspectives on Jerusalem is Robert Wilken's book *The Land Called Holy*. Wilken's goal is to prove that Jerusalem never lost its spiritual primacy in ancient Christianity, and, in so doing, he points out that Justin located the eschatological kingdom in a restored earthly Jerusalem.[50] Since the purpose of the present essay differs from Wilken's, however, it must be observed that for Justin the Jerusalem-based phase of salvation history was not to be eternal. In the *Dialogue with Trypho* Justin, citing the prophets Ezekiel and Isaiah as well as the book of Revelation, expresses his belief in a temporary reign of Christ in a rebuilt Jerusalem—a reign that would be followed by the final judgment and resurrection—a resurrected state that does not simulate carnal existence.[51] Thus, although Jerusalem will

---

47. Justin, *Trypho*, trans. Falls, rev. Halton, ed. Slusser.
48. *Trypho* 47.1–2, trans. Falls, 71.
49. E.g., *Trypho* 16.2, 22.11, 40.2, trans. Falls, 27, 36, 61.
50. Wilken, *The Land Called Holy*, 57.
51. *Trypho* 80–81, trans. Falls, 125–27.

continue to be necessary for a while longer, it is not the eternal, heavenly home promised to Christians. Moreover, the Jerusalem of the thousand-year reign will feature wolves enjoying fellowship with lambs, and a total absence of pain and destruction, as Isaiah 65 prophesies in the verses that Justin quotes; thus the eschatological city is the radically transformed Jerusalem (*sans* temple) that is described in Revelation—not the Jerusalem of the Old Testament or of Justin's day.

What of the land in which Jerusalem resides? Like the author of *Barnabas*, Justin interprets typologically the entrance into the promised land, distinguishing between, on the one hand, the temporary allocation of the land by Joshua (Greek, *Iēsous*) and, on the other, the "inheritance for eternity" bestowed by Jesus (also *Iēsous* in Greek) in the New Testament.[52] The entrance into the promised land represents a personal transformation for all Christian believers, who, having "renounced all worldly things,"[53] will enjoy Christ forever in "the land of all the saints."[54] The heirs of Abraham are all people "from every land, whether slaves or free men, who believe in Christ and recognize the truths of his words and those of the prophets," and it is the church's ethnic diversity that God foretold in promising Abraham that he would be a father of many nations.[55]

Thus Justin has assigned symbolic meanings to Old Testament narratives in such a way as to expand the scope of salvation to embrace all people and places. This expansion would be further developed in the writing of Irenaeus. Both Justin and Irenaeus upheld the concept of a physical restoration of the creation, including the resurrection of the human body,[56] and for Irenaeus this concept was intrinsic to his refutation of the Gnostic disparagement of the material creation.

---

52. *Trypho* 113.3–4, trans. Falls, 169. The identity of these two names in the Greek and Latin OT and NT is a not uncommon means employed by the church fathers for setting up parallels and contrasts, as seen in *Barnabas* (mentioned previously) as well as Origen and Tertullian (see below).

53. *Trypho* 119.5–6, trans. Falls, 179.

54. *Trypho* 139.5, trans. Falls, 209. Wilken, *The Land Called Holy*, 58, believes that Justin foretells an eschatological apportionment of a physical landscape rather than a heavenly home, but this prediction is ambiguous in light of Justin's view that the thousand-year reign of Christ will be temporary, as described above. Either way, the theology of Justin does not support a specifically Jewish occupation of the land, but clearly includes all peoples.

55. Ibid.; also *Trypho* 119.4, trans. Falls, 179. See Gen 17:4–5 and Rom 4:17–18.

56. For Justin's declaration that authentic Christianity includes the resurrection of the body, see *Trypho* 80.4–5, trans. Falls, 126.

Irenaeus

At the end of the second century, Irenaeus, the Bishop of Lyons, proposed a theology that encompassed a variety of questions, including the goodness of God's physical creation, the fall of Adam and Eve, the canon of holy Scripture, and the ultimate state of the world at the end of time. He exercised leadership in a time and place where savage persecution had recently occurred. As immigrants from Asia Minor living in Gaul, the Christian community had become the target of a local mob and of the imperial authority there.[57] Apparently, however, the violence had subsided, allowing Irenaeus to address the theological controversies resulting from the teachings of heterodox groups.

Writing in Greek against the Gnostics and the Marcionites, Irenaeus revealed his eschatological vision of renewal for the whole world. Unlike his theological opponents, who rejected the Old Testament with its creation story and Creator God, and unlike the Montanists, who envisioned the New Jerusalem descending from heaven onto a particular location in Asia Minor, Irenaeus drew on both Testaments in presenting his all-embracing view of salvation history, which promised the renewal of God's entire creation, including even animals.[58] Thus Irenaeus's theology of "restoration" or "recapitulation" (*anakephalaiōsis*) promises a transformative renewal of the entire universe, "new heavens and a new earth,"[59] as the fulfillment of God's promises in both Testaments.

In supporting his view Irenaeus interprets two events related in Genesis. One is God's promise of land to Abraham and his "seed," quoted by Irenaeus from Gen 13:14–17 and Gen 15:18. In a line of reasoning reminiscent of, but not utilizing, Heb 11:8–10 (discussed above), Irenaeus states in regard to Abraham:

> Yet he received no inheritance in it, not even a footprint, but was always a pilgrim and a stranger in it. And when Sarah his wife was dead, and the Hittites wanted to give him freely a place for her burial, he would not accept it, but bought a tomb [Gen 23]. ... If, then God promised him the inheritance of the [promised] land, but in all his sojourning there he did not receive it, it must

---

57. See the narrative of the martyrs of Lyons and Vienne in a letter from the churches of those cities to Asia Minor, preserved by Eusebius, *The History of the Church* 5.1–2, trans. Williamson, 193–205.

58. Irenaeus, *Against Heresies* (*Adversus haereses*) 5.33.4. See the translation by Hardy, 395–96.

59. Irenaeus cites Isa 66:22 in *Against Heresies* 5.36.1, trans. Hardy, 396.

be that he will receive it with his seed, that is, with those who fear God and believe in him, at the resurrection of the just. For his seed is the Church, which receives through the Lord adoption to God, as John the Baptist said, "That God is able from these stones to raise up sons of Abraham" [Luke 3:8; Matt 3:9].[60]

The exegesis here displays the characteristic patristic method of interpreting one part of the Bible by means of another, with the assumption that the Scriptures form a unity. The result is a redefinition of Abraham's "seed," expanding its meaning from a particular genealogical line of descent to include all Christian believers without regard to ethnicity. In support of this redefinition Irenaeus cites relevant passages from Paul's Epistle to the Galatians, concluding with Gal 3:9: "Now the Scripture, foreseeing that God would justify the Gentiles by faith, foretold to Abraham, In you will all nations be blessed. Therefore those who are of faith are blessed with faithful Abraham."[61] Faith, not biological ancestry, is the criterion identifying the heirs of the promise.

The other Genesis passage that Irenaeus applies to the legacy of the Old Testament patriarchs is the blessing of Isaac upon his son Jacob in Gen 27:27–29. The words of the blessing, as quoted by Irenaeus from the Septuagint, are as follows:

> Behold, the smell of my son is as the smell of a rich field, which God has blessed. God give you of the dew of heaven, and of the fertility of the earth, abundance of grain and of wine. And the nations will serve you, and princes will worship you, and you will be lord over your brother, and the sons of your father will worship you. He who curses you will be accursed, and he who blesses you will be blessed.[62]

Between the first and second sentences of this blessing, Irenaeus interjects his own interpretation of the "rich field" as "the world," saying, "The field is the world." Again we see his expansion of the language of particularity, here extended to cosmic dimensions. After quoting the rest of the Genesis passage, he demonstrates that the predictions stated in Isaac's blessing were not fulfilled in Jacob's lifetime, concluding, "So the aforesaid benediction undoubtedly refers to the times of the Kingdom, when the just, rising from the dead, will reign, when the created order will be made new

---

60. Irenaeus, *Against Heresies* 5.32.2, trans. Hardy, 392. Bracketed material represents translator's notes.

61. Ibid., 392–93. Translation of the Epistle text as quoted by Irenaeus is Hardy's.

62. *Against Heresies* 5.33.3, trans. Hardy, 394.

and set free, and will produce an abundance of all kinds of food, from the dew of heaven and of the fertility of the earth."[63] Thus the eschatological reign of Christ on earth (which Irenaeus proceeds to explicate at greater length, adding several Scripture texts) is the fulfillment of promises ostensibly made to one man in a specific setting, but actually embracing the entire creation. Plants, animals, and humans will flourish everywhere in the transformed and renewed creation in such a way that the creation's final state will conform to God's original intention.[64]

Irenaeus observes that his opponents are guilty of trying to disinherit Abraham. Irenaeus exclaims, "Vain, too, is [the effort of] Marcion and his followers when they [seek to] exclude Abraham from the inheritance," and he subsequently remarks that God "introduces, through Jesus Christ, Abraham to the kingdom of heaven . . ."[65] Repeatedly he tells us that the old covenant prefigures the new, that the prophets foretold Christ, that Abraham was heir to the promises of Christ, and, above all, that the same God is revealed in both Testaments.[66] While rejecting allegory (the interpretation of tangible phenomena or narratives about earthly happenings as symbols of spiritual realities),[67] he creatively finds ways to integrate his Christocentric faith with the continuing validity of the Hebrew Scriptures, interpreting each of the two Testaments as revealing physical realities, the past events of the Old pointing to the yet-to-be-materialized but certain future. Marcion, on the other hand, is taking the easy route of simply dismissing those Scriptures altogether. In twenty-first century terms, it is legitimate to say that the true "supersessionists" were the heterodox adversaries of Irenaeus and other church fathers.

Origen

The dawn of the third century saw the end of Irenaeus's career. It was in the middle of the ensuing century that pre-Constantinian biblical exegesis reached its zenith in the work of the Alexandrian scholar Origen, whose

---

63. Ibid.

64. Wilken remarks, "In Irenaeus the land promise remains earthbound. . . . though 'land' is extended beyond the land of Israel to embrace the earth as a whole"; *The Land Called Holy*, 61.

65. Irenaeus, *Against Heresies* 4.8.1, *Ante-Nicene Fathers* 1:470–71.

66. Ibid.; also, e.g., *Against Heresies* 4.5.2–5, 4.7.1–3, 4.9.3, 4.11.1, *Ante-Nicene Fathers* 1:467, 469–70, 472–73, 474.

67. *Against Heresies* 5.35.1–2, *Ante-Nicene Fathers* 1:565–66.

passion for God's word led him to study the Hebrew language with a former rabbi, whom he referred to as "the Hebrew."[68] Despite this Jewish connection and his immersion in the Hebrew Scriptures, Origen makes a blistering remark about the Jews in his polemical work *Against Celsus*. In this treatise, which is Origen's rebuttal of the mocking disparagement of Christianity by the pagan Celsus, Origen responds harshly to the anti-Christian polemic that Celsus attributes to Jews by firing off an accusation against the Jews for allegedly killing Christ.[69] This was not the first time that a Christian had made this charge,[70] but it is distressing that a theologian of Origen's depth and creativity has continued this hideous tradition.

It must be noted in his favor, however, that in the same treatise Origen defends the Jews against Celsus, saying that "they were men who manifested a shadow of the heavenly life upon earth. Among them none was regarded as God other than the supreme God."[71] Elsewhere he remarks:

> What an admirable thing it was for [the Jews] that they were taught even from childhood to ascend above all sensible nature and not to think that God is established in any part of it, but even to seek for Him beyond material things! . . . These truths were proclaimed still under the form of a story because they were children and only had the understanding of children.[72]

Origen's goal of defending his own faith, therefore, prompts him to praise the people of the Old Testament (even though they had only received an incomplete revelation, he believes) while criticizing harshly those of his own day who rejected Christian beliefs. This same apologetic goal mandates the view that the Old Testament points to the New by means of typology, just as the author of the *Epistle of Barnabas* had done a century before Origen, and Paul too, in his interpretation of Sarah and Hagar (Gal 4:21–24), several decades before pseudo-Barnabas. Origen makes use of this approach in *Against Celsus*.

In his homiletic and exegetical works, however, Origen focuses on Scripture and the spiritual life. He is renowned for his perception of three

---

68. Trigg, *Origen*, 80–81, referring to Origen's *Homilies on Jeremiah* 20.2. See also Eusebius, *The History of the Church* 6.16.1, trans. Williamson, 256.

69. Origen, *Against Celsus* 4.32, trans. Chadwick, 209.

70. Melito of Sardis, a contemporary of Irenaeus, had declared the Jews to be guilty of murder in his paschal speeches; see *On Pascha* 72, 73, 74, 79, 86, trans. Stewart-Sykes, 56–59, 61.

71. *Against Celsus* 4.31, trans. Chadwick, 207.

72. *Against Celsus* 5.42, trans. Chadwick, 298.

levels of meaning in the Scriptures: the literal, the moral, and the spiritual. The spiritual level is that of typology and allegory, and Origen specifically cites the Epistle to the Galatians as his scriptural justification for this exegetical method.[73] We can see him employing it in his homilies on Joshua, where he interprets the symbolism of the promised land.[74]

Origen states that the God-given land into which Joshua led the people is the same as the land mentioned in Matt 5:5 ("Blessed are the meek, for they shall inherit the earth [or land]").[75] Entering the promised land, he says, signifies the attainment of spiritual perfection, whereas wandering in the wilderness is an allegory for sinning, for living without virtue.[76] Thus the occupation of the promised land by the Hebrews is significant only as a symbol for a spiritual state to be sought, not as an historical fact. As Wilken notes, Origen, like other writers before and after him, calls attention to the names of Joshua and Jesus (both *Iēsous* in Greek, as noted previously),[77] thus ascribing a Christocentric significance to Joshua's role.

Origen also quotes Josh 1:3, which on the literal level is a divine bestowal of land, and interprets this passage as a symbolic exhortation to Christians to understand Scripture on the spiritual level instead of the literal, as follows:

> "Every place, wherever you will ascend with the soles of your feet, I shall give to you." What are the places we ascend with the soles of our feet? The letter of the Law is placed on the ground and lies down below. On no occasion, then, does the one who follows the letter of the Law ascend. But if you are able to rise from the letter to the spirit and also ascend from history to a higher understanding, then truly you have ascended

---

73. Origen, *On First Principles* 4.2.4, 4.2.6, trans. Butterworth, 275–76, 280–81. Origen cites Gal 4:21–24, in which the verb "allegorize" appears in participial form; thus Scripture itself is seen to support the allegorical interpretation of it.

74. Wilken presents a fuller discussion of Origen's homilies on Joshua, adding evidence from the homily on Psalm 36 (37), another text where Origen interprets the promised land as eternal life in heaven rather than as an earthly territory. See *The Land Called Holy*, 76. Wilken's entire discussion of Origen on this topic, 65–78, is helpful in demonstrating that Origen's exegesis functioned as a watershed by spiritualizing Jerusalem and the promised land.

75. Origen, *Homilies on Joshua* 2.2, trans. Bruce, ed. White, 39. The Greek word for "land" in Josh 1:3 and for "earth" or "land" in Matt 5:5 is the same: *gē*. Robert Wilken, too, has noted that the Septuagint term for "the land" is the same as the word appearing in this beatitude; see *The Land Called Holy*, 47–48. Wilken, 75, also points out that for Origen "the land" was a heavenly realm.

76. *Homilies on Joshua* 4.4, trans. Bruce, ed. White, 56–58.

77. Wilken, *The Land Called Holy*, 75.

> the lofty and high place that you will receive from God as your inheritance.[78]

Here the Scripture itself is an instruction, couched in symbolic terms, concerning the optimal approach to understanding Scripture; that is, the spiritual meaning of the Scripture points to itself by advising an allegorical approach to exegesis. Any relevance of this Old Testament text to territorial claims has evaporated.

In one of his homilies on Genesis, Origen preaches on Gen 22:15–17, which is God's reiteration of his promise of innumerable offspring to Abraham, spoken from heaven immediately after Abraham's near-sacrifice of Isaac. Here Origen perceives Isaac as a type of Christ, and therefore the promise of offspring in Genesis 22 must be addressed to the church, which, like Abraham, will gain many children. Gen 22:17 foretells that Abraham's seed will conquer and occupy their enemies' cities. Origen applies this verse to the spiritual life, identifying Christ as Abraham's seed (as does Paul in Gal 3:16, remarks Origen), the enemies as sins, and the cities as human souls. Christ will conquer sin in the human soul if we cooperate with him.[79] The Hebrews' conquest of the Canaanite cities has become the personal victory of the Christian in combat against his or her own sins.

Origen's exegesis of the promised land in the Old Testament runs counter to any thought of achieving moral or spiritual progress by means of occupying any particular territory on earth. The land does not belong exclusively to any specific population because it is a symbol of life in Christ, which is accessible to all people. Origen's hope for the Jewish people is the same as his hope for all of humanity.

Tertullian

Tertullian, a contemporary of Origen's, produced an abundance of apologetic, polemical, and moral treatises in Latin-speaking North Africa. Though belonging to a different linguistic sphere, Tertullian expresses the same concepts as the Greek writers do. He, too, redefines the promised land, identifying it as "eternal life" and connecting the two names Joshua and Jesus, which are the same name, *Iesus,* in Latin (identical also in

---

78. *Homilies on Joshua* 2.3, trans. Bruce, ed. White, 39–40.

79. Origen, *Homilies on Genesis* 9, trans. Heine, 148–50, 153–56; quoted by Sheridan in *Genesis 12–50,* 114.

Greek, as mentioned above). The grace of Christ is now the path into the promised land, rather than the Law of Moses.[80]

Summary: Pre-Constantinian Perspectives

It is clear that the early Christian writers, though disparaging the Jews of their own day, were engaged in a much broader agenda than opposition to Judaism alone. In confrontation with factions calling themselves "Christian," namely, the Marcionites and various schools of Gnosticism, who insisted on jettisoning the Old Testament, the orthodox bishops had to prove its indispensability and its relevance to salvation in Christ, and they accomplished this by offering a distinctively Christocentric exegesis. Moreover, in order to defend the credibility of Christianity in a pagan culture that venerated ancient writings and suspected innovation, it was necessary to demonstrate that the church was the legitimate heir to the ancient and venerable legacy of Moses.[81] The redefinition of Old Testament language (such as "seed of Abraham") by means of typological and allegorical exegesis was the method by which the church appropriated the Old Testament and integrated it with Christocentric faith.[82]

But if the church was the owner and correct interpreter of the Old Testament, where did that leave the Jews of the patristic era? The early Christian answer was to present the church as the successor to ancient Israel, a transformed and expanded Israel that now welcomed both Jews and Gentiles and that held faith rather than genealogy as the criterion of membership. The corollary was that Jews who chose not to embrace faith in Christ had rejected membership in the new Israel with its path to

---

80. Tertullian, *Answer to the Jews* 9.22, quoted from *Ante-Nicene Fathers* 3 by Lienhard and Rombs, 19.

81. For example, Justin Martyr goes to great lengths to establish the antiquity of Christianity in his apologetic work addressed to pagans. He produces evidence from the Old Testament that Moses and the prophets predicted the coming of Christ, and then presents the claim (not unique to Justin) that Plato borrowed material from Moses, his predecessor; see his *First Apology* 30–53, 59; trans. Hardy, 260–77, 280. Athenagoras in his *Legatio* turns the tables on the pagans by arguing that their gods are more recent than the Christian God; see *A Plea Regarding Christians* 18, trans. Richardson, 316.

82. Typology is the perceived foreshadowing in the Old Testament of New Testament teachings, whereas allegorical exegesis in general discerns spiritual truths symbolized in biblical narratives. The two methods are closely related, but typology has a narrower scope than does allegory.

salvation. (This negative choice was of course reversible upon profession of faith.)

The implication of this perspective for the land of Palestine was that the land must represent symbolically some aspect of life in Christ. Justin Martyr foresaw a restoration of the land for all peoples of the world as a prelude to the final judgment. Irenaeus perceived it as representing the eschatological renewal of the entire earth, whereas Origen considered it to symbolize the individual's new life in Christ, and Tertullian equated it with the Christian's immortal after-life. These interpretations seemed to be supported by the events that had occurred in Judea, the destruction of the Jewish temple and of Jerusalem. When we combine these interpretations with the emotional detachment from home and hearth associated both with the ethos of martyrdom and with Stoic influences, the conclusion can only be that the general tenor of pre-Constantinian Christian thought does not support today's Zionist impulse toward settlement.

AFTER THE ACCESSION OF CONSTANTINE: PERSPECTIVES ON HOMELAND AND PROMISED LAND

Emperor Constantine (who reigned 312–337) put an end to persecution, bestowed magnificent gifts upon churches, and was finally baptized shortly before his death. It is plausible to assume that the conversion of the emperor, with the security that was now afforded to Christians, made it easier for Christians to engage in civic life and to sink deep roots into their local soil. As bishops became enmeshed with the imperial government and assumed positions of public leadership in their municipalities, the boundaries between the Christian community and the secular society tended to fade. A Christian could now take pride in his or her native city, as did Bishop Damasus of Rome in the middle of the fourth century, when he sponsored the construction of lavishly appointed shrines and churches in his city to transform it from a secular to a Christian capital.[83] An even more striking example of the entwinement of Christian faith and civic pride is the mass conversion of the residents of Majuma, the seaport of Gaza, which Constantine rewarded by granting it the status of a self-governing city and renaming it Constantia.[84]

---

83. See Trout, "Damasus and the Invention of Early Christian Rome," 517–36; also Henry Chadwick, *The Early Church*, 160–63, 215.

84. Sozomen, *Ecclesiastical History* 2.5 and 5.3, *Nicene and Post-Nicene Fathers*, 2nd Series, 2:262, 328.

Even in the face of these human realities, the earlier ideal, that of belonging nowhere in particular while being everywhere at home with the Lord, did not vanish, but was kept alive in the burgeoning monastic movement. *The Life of Antony,* Athanasius's hagiographic account of the ascetic piety and orthodoxy of Antony of Egypt (d. ca. 356 CE), describes Antony's withdrawal from areas of human habitation, beginning with his youthful decision to obey the gospel injunction "If you would be perfect, go, sell what you possess..."[85] This renunciation of home and possessions became one of the foundational principles of the monastic life for centuries to come, as it had been for the ethos of martyrdom earlier. This was the path to perfection.

But what of the Christians left behind in the cities? Their bishops continued to debate theological issues, to compose commentaries on Scripture, and to preach. The use of typology and allegory continued throughout late antiquity and on through the Middle Ages, and thus the New Testament was the indispensable lens through which the Old Testament could be comprehended. Thus the stories of Abraham and Moses were seen to symbolize Christian truths.[86]

Eusebius of Caesarea

An especially striking example of the christianization of the Old Testament promises to Abraham is the perspective of Eusebius of Caesarea, a prominent contemporary of Constantine, who pondered the correct way to classify Abraham, whether as a Jew or as a Hellenist. Eusebius concludes that, since all the nations are to be blessed in Abraham (Gen 12:1–3), he and the rest of "those holy men who lived before Moses and before Judaism" must be regarded as neither Jewish nor Hellenist but as belonging to "a third way of piety" that is the direct source of the Christian church, which preaches the gospel to all humankind. Because the Mosaic Law of

---

85. Athanasius, *The Life of Antony* 2, trans. Gregg, 31. The Scripture text is Matt 19:25.

86. Gregory of Nyssa (died ca. 395), like the Jewish scholar Philo more than three centuries earlier, interpreted elements of the Exodus story allegorically; for example, the hasty departure from Egypt represents the fleeting nature of this earthly life; the Egyptian army, the sinful passions; and the manna, the virgin birth of Jesus. See Gregory's *The Life of Moses* 106, 122, 139, trans. Malherbe and Ferguson, 79, 83, 88. For Didymus the Blind, an Alexandrian exegete of the late fourth century, God's promise to Abraham referred to the Christian virtues; see the comment on Gen 15:18 from his *On Genesis,* trans. and quoted by Sheridan in *Genesis 12–50,* Ancient Christian Commentary on Scripture, 40.

Zionism and Ancient Christianity

Judaism requires regular visits to Jerusalem, it is impossible for Diaspora Jews and for other nations to obey the Law, and it is precisely for this reason that Christ sent his disciples to teach all nations everywhere (Matt 28:19–20).[87] Thus Eusebius recognized the limitation of religious doctrines based on geography.

Ambrose

A homiletic emphasis in the recently christianized empire was that both lay people and clergy, while not expected to uproot themselves from their homes, were urged to avoid avarice, especially in the form of amassing money and land. The church now had many more Christians of higher social status, and their attachment to land was problematic to preachers. Land ownership could be associated with greedy acquisition and hoarding. Ambrose, Bishop of Milan in the late fourth century, wrote decisively on the topic of private property. In his comments on Naboth's vineyard[88] Ambrose repeatedly deplores the continual re-enactment of this story in his own day, as the wealthy greedily gobble up the property of the poor, feeling entitled to do so in spite of the fact that the land was created for all people.[89] In his advice to clergy, Ambrose, invoking Stoic philosophy but claiming that the Stoics derived their ideas from the Old Testament, says that private property is "not even in accord with nature, for nature has poured forth all things for all men for common use"—an idea, he says, whose ultimate source is Gen 1:26 (human beings sharing dominion over the earth) and Ps 8:7–8, which echoes the same concept.[90] In these examples, however, there is no reference to Abraham and the promised land.

We see Ambrose directly addressing exegetical questions concerning Abraham and his land in the treatise *On Abraham*. Here Ambrose interprets the Genesis narrative regarding Abraham both as moral instruction and as allegory. To be a son of Abraham consists in imitating his moral

---

87. Eusebius, *The Proof of the Gospel,* trans. Luibhéid, 39–45. The contribution of this treatise to the growth of Christian monasticism is discussed by Hollerich, "Hebrews, Jews, and Christians: Eusebius of Caesarea."

88. See 1 Kgs 21:1–24, where King Ahab of Israel seizes the ancestral land of the peasant Naboth the Jezreelite, and Naboth is murdered in the process. For the contemporary relevance of this story see Burge, *Whose Land? Whose Promise?* 91–92, 100, 197, and 217.

89. Ambrose, *De Nabuthae* 1.1.1—3.4.12, ed. C. Schenkl, 469–74.

90. Ambrose, *On the Duties of the Clergy* (*De officiis*) 1.132–33, *Nicene and Post-Nicene Fathers,* 2nd Series, 10:23.

virtues, and the descendants of Abraham are the church. Abraham's total devotion to God in departing from his homeland to encounter the unknown is an example for us to imitate. Furthermore, his freedom from the vice of greed is evident in his sharing the land with Lot, to whom he even gave the choice of territorial possessions, contenting himself with the land left over after Lot made his selection. Allegory appears in the varieties of Abraham's riches, specified as cattle, silver, and gold in Gen 13:2; these are, for Ambrose, allegorical representations of the corporeal senses (as brute beasts), the faculty of speech (as silver), and the mind (as gold). Thus Abraham's wealth did not consist in worldly goods. God's bestowal of land in Gen 13:14–15 comprises a vast expanse in all directions, that is, a geographic immensity that symbolizes the totality of creation, namely, nature. As in his comments on Naboth and in his advice to clergy, Ambrose states that nature is the possession of all human beings, even the penniless and the homeless, and the wise man must live in accord with it.[91]

John Chrysostom

A further contrast between greed in the late Roman Empire and the virtue of Abraham appears in the preaching of Ambrose's younger contemporary, John (later called "Chrysostom" or "Golden-Mouth"), Bishop of Constantinople at the turn of the fifth century. In one of his homilies on Genesis, John Chrysostom characterizes Abraham as "an alien and a nomad" on the basis of the fact that, not owning a family burial plot, he had to purchase a tomb for Sarah, and then Chrysostom goes on to say, "[Abraham] could not call a place his own, unlike many people today, who give all their attention to acquiring land, whole towns, and great wealth beyond telling. You see, he had sufficient riches in his attitude, and he put no store by these other things." After this, Chrysostom quotes Heb 11:9, which also describes Abraham as a foreigner.[92] The present life is a "foreign country," and our "true homeland" is the after-life.[93]

---

91. Ambrose, *De Abraham* 1.2.3–5, 1.3.10–12, 2.1.1–2, 2.1.4, 2.5.20, 2.7.37–38; ed. C. Schenkl, 502–5, 509–11, 564–66, 567, 578–79, 592–94.

92. John Chrysostom, *Homilies on Genesis* 48.2–4, trans. Hill, 25–27; quoted by Sheridan in *Genesis 12–50*, Ancient Christian Commentary, 117–18.

93. *Homilies on Genesis* 48.6, trans. Hill, 28. "Homeland" is *patris*, as in previous quotations; this Greek text in Migne, ed., Patrologia graeca 54:436.

Augustine

This belief in the heavenly homeland is illustrated in Augustine's *Confessions*, written in 397, by the moving episode of his mother's death. Having followed her son Augustine from their native North Africa to Italy, and having yearned and prayed for his conversion to Christianity, Monica, thrilled by the fulfillment of her longing, is then content to relinquish this earthly life. Dying far from home, Monica instructs her sons not to bother themselves with the task of transporting her body home for burial, but asks only to be remembered at the Eucharist.

> [Monica says,] "It does not matter where you bury my body. Do not let that worry you. All I ask of you is that, wherever you may be, you should remember me at the altar of the Lord." . . . [Augustine recalls] I had always known, and well remembered now, my mother's great anxiety to be buried beside her husband's body in the grave which she had provided and prepared for herself. . . . I did not know when it was that your [God's] good gifts had borne their full fruit and her heart had begun to renounce this vain desire, but I was both surprised and pleased to find that it was so. . . . [Augustine's friends] asked whether she was not frightened at the thought of leaving her body so far from her own country. "Nothing is far from God," she replied, "and I need have no fear that he will not know where to find me when he comes to raise me to life at the end of the world."[94]

In another book Augustine stresses the transitory nature of earthly phenomena, which mandates that we should fix our gaze on God, seeking to "enjoy" only God. To enjoy (Latin: *frui*) something is to love it for its own sake, and only God merits such love. Everything else on earth, even our closest human relationship, is a vehicle to convey us toward God, and we utilize (Latin: *uti*) these things without becoming permanently attached to them. We are travelers returning to our homeland, which is God, and we must not be distracted by the transitory pleasures of the journey.[95]

Apparently with this dichotomy in mind between the transitory and the eternal, Augustine wrestles with the meaning of "eternal" in regard to God's gift of the promised land to the ancient Israelites. Proceeding on the assumption that nothing on earth will endure forever, Augustine

---

94. Augustine, *Confessions* 9.11, trans. Pine-Coffin, 199–200. Bracketed material has been added by the present author.

95. Augustine, *On Christian Teaching* 1.3.3–1.5.5, trans. Green, 9–10. The Latin word for "homeland" here is *patria*; see *De doctrina Christiana* 1.4.4, ed. Martin.

concludes that the stones of the promised land as well as the possession of the land itself, must signify only figuratively an eternal verity. Here he interprets Josh 4:7:

> "And these stones will be for you a memorial to the sons of Israel unto eternity" [Josh 4:7]. How can it be "unto eternity," since heaven and earth will pass away? Can it be that these stones signify something eternal, since they themselves cannot be eternal?[96]

His exegesis of Gen 17:8 pursues the topic further:

> "I will give to you and your seed after you the land in which you are living, all the inhabited land for an eternal possession" [Gen 17:8]. The question is how he meant "eternal," since the land was given temporarily to the Israelites, that is, whether "eternal" was spoken in reference to this age. Thus, just as from the Greek [noun] *aiōn*, which means "age" [*saeculum*] is derived the [Greek adjective] *aiōnion*, likewise in Latin we can say "of the age" [*saeculare*].[97] From this are we compelled to understand here some kind of spiritual promise, accounting for the use of the word "eternal," from which something eternal is signified? Or is it the Scriptures' manner of speaking?[98]

Clearly Augustine finds it unthinkable that any territory could have been given to anyone as an eternal legacy. He has approached the text with the Platonic preconception that the unchanging realm of Being is an order of existence entirely different from the realm of Becoming, which is the world of human events. The mutable, impermanent features of earthly life can, however, operate as signs of the true realities in heaven, as Augustine states in reference to Josh 24:3:

> Here is what the seventy translators have: "And I have taken your father Abraham from across the river and I have led him into all the land" [Josh 24:3], which is an interpretation from what the Hebrew has: "And I have led him into the land of Canaan." It would be thus amazing if the seventy decided to substitute "all the land" for "the land of Canaan" without being aware of prophecy. Through prophecy this passage is to be understood

---

96. Augustine, *Quaestionum in Heptateuchum, Libri VII*, Book 7, Question 4, ed. Fraipont, 313–14; trans. mine.

97. The Greek version is determinative for Augustine because he is using the Septuagint.

98. *Quaes. in Hept.*, Book 1, Question 31, ed. Fraipont, 13; trans. mine.

Zionism and Ancient Christianity

as a promise of God more than as a fact because what will most surely come to be in Christ and in the church was announced ahead of time, and because the true seed of Abraham is not in the sons of the flesh, but in the sons of the promise.[99]

Augustine has redefined the progeny of Abraham as Christ and the church, just as the *Epistle of Barnabas,* Justin Martyr, and Irenaeus had done in the second century, and Origen in the third. By the time of Augustine, this interpretation was well established. The implications of the patristic tradition for Christians considering the dilemma of Israel and Palestine today will be explored immediately below.

ANCIENT CHRISTIAN TRADITION AND MODERN ZIONISM

Unlike today's Christian Zionists, our forebears in the Christian faith did not advocate a restoration of King Solomon's glorious city, or even the Jerusalem of King Herod. In fact, pagan proposals for reconstructing the temple worried early Christian thinkers[100] whose Christocentric exegetical approach regarded the Old Testament narratives of election, exodus, and conquest as pointing toward eternal salvation in Christ for the entire human race. As Wilken has observed (in regard to Origen),[101] a restoration of the Jerusalem of the Old Testament would contradict the belief that the Old Testament prophecies of return from exile and of renewal had already been fulfilled in the advent, ministry, and sacrifice of Jesus Christ.

The Christocentric perspective of ancient Christian exegetes did not regard the Old Testament as meaningful apart from the New Testament and did not identify God's people as any particular ethnic group. Nor did the patristic theologians point to any specific territory on earth as an indispensable locus for attaining knowledge of God; in fact, the ultimate

---

99. *Quaes. in Hept.*, Book 7, Question 25, ed. Fraipont, 330; trans. mine.

100. The *Epistle of Barnabas* 16.3–5, trans. Kleist, 60, forecasts failure for a Roman attempt to rebuild the Jerusalem temple; Kleist, 180 n. 166, connects these words to the policies of Emperor Hadrian prior to the Jewish revolt of 132–135. In the fourth century the bitterly anti-Christian Emperor Julian ("the Apostate") planned a restoration of a Jewish Jerusalem, probably including its temple. See Marcus, *The Jew in the Medieval World,* 8–12. The ancient Christian historian Sozomen connected Julian's favor toward the Jews with his antagonism toward Christians, and attributed to pagans a desire "to falsify the prophecies of Christ" by rebuilding the temple; see Sozomen, *Ecclesiastical History* 5.22, *Nicene and Post-Nicene Fathers,* 2nd Series, 2:343–44.

101. Wilken, *The Land Called Holy,* 76–78.

destination awaiting God's servants at the end of their journey of faith, in the view of the church fathers, is not of this world. Why, then, should we Christians urge our Jewish brothers and sisters to seek God through avenues that we ourselves do not pursue—for example, through imitating ancient Israelite conquests by seizing and occupying the lands of the West Bank? To promote such activity would be to compromise our Christian love for humanity by pushing God's Jewish servants into a blind alley.

We have seen that early Christians characterized an acquisitive attitude toward land (such as that which is displayed by the Israeli settlement movement) as avarice and therefore as sinful. Should today's Christians exempt from moral scrutiny the ongoing land confiscation in the West Bank? Christian moral criteria are not selectively applied to some people's actions and held aloof from the behavior of others, for "God shows no partiality" (Acts 10:34). Why, then, should we Christians urge our Jewish brothers and sisters to indulge in sinful behavior that we ourselves are admonished to avoid?

The stories of Christians enduring the challenges of life under persecution as well as the examples of monastic Christians direct our attention to the gospel texts in which Jesus urges his followers to detach themselves from homes and possessions. Moreover, early Christianity was a missionary religion, for the sake of which the faithful were asked to "Go, make disciples of all nations" (Matt 28:19) and to be "witnesses through Judea and Samaria and to the ends of the earth" (Acts 1:8). Given that the earliest traditions of our faith involve detachment from homeland,[102] as expressed, for example, in the *Epistle to Diognetus* (quoted at the beginning of this essay), why should we Christians attempt to convince either our Christian or our Jewish brothers and sisters that the path to God for anyone is to become passionately, inseparably attached to a particular geographical area?

Waggish opponents may mischievously propose that Palestinian Christians should exercise virtuous detachment by willingly relinquishing their lands in submission to Zionist initiatives. The response to this ludicrous suggestion can only be that King Ahab's infamous deed (of seizing Naboth's vineyard) remains heinous regardless of the victim's reaction to it—as is the case with all acts of theft from the poor. Voluntary submission to a usurper's greed, therefore, would amount to facilitation of, and

---

102. Detachment from homeland does not necessarily indicate rejection of political philosophy. For example, the author of the present essay, a Christian, is also an ardent proponent of the ideals of American democracy. The particular locale in which these ideals are to be implemented is another issue.

collusion in, a grievous sin—especially grievous since the seizure of ancestral land is, for many Palestinians, the deprivation of their only livelihood.

Rabbi Daniel F. Polish has compared the relationship between the land of Israel and Jewish spirituality to the role exercised by the sacrament of the Eucharist in the Christian life.[103] What he overlooks is that Christian sacraments employ common, ordinary materials (water, bread, wine, oil) that are available everywhere; thus our omnipresent Lord may be sacramentally present to us in any location where Christians may gather. Moreover, the Holy Spirit "blows where it wills" (John 3:8), and God's love extends to all people—Jewish and Gentile, male and female—in every place at every time. If we truly love our fellow human beings of all faiths, we will not dilute this message.

BIBLIOGRAPHY

The English version of the Bible utilized in this essay is *The Oxford Annotated Bible: Revised Standard Version*. This source has not been employed for biblical quotations appearing within extracts from patristic writings.

Texts and Translations

A Diognète. Edited by Henri Irénée Marrou. In Sources Chrétiennes 33bis, 2nd ed. 1951. Reprint. Paris: Cerf, 1997.
Ambrose. *De Abraham*. Edited by C. Schenkl. In Corpus Scriptorum Ecclesiasticorum Latinorum 32.1:501–638. Leipzig: Tempsky and Freytag, 1897.
———. *De Nabuthae*. Edited by C. Schenkl. In Corpus Scriptorum Ecclesiasticorum Latinorum 32.2:469–516. Leipzig: Tempsky and Freytag, 1897.
———. *On the Duties of the Clergy*. In vol. 10, 1–89, of *The Nicene and Post-Nicene Fathers*. Series 2. Edited by Philip Schaff. 14 vols. 1886–89. Reprint. Peabody, MA: Hendrickson, 1994.
Athanasius. *The Life of Antony*. In *Athanasius: The Life of Antony and The Letter to Marcellinus*, translated with introduction by Robert C. Gregg, 29–99. The Classics of Western Spirituality. New York: Paulist, 1980.
Athenagoras. *A Plea Regarding Christians*. Translated by Cyril C. Richardson. In *Early Christian Fathers*, edited by Cyril C. Richardson, 300–340. New York: Macmillan, 1970.
Augustine. *Confessions*. Translated by R. S. Pine-Coffin. New York: Penguin, 1961.
———. *De doctrina Christiana*. Edited by Joseph Martin. In Corpus Christianorum, Series Latina 32:1–167. Turnholt: Brepols, 1962.
———. *On Christian Teaching*. Translated by R. P. H. Green. Oxford: Oxford University Press, 1997.

---

103. Polish, "A Spiritual Home," 15.

———. *Quaestionum in Heptateuchum, Libri VII.* Edited by I. Fraipont. In Corpus Christianorum Series Latina 33:1–377. Turnholt: Brepols, 1958.
Cyprian. *Epistle 74.* Translated by G. W. Clarke. In Ancient Christian Writers 47:69–78. Mahwah, NJ: Newman, 1989.
Didache. In *The Apostolic Fathers,* vol. 1, edited and translated by Bart D. Ehrman, 416–43. 2 vols. Loeb Classical Library. Cambridge: Harvard University Press, 2003.
Didache. Edited and translated by James A. Kleist. In Ancient Christian Writers 6:3–25. Mahwah, NJ: Newman, 1948.
Epistle of Barnabas. In *The Apostolic Fathers,* vol. 2, edited and translated by Bart D. Ehrman, 12–83. 2 vols. Loeb Classical Library. Cambridge: Harvard University Press, 2003.
Epistle of Barnabas. Edited and translated by James A. Kleist. In Ancient Christian Writers 6:29–65. Mahwah, NJ: Newman, 1948.
Epistle to Diognetus. Edited and translated by Eugene R. Fairweather. In *Early Christian Fathers,* edited by Cyril C. Richardson, 213–24. New York: Macmillan, 1970.
Eusebius of Caesarea. *The History of the Church.* Translated by G. A. Williamson. New York: Penguin, 1965.
———. *The Proof of the Gospel.* In *The Essential Eusebius,* edited and translated with commentary by Colm Luibhéid, 39–58. New York: The New American Library, 1966.
The Greek New Testament. Edited by K. Aland, M. Black, C. Martini, B. Metzger, and A. Wikgren. 3rd ed. London: United Bible Societies in cooperation with the Institute for New Testament Textual Research, 1975.
Gregory of Nyssa. *Life of Moses.* In *Gregory of Nyssa: The Life of Moses.* Translated by Abraham J. Malherbe and Everett Ferguson. Preface by John Meyendorff. New York: Paulist, 1978.
Irenaeus. *Against Heresies.* In *The Ante-Nicene Fathers,* vol. 1, edited by Alexander Roberts and James Donaldson, 315–567. 10 vols. 1885–87. Reprint. Peabody, MA: Hendrickson, 1994.
———. *Against Heresies* (Selections). Translated by Edward Rochie Hardy. In *Early Christian Fathers,* edited by Cyril C. Richardson, 358–97. New York: Macmillan, 1970.
John Chrysostom. *Homilies against Judaizing Christians.* Translated by Paul W. Harkins. Fathers of the Church 68. Washington, DC: Catholic University of America Press, 1979.
———. *Homilies on Genesis.* Translated by Robert C. Hill. Fathers of the Church 87. Washington, DC: Catholic University of America Press, 1992.
———. *Homilia XLVIII.* Patrologia graeca 54:434–43. Edited by J.-P. Migne. 162 vols. Paris, 1857–1886.
Justin Martyr. *St. Justin Martyr: Dialogue with Trypho.* Translated by Thomas B. Falls. Revised with new introduction by Thomas P. Halton. Edited by Michael Slusser. Selections from the Fathers of the Church 3. Washington, DC: Catholic University of America Press, 2003.
———. *First Apology.* Translated by Edward Rochie Hardy. In *Early Christian Fathers,* edited by Cyril C. Richardson, 225–89. New York: Macmillan, 1970.
The Martyrdom of Perpetua and Felicitas. In *Acts of the Christian Martyrs,* edited and translated by Herbert Musurillo, 106–31. Oxford: Clarendon, 1972.

Zionism and Ancient Christianity

The Martyrdom of Saints Agapē, Irenē, and Chionē at Saloniki. In *Acts of the Christian Martyrs,* edited and translated by Herbert Musurillo, 280–93. Oxford: Clarendon, 1972.
Melito of Sardis. *On Pascha*. Translated with introduction and notes by Alistair Stewart-Sykes. Popular Patristics Series. Crestwood, NY: St. Vladimir's Seminary Press, 2001.
Origen. *Against Celsus*. Translated by Henry Chadwick. *Origen: Contra Celsum*. Cambridge: Cambridge University Press, 1953.
———. *Exhortation to Martyrdom*. Translated by John J. O'Meara. Ancient Christian Writers 19:141–96. Westminster, MD: Newman, 1954.
———. *Homilies on Genesis*. Translated by Ronald E. Heine. Fathers of the Church 71. Washington, DC: Catholic University of America Press, 1982.
———. *Homilies on Joshua*. Translated by Barbara J. Bruce. Edited by Cynthia White. Fathers of the Church 105. Washington, DC: Catholic University of America Press, 2002.
———. *On First Principles*. Translated by G. W. Butterworth. Gloucester, MA: Smith, 1973.
The Oxford Annotated Bible. Edited by Herbert G. May and Bruce M. Metzger. New York: Oxford University Press, 1962.
Philo. *On Abraham*. In *Philo,* vol. 6, translated by F. H. Colson, 4–135. 10 vols. Loeb Classical Library. Cambridge: Harvard University Press, 1935
Sozomen. *Ecclesiastical History*. In *The Nicene and Post-Nicene Fathers*. Series 2. Vol. 2, edited by Philip Schaff, 239–427. 14 vols. 1886–1889. Reprint. Peabody, MA: Hendrickson, 1994.
Tertullian. *On Idolatry*. In *The Ante-Nicene Fathers,* vol. 3, edited by Alexander Roberts and James Donaldson, 61–76. 10 vols. 1885–1887. Reprint. Peabody, MA: Hendrickson, 1994.
———. *To the Martyrs*. Translated by Rudolph Arbesmann. Fathers of the Church 40:17–29. New York: Fathers of the Church, 1959.

Modern Sources

Ateek, Naim Stifan. *Justice and Only Justice: A Palestinian Theology of Liberation*. Foreword by Rosemary Radford Ruether. Maryknoll, NY: Orbis, 1989.
Bauckham, Richard, Daniel R. Driver, Trevor A. Hart, and Nathan MacDonald, editors. *The Epistle to the Hebrews and Christian Theology*. Grand Rapids: Eerdmans, 2009.
Bockmuehl, Markus. "Abraham's Faith in Hebrews 11." In *The Epistle to the Hebrews and Christian Theology,* edited by Richard Bauckham, et al., 364–73. Grand Rapids: Eerdmans, 2009
Boyarin, Daniel. "Semantic Differences; or, 'Judaism'/'Christianity.'" In *The Ways that Never Parted,* edited by Adam H. Becker and Annette Yoshiko Reed, 65–85. Minneapolis: Fortress, 2007.
Burge, Gary M. *Jesus and the Land: The New Testament Challenge to "Holy Land" Theology*. Grand Rapids: Baker Academic, 2010.
———. *Whose Land? Whose Promise? What Christians are Not Being Told about Israel and the Palestinians*. Cleveland, OH: Pilgrim, 2004.
Chadwick, Henry. *The Early Church*. New York: Penguin, 1967.

Chapman, Colin. *Whose Promised Land? The Continuing Crisis over Israel and Palestine.* Grand Rapids: Baker, 2002.
Church, Philip. "'Here We Have No Lasting City' (Heb 13:14): The Promised Land in the Letter to the Hebrews." In *The Gospel and the Land of Promise*, edited by Philip Church et al., 45–57. Eugene, OR: Pickwick, 2011.
Church, Philip, Peter Walker, Tim Bulkeley, and Tim Meadowcroft, eds., *The Gospel and the Land of Promise: Christian Approaches to the Land of the Bible.* Eugene, OR: Pickwick, 2011.
Hays, Richard B. "'Here We Have No Lasting City': New Covenantalism in Hebrews." In *The Epistle to the Hebrews and Christian Theology*, edited by Richard Bauckham et al., 151–73. Grand Rapids: Eerdmans, 2009.
Heen, Erik M., and Philip D. W. Krey. "Introduction to Hebrews." In *Hebrews*, xvii-xxvi. Ancient Christian Commentary on Scripture: New Testament X. Downers Grove, IL: InterVarsity, 2005.
Hollerich, Michael J. "Hebrews, Jews, and Christians: Eusebius of Caesarea on the Biblical Basis of the Two States of the Christian Life." In *In Dominico Eloquio, In Lordly Eloquence: Essays on Patristic Exegesis in Honor of Robert Louis Wilken*, edited by Paul M. Blowers, et al., 172–84. Grand Rapids: Eerdmans, 2002.
Hooker, Morna D. "Christ, the 'End' of the Cult." In *The Epistle to the Hebrews and Christian Theology*, edited by Richard Bauckham et al., 189–212. Grand Rapids: Eerdmans, 2009.
Lienhard, Joseph T., S.J., in collaboration with Ronnie J. Rombs. *Exodus. Leviticus, Numbers, Deuteronomy.* Ancient Christian Commentary on Scripture: Old Testament III. Downers Grove, IL: InterVarsity, 2001.
Marcus, Jacob. *The Jew in the Medieval World: A Sourcebook, 315–1791.* New York: Sinai, 1938.
Nanos, Mark D. "*New* or *Renewed* Covenantalism? A Response to Richard Hays." In *The Epistle to the Hebrews and Christian Theology*, edited by Richard Bauckham et al., 183–88. Grand Rapids: Eerdmans, 2009.
Parmentier, Martin. "No Stone Upon Another? Reactions of the Church Fathers against the Emperor Julian's Attempt to Rebuild the Temple." In *The Centrality of Jerusalem: Historical Perspectives*, edited by M. Poorthuis and Ch. Safrai, 143–59. Kampen: Kok Pharos, 1996.
Polish, Daniel F. "A Spiritual Home: What Christians Should Know About Jewish Identity." *America* 204.12, whole no. 4929 (April 11, 2011) 12–15.
Scott, Sir Walter. "The Lay of the Last Minstrel." In *One Hundred and One Famous Poems, With a Prose Supplement*, rev. ed., edited by Roy J. Cook, 110. Chicago: Reilly & Lee, 1958.
Shepardson, Christine. "Controlling Contested Places: John Chrysostom's *Adversus Iudaeos* Homilies and the Spatial Politics of Religious Controversy." *Journal of Early Christian Studies* 15:4 (2007) 483–516.
———. "Paschal Politics: Deploying the Temple's Destruction against Fourth-Century Judaizers." *Vigiliae Christianae* 62:3 (2008) 233–60.
Sheridan, Mark. *Genesis 12–50.* Ancient Christian Commentary on Scripture: Old Testament II. Downers Grove, IL: InterVarsity, 2002.
Simon, Marcel. *Verus Israel: A Study of the Relations between Christians and Jews in the Roman Empire (135–425).* Translated by H. McKeating. The Littman Library of Jewish Civilization. 1948. Reprint. Oxford: Oxford University Press, 1986.

Simonetti, Manlio. *Biblical Interpretation in the Early Church: An Historical Introduction to Patristic Exegesis*. Translated by John A. Hughes. Edinburgh: T. & T. Clark, 1994.

Sizer, Stephen. *Zion's Christian Soldiers? The Bible, Israel and the Church*. Downers Grove, IL: InterVarsity, 2008.

Skarsaune, Oskar. "Does the Letter to the Hebrews Articulate a Supersessionist Theology? A Response to Richard Hays." In *The Epistle to the Hebrews and Christian Theology*, edited by Richard Bauckham et al., 174–82. Grand Rapids: Eerdmans, 2009.

Tarazi, Paul Nadim. *Land and Covenant*. St. Paul, MN: Orthodox Center for the Advancement of Biblical Studies, 2009.

Trigg, Joseph Wilson. *Origen: The Bible and Philosophy in the Third-century Church*. Atlanta: John Knox, 1983.

Trout, Dennis E. "Damasus and the Invention of Early Christian Rome." *Journal of Early Medieval and Modern Studies* 33.3 (2003) 517–36.

Wilken, Robert L. *John Chrysostom and the Jews: Rhetoric and Reality in the Late 4th Century*. 1983. Reprint. Eugene, OR: Wipf and Stock Publishers, 2004.

———. *The Land Called Holy: Palestine in Christian History & Thought*. New Haven: Yale University Press, 1992.

Zionism and
Modern Christianity

4

"Why the Caged Bird Sings"
Faithfulness in Exile[1]

Beverly Eileen Mitchell

Men and women of African descent have had their own experience of exile—forced to live in a land that was not their home. Their geographic displacement from the home of their ancestors was traumatic and wrought much grief. In this strange land they *heard* a religious message that was intended to leave them complacent about their bondage. By the power of the Holy Spirit, however, they *received* a message of liberation that stirred them in their fight for emancipation and the recognition of their dignity as full human beings. Their struggle for justice was arduous in a land where liberty was claimed as a natural birthright and a Judeo-Christian religious foundation inspired its first settlers. Nevertheless, these sons and daughters of Africa affirmed the faithfulness of God and were given the strength to "sing the Lord's song in a foreign land" (Ps 137:4).

---

1. The phrase "why the caged bird sings" is taken from the title of Maya Angelou's autobiographical work *I Know Why the Caged Bird Sings* (1970; copyright, 1969), which in turn was taken from Paul Laurence Dunbar's poem "Sympathy."

Zionism and Modern Christianity

THE AFRICAN-AMERICAN CONTEXT[2]

The exodus has been a prominent theme in the history of African-American religion and also in current black theological reflection. Early on, African Americans identified themselves with the enslaved Hebrews, and came to believe that just as God delivered the Hebrew slaves from their Egyptian oppressors, God would also liberate them from their American captors and deliver them into a promised land—or at least a rightful place in America. The second most notable experience of the Hebrews (by then called the Israelites) was their exile into Babylonian captivity. The exile of the Israelites was another paradigmatic experience that resonated profoundly in the collective psyche of the African-American religious community. The devastating journey to slavery in the New World was the exile experience for the slaves of African ancestry. While the Hebrew/Israelite people experienced their exodus deliverance before their painful exile, African Americans were "exiled" before they harbored any hope of divine deliverance in an exodus.

The survival of black slaves was determined by how well they could forge a new identity after being granted strange-sounding names, held captive in a hostile environment, and forced to perform back-breaking, uncompensated labor until their bodies wore out. Although they may have struggled at times with the notion of God's providential care, they did learn to "sing the Lord's song" (Ps 137:4) in a context of unjust suffering. Despite their involuntary "exile," the slaves encountered the Christian Gospel, perceived and embraced its liberating message, and their very existence would trouble the conscience of white Christian Americans.

Involuntary Exile

There are very few written accounts of the African men, women, and children who survived their abduction and the subsequent journey of the Middle Passage. There are, however, extant accounts of their transport by their captors. Even these secondhand accounts leave no doubt that the experience of capture and transport on the slave ships was, as John Hope Franklin put it quite baldly, "a veritable nightmare."[3] Even in less egregious

---

2. The discussion in the section subtitled "The African-American Context" is adapted from my chapter, "Black Abolitionists, Faithful Voices in Exile," in *Strangers in a Strange Land*, ed. Hogan and Faupel, 105–11.

3. Franklin, *From Slavery to Freedom*, 41.

circumstances, abrupt departure from one's homeland to a foreign country would evoke a sense of alienation, isolation, and disorientation. But in the case of African slaves, their suffering was compounded by the *manner* of exile—a journey of horrors steeped in brutality and degradation.

Prior to boarding a slave ship, some captives were forced to march their way to the coast from the interior of Africa. Others were bound and taken on long rides on river canoes to meet the waiting slave ships.[4] Slavers warehoused the captives in filthy holding cells until a full cargo was ready to depart. Once aboard the slave ship, the nightmare reached even greater proportions. Male slaves were manacled and shackled together, unable to position themselves comfortably, as they lay pressed together in their own filth, hardly able to breathe.[5] The chains and shackles often cut into the flesh of their wrists and ankles, as the slaves tried to lessen their discomfort. Under heavy guard by crewmen poised at strategic locations throughout the ship to prevent escape and mutiny, the slaves were forced to live in the cargo area for weeks and months in conditions unfit even for animals.[6] Those slaves who survived disease, suicide attempts, brutality, and attempted revolts landed on the shores of the New World, where they were prepared for auction. Bereft of family, homeland, and bodily liberty, it was not entirely certain whether and for how long they would survive. It is even less conceivable that they could sing *any* god's song in this foreign land. Progeny of the survivors of the Middle Passage, however, did come to sing the song of the God of Abraham, Sarah, Isaac, Rebecca, Mary, and the Son of Man, Jesus.

Evangelization

The fires of revivalism during the first and second Great Awakenings extensively shaped Christianity in the United States in the late eighteenth and early nineteenth centuries. The form of Christianity that emerged was "experiential, revivalistic, and biblically oriented,"[7] and attracted black slaves in large numbers.[8] What made evangelical Christianity appealing to blacks, in contrast to the arid, catechetically-oriented Anglican missionary

---

4. Mitchell, *Plantations and Death Camps*, 24, citing Harding, *There Is a River*, 3.
5. Ibid., 25, citing Rediker, *The Slave Ship*, 72.
6. Ibid., citing Harding, *There is a River*, 11.
7. Albert J. Raboteau, "The Black Experience," in Fulop and Raboteau, eds., *African American Religion*, 91.
8. As Albert Raboteau indicates, not all slaves converted to Christianity, nor were

efforts of the Society for the Propagation of the Gospel in Foreign Parts, was that the former method of evangelization placed much emphasis on the importance of having a dramatic conversion experience. For the slaves, evangelical Christianity meant conversion of sinners, extension of church membership, and reformation of society.[9] As African Americans struggled with the incongruity between the message of the gospel of freedom and the proclamation of that same gospel by slaveholders, the slaves were able to find meaning and value for their lives and to sustain their confidence that the Christian God did not condone their enslavement. Despite the fact that they shared many of the same doctrines, beliefs, and rituals, white and black Christians held fundamentally different views about God's will for black people and the meaning of the presence of blacks in America.[10] Evangelized blacks whose faith aroused resistance to slavery were disturbing prophetic witnesses. These witnesses pricked the conscience of white Americans as they rebuked not only the political hypocrisy of slavery in the land of liberty, but also the religious hypocrisy of a slaveholding nation shaped by the Judeo-Christian principle of the sacredness of human beings created in the image of God.

Evangelical Christianity forged an identity for the black community, strengthened their prophets for bold witness, and perfected their praxis with a notion of servanthood. God was praised because God the Liberator was seen as faithful. Implicit trust was placed in God despite the calamity of slavery. Although the Israelites under Babylonian captivity were called to repentance for their failure to remain faithful to God in the promised land, African Americans did not attribute their own exile and captivity to sins of their own making. They understood that in this instance, they were the ones sinned against. They also, however, accepted their dependence upon God and sought to be pruned of anything that would hinder God's work in them. Their fight for liberty and for the restoration of their dignity as full human beings was fueled neither by hatred nor by a desire for retribution. Black slaves, fugitive slaves, and freeborn blacks who encountered the gospel message formed a new community that gave them an identity as a people of God. They clung to the knowledge that they were saved, sanctified, and filled with God's Spirit. The challenge of faithful witness in the context of exile was borne in a spirit of humility, for the One whom

---

all of those who accepted the faith members of a church, but the teachings and worldview were familiar to most. See Raboteau, *Slave Religion*, 212.

9. Raboteau, "The Black Experience," 91.

10. Ibid., 98.

African-American Christians followed was Jesus, the ultimate Suffering Servant. It is out of the African encounter with evangelical Christianity on American shores that a distinct and vibrant expression of African-American spirituality[11] was born.

AFRICAN-AMERICAN SPIRITUALITY

Spirituality is life in the Spirit.[12] If the Holy Spirit is the "Giver of life,"[13] then the Holy Spirit is the foundation of Christian spirituality. Spirituality arises in the context of one's experiences of God. Spirituality emerges within specific socio-historical contexts. It is forged and shaped, not only by worship practices, but also by the believer's economic, social, and political realities. The spirituality of black slaves was formed in the crucible of slavery, African traditional religion,[14] and their encounter with Christianity in America. The fusion of elements of African traditional religious practices and the liberating gospel of Jesus Christ, in the context of human bondage, wrought a new expression of Christianity that not only supported and enlivened the faith of African Americans, but contributed as well to the tenor and spirit of Christianity in the United States as a whole.[15]

---

11. Because the term "spirituality" is so overly used and broadly applied today, I find it necessary to establish here that I define it in relation to Christianity. To do so, I draw upon the works of both Jürgen Moltmann and José Comblin for my conception of spirituality. Moltmann's *The Spirit of Life, A Universal Affirmation* and *The Source, The Holy Spirit and the Theology of Life*, and Comblin's *The Holy Spirit and Liberation*, provide insights on the work of the Holy Spirit that seem particularly fitting for discerning the nature of spirituality in the context of Christian black slaves.

12. In a Christian context "Spirit" refers to the *Holy* Spirit.

13. As described in the Niceno-Constantinopolitan Creed ("the Nicene Creed," as it is known).

14. The degree to which the slaves retained elements of African traditional religious beliefs and practices is difficult to assess definitively. Albert Raboteau addresses the debate on this issue between E. Franklin Frazier and Melville Herskovits, in *Slave Religion*, 48–87. Herskovits maintained that elements of African culture survived slavery in the United States. Frazier maintained the unlikelihood that elements of African culture survived slavery in the United States in any significant way. Raboteau takes the position that some elements of African culture did survive slavery in the United States, but to a lesser degree than Herskovits suggests. In their respective discussions of African-American spirituality, Bridges, in *Resurrection Song*, and Stewart, in *Black Spirituality & Black Consciousness*, take for granted the retention of African cultural influences on the slaves. I lean toward Raboteau's measured assessment of this retention, based on his evaluation of the available scholarship.

15. Lincoln and Mamiya, "The Religious Dimension," in *Down by the Riverside*, ed. Murphy, 32.

Central to understanding the nature of African-American (Christian) spirituality is the recognition of the presence and activity of the Holy Spirit in the life of the individual believer and the community as a whole. Because the Holy Spirit is the Giver of life, the Holy Spirit lifts up what has been debased, saves what has been lost, and rebuilds the people of God.[16] The action of the Holy Spirit can be seen as the oppressed are led to struggle against the forces that rob them of their vitality and compromise their lives through deadly economic, social, and political oppression. I maintain that the emergence of the African-American *community*, as an alternative to the collective of non-persons that perpetrators of slavery conceived the slaves to be, is itself an effect of the work of the Spirit in the lives of the slaves.

An examination of the development of Christianity within the slave community reveals several markers that are constitutive of early African-American spirituality: transformation, a sense of sacred worth, freedom, discernment of truth, and a notion of justice tempered by mercy.

Transformation

As José Comblin maintains, the Spirit of God "animates, purifies, and strengthens" those longings in which one tries to make life more human.[17] Life in the Spirit contributes energy, vitality, and an appetite for the quality of life that God desires for human beings. In the context of wanton dehumanization, the slaves did yearn to have their dignity as human beings acknowledged. They would have fought any impulse to acquiesce to their dehumanization. Life in the Spirit strengthened them whereby they were "never wholly defined or determined by their oppressors."[18] Human beings, whether slave or free, long for liberation, and the Holy Spirit is present in that longing. In the context of the slaves' conversion to Christianity, a "new humanity" was formed in their liberation from the power of sin and death. This new humanity, an inner transformative phenomenon, was manifested outwardly in the creation of the black community itself. Powerless and marginalized in American society, slaves, fugitive slaves, and free blacks were transformed by their life in the Spirit to work toward the betterment of the whole community.[19]

16. José Comblin, *The Holy Spirit and Liberation*, 69.
17. Ibid., 48.
18. Bridges, *Resurrection Song*, 5.
19. Comblin, *The Holy Spirit and Liberation*, 23.

Without the transformative power of the Spirit, it is difficult to imagine that such a community could have emerged, let alone have survived. The slaves' longing for right relationships, their struggle against an economic, social, and political arrangement that fostered death not life, reflected the presence of the Holy Spirit. This Spirit of Life gave them the impetus to resist their dehumanization.

Sense of Sacred Worth

The power of the Holy Spirit in the lives of those slaves who embraced Christianity enabled them to find solace and inner well-being despite their context. The enlivening work of the Spirit also served as a radicalizing force to enable them to resist complete psychological, spiritual, and physical subjugation by giving voice, power, and transcendence to the matters of their ultimate concern.[20] As Carlyle Stewart notes, what kept the slaves from destroying themselves "and their oppressors through unmitigated rage, such animus [was] often sublimated into cultural and spiritual inventions that [augmented] the quality of black life." The slaves were able to direct that energy to higher purposes.[21] African-American spirituality enabled blacks to affirm their self-worth as children of God, despite their condition. This ability to affirm their reality in the eyes of God, in a context bent toward eradicating any sense of their sacred worth, is probably the most powerful indication of spiritual creativity and genuine freedom.[22]

Freedom

As the Apostle Paul asserted in his letter to the church at Corinth, "Now the Lord is the Spirit, and where the Spirit of the Lord is, there is freedom" (2 Cor 3:17). If that insight is true, bondage, interior and/or exterior, is the enemy of life in the Spirit. True life in the Spirit will not permit us to rest easy in the bondage we impose upon ourselves or the bondage we impose upon others. The presence of the Spirit in the African-American community fueled the spirit of resistance that energized slaves to long for

---

20. Stewart, *Black Spirituality & Black Consciousness*, 42. In his discussion, Stewart refers to African-American spirituality as the active agent. I prefer to attribute this activity to the Holy Spirit.

21. Ibid., 48–49.

22. Ibid, 69.

their economic, social, and political freedom. The freedom they sought was both a gift and condition to be sought. As Comblin asserts,

> This freedom is a gift of the Spirit, an effect of the Spirit's presence in men and women. But as gift, it is also a human work, since the property of the Spirit is not to act of itself, but to tell creatures what to do, or to work through what they do.[23]

The tireless agitation of black abolitionists and the attempts of some slaves to flee their enslavement were an embodiment of the activity of the Holy Spirit—the One who engenders freedom.

Discernment of Truth

It is through the work of the Spirit that the slaves could appropriate the liberating gospel from the distorted gospel of the slaveholders. The Spirit, the Illuminator of truth (John 16:13), reinforced the reality of the slaves' God-given dignity. Despite all attempts by slaveholders to assert that the slaves were content with their lot, the slaves themselves knew that the way they were treated under chattel slavery denied their humanness. The slave system denied that they were made in the image of God. Nevertheless, the slaves discerned that the quality of their life in slavery was less than what God desired for them. Their conversion to a new humanity enabled them to envision and strive for a reality in which they could live as full human beings before others as well as God. This striving engendered resistance, and the power of that resistance thwarted their complete domestication for purposes of subjugation, domination, and annihilation.[24] The Holy Spirit moved within the spirit of black people and gave them not only the will to survive but also the courage to confront and surmount the threats to their existence. The Spirit empowered them to form their own sense of identity.[25]

---

23. Comblin, *The Holy Spirit and Liberation*, 63.
24. Stewart, *Black Spirituality & Black Consciousness*, 2.
25. Bridges, *Resurrection Song*, 5. In her discussion, Bridges refers to African-American spirituality as the active agent. I prefer to attribute this activity to the Holy Spirit.

Justice Tempered by Mercy

As Flora Wilson Bridges indicates, African-American spirituality was determined less by attendance to rituals, creeds, and doctrine than by whether one had actually had an encounter with God and been transformed in such a way that one sought to "treat everyone right."[26] This transformation could not have happened apart from the working of the Spirit, for the Holy Spirit works in and through humans to form them into the image of Christ, so that they are able to live according to the commandment to love not only their neighbors but their enemies as well. This transformation also convinced them of the justice of God. Affirmation of the justice of God made it easier to relinquish the urge for revenge. It also made it possible for African Americans to be forgiving, for they understood that those who hated them were also expressing a hatred of God. Because of their belief in a moral and just universe—wherein one reaps what one sows (Gal 6:7)—they could leave matters of restitution "in God's hand."[27] Their spirituality, grounded in the conviction of the sovereignty of God, assured them that the God of justice would give them total liberation from all dehumanizing sources.[28]

Out of the wellsprings of African-American spirituality, Christian slaves learned to truly pray. Such prayers did not need to be forced out of them; rather, their prayers sprang naturally from the reality of their life of enlivened faith.[29] The Negro spirituals sprang from that same Spirit.

THE NEGRO SPIRITUALS: THE CAGED BIRD'S SONGS

It is understandable that a time of defeat and disaster, such as the Israelites experienced in their exile, might lead a faith community to question the possibility of "singing the Lord's song" in a strange land. Enslaved Africans who found themselves on foreign soil were granted the grace to sing the Lord's song, *literally*. In the context of servitude that threatened to extinguish their past, rendered their present uncertain, and made their future doubtful, the Negro spirituals emerged from the hearts of the enslaved as

---

26. Ibid., 2.
27. Ibid., 168.
28. Stewart, *Black Spirituality & Black Consciousness*, 41.
29. Comblin, *The Holy Spirit and Liberation*, 137.

a testimony to the possibility that one could indeed sing the Lord's song in a strange land.[30]

Scholars who have reflected on the Negro spirituals have identified this genre of music as both life-affirming and faith-engendering.[31] For Howard Thurman the spirituals were "an expression of the slaves' determination to *be* in a society that [sought] to destroy their personhood."[32] The songs were "an affirmation of the dignity of the black slaves, the essential humanity of their spirits."[33] These songs were a way of holding their personhood together. W. E. B. Du Bois saw these "sorrow songs" as an affirmation of life.[34]

Not only were the spirituals an affirmation of life, but they were also an affirmation of faith. As Du Bois maintained, "Through all the sorrow of the Sorrow Songs there breathes a hope—a faith in the ultimate justice of things."[35] Concurring with Du Bois' assessment, Christa Dixon affirmed these songs as "songs of faith by the people, of the people, [and] for the people."[36] The slaves were granted a faith that allowed them to believe that they were sheltered by God, and they trusted in God's justice and ultimate goodness.[37] Such faith emerged as a result of their *experience* of God's presence. This sense of the presence of God gave them the strength to endure suffering and to transform that suffering into an event of redemption.[38] Because they did not question God's existence, justice, or goodness, these songs were sung to exhort the community of hearers to remain faithful in a world of trouble.[39] By rehearsing the mighty deeds of God in song, they

---

30. It has often been maintained that the lyrics of the spirituals were sometimes interpreted in multiple ways, beyond a religious sense. Sometimes the spirituals were used as a code to announce a secret meeting or to announce an impending opportunity to escape enslavement. Albert J. Raboteau favors a more nuanced view of the ambiguity of the meaning of the spirituals. Acknowledging that there were spirituals that were used to announce secret meetings or to warn of the overseer's approach, he contends that "the relevance of most spirituals to the situation of slavery was both more ambiguous and more profound." See Raboteau, *Slave Religion*, 246–47. In the discussion here, the spirituals have been interpreted in their religious sense.

31. Dixon, *Negro Spirituals*, x.

32. Cone, *The Spirituals and the Blues*, 16.

33. Ibid.

34. Ibid., 13.

35. Ibid.

36. Dixon, *Negro Spirituals*, 113.

37. Cone, *The Spirituals and the Blues*, 60, 61.

38. Ibid., 56.

39. Ibid., 57.

"'remembered' the Exodus, the Covenant, the prophets, and, most of all, Jesus' life, death, and resurrection."[40] The spiritual "Let My People Go" is an example of such a rehearsal of the mighty acts of God in the deliverance of the Hebrews from Pharaoh:

> When Israel was in Egypt's land,
> Let my people go;
> Oppressed so hard they could not stand,
> Let my people go;
> Go down, Moses, 'way down in Egypt's land
> Tell ole Pharaoh
> Let my people go.[41]

The spirituals were also an important vehicle of self-expression in a context in which the thoughts and feelings of a slave were of little or no importance to those wedded to sustaining the institution of slavery. Singing the spirituals allowed the slaves to give voice to their true feelings; they were a true faith response to a God who loved and cared for them just as they were.[42] The slave songs imparted the truth of the slaves' existence on earth despite the efforts to portray the institution of slavery as benign and God-ordained. The theological assumption of black slave religion, as expressed in the spirituals, was that "slavery contradicts God, and God will therefore liberate black people."[43] Central to them was a notion of God's involvement in history and the liberation of the oppressed from bondage.[44] In a profound way, the slaves knew that this world would never be their home:

> Deep River, my home is over Jordan;
> Deep River, my home is over Jordan.
> O don't you want to go to that Gospel Feast,
> That promised Land where all is peace?
> Deep River, I want to cross over into camp ground.[45]

They also knew that trouble would not last always.

> Soon-a-will be done with troubles of the world;
> Soon-a-will be done with troubles of the world;

40. Ibid., 60.
41. Thurman, *Deep River*, 13.
42. Dixon, *Negro Spirituals*, 113.
43. Cone, *The Spirituals and the Blues*, 65.
44. Ibid., 66.
45. Thurman, *Deep River*, 66.

Going home to live with God.[46]

These songs were a testimony to God's faithfulness to the slaves and an exhortation for the slaves to be faithful to God.

The spirituals were not only affirmations of life and faith, but also a record of a people's history. Mark Miles Fisher reminds us that the chief aim of African music was to articulate the history of the people.[47] Descendants of those Africans rendered the spirituals as historical documents of the people of the African Diaspora.[48] In the context of the African slave in America, where the perpetrators fought mightily to "de-historicize black existence" and "foreclose the possibility of a future defined by their African heritage," the spirituals affirmed their rightful existence and posited a future that reaffirmed their existence as children of God.[49] As James Cone maintains,

> The spirituals are historical songs which speak about the rupture of black lives; they tell us about a people in the land of bondage, and what they did to hold themselves together and to fight back. . . . In Africa and America, black music was not an artistic creation for its own sake; it was directly related to daily life, work, and play. In the spirituals, black slaves combined the memory of their fathers with the Christian gospel and created a style of existence that participated in their liberation from earthly bondage.[50]

In their history-telling, life-affirming, faith-engendering task, the spirituals also were an expression of resistance. By affirming that they were children of God, the people asserted their resistance to their oppressors' assault on their humanity and sacred worth. They steadfastly refused to accept that their enslavement was God's will for them, despite the attempt of their masters to indoctrinate them otherwise.

Not surprisingly, the theme of liberation loomed large in the spirituals. Probably the best-known spiritual that illustrates this is:

> O freedom! O freedom!
> O freedom over me!
> An' befo' I'd be a slave,

---

46. Thurman, *The Negro Spiritual Speaks*, 28.
47. Fisher, *Negro Slave Songs*, 1.
48. Ibid., 25.
49. Cone, *The Spirituals and the Blues*, 23.
50. Ibid., 30.

> I'll be buried in my grave,
> An' go home to my Lord an' be free.[51]

The slaves dared to believe that at some point in time they would be free. As Cone observes, their resistance to their masters, whether subtly through secret worship or boldly as in the Nat Turner revolt, enabled them to "create beauty and worth out of the ugliness of slave existence."[52]

The Negro spirituals were songs sung unto the Lord. They reveal why the caged bird sings. Mark Miles Fisher states that these songs were "the aching, poignant cry of an entire people."[53] The spirituals held a reservoir of emotion and served multiple purposes. As Cone explains about the role of song in the African-American community,

> We sing when we are happy and when we are sad; when we get a job and when we lose one; when we protest for our rights and when the formal achievement of them makes no difference in the quality of our life. Singing is the medium through which we talk to each other and make known our perspectives on life to the world.[54]

Howard Thurman, yet another interpreter of the genre, is particularly insightful in summing up the significance of the spirituals:

> They express the profound conviction that God was not done with them; that God was not done with life. The consciousness that God had not exhausted His resources or better still that the vicissitudes of life could not exhaust God's resources, did not ever leave them. This is the secret of their ascendancy over circumstances and the basis of their assurances concerning life and death.[55]

These songs in a strange land were a testimony to the creativity and the resilience of the slaves. They give evidence of their confidence in God's providential care and are an affirmation of the presence of grace in exile.

---

51. Thurman, *Deep River*, 29.
52. Cone, *The Spirituals and the Blues*, 27, 28, 29.
53. Fisher, *Negro Slave Songs*, 25, quoting V. F. Calverton.
54. Cone, *The Spirituals and the Blues*, 129.
55. Thurman, *The Negro Spiritual Speaks*, 37–38.

GRACE IN EXILE

The experience of being stolen from one's homeland or driven away by economic, social, or political oppression will always evoke a deep sense of loss and profound grief. Nevertheless, the experience of Africans in America indicates that even though the road they trod was "stony,"[56] they encountered the grace of God in a strange land. That experience of grace came through the strength and creativity they were given to fashion themselves as a new people. Partly African, partly "American," they managed to forge an identity, a culture, and a way of being in an environment that was hostile to their well-being. *Can there be grace in exile?* African Americans answered with a faith-filled "yes." As Yvonne Delk asserts,

> For the exiles there were no songs of Zion but the Lord's songs. The songs of Zion were not the songs of patriotism or nationalism. They were the songs of the Creator, who alone calls worlds into being and sets before us the ways of life and death. It was this recognition that forced the exiles to cry out, "How shall we sing the Lord's song in a foreign land?" . . . We can sing the Lord's song if we understand a simple but very basic truth. The Lord's song was created not only for Zion but for Babylon as well. We are called to sing God's song wherever people feel trapped, wherever they are hurting. The most powerful song that was ever sung was heard from a cross.[57]

Not only is it possible to sing a new song in exile, but these songs of praise were designed to be sung particularly when praise was most difficult to muster.

Does the ability, however, to sing songs of praise in exile mean that one can or even should "seek the welfare of the city" (Jer 29:7) in the context of forced abduction? As African Americans struggled under slavery and labored under the burden of Jim Crow, they never gave up on the notion that this strange land could one day be their temporal home. Even as they fought for their own emancipation, their sights were set on the welfare of a nation they believed held promise and blessing for all. Even in their strongest condemnation of the political and religious hypocrisy of America, black slaves and their descendants always kept in mind that the freedom and social harmony for which they fought were a reality they

---

56. An allusion to stanza 2 of James Weldon Johnson's famous anthem "Lift Ev'ry Voice."

57. Delk, "Singing the Lord's Song," in *Can I Get a Witness?* 94, 98.

hoped to share in *with* repentant oppressors. The welfare of innumerable cities rested on a reconciliation that followed justice.

David Walker, the author of one of the most passionate, prophetic appeals to the conscience of America, warned against this nation's insistence on upholding an institution that dehumanized both the slave *and* the slaveholder. He exhorted:

> Remember Americans that we must and shall be free and enlightened as you are, will you wait until we shall, under God, obtain our liberty by the crushing arm of power? Will it not be dreadful for you? I speak Americans for your good. . . . Treat us like men, and there is no danger but we will all live in peace and happiness together. . . . What a happy country this will be, if the whites will listen. What nation under heaven will be able to do any thing with us, unless God gives us up into its hand? But Americans, I declare to you, while you keep us and our children in bondage, and treat us like brutes, to make us support you and your families, we cannot be your friends. You do not look for it, do you? Treat us then like men, and we will be your friends. And there is not a doubt in my mind, but that the whole of the past will be sunk into oblivion, and we yet, under God, will become a united and happy people. The whites may say it is impossible, but remember that nothing is impossible with God.[58]

Although Walker's *Appeal* is sometimes perceived as harsh, but certainly always as uncompromising, he, too, offers a vision of a peace between the races that would ensure the welfare of the entire country. Even in his entreaty to his oppressors for repentance, he makes an astonishing offer of friendship and indicates a willingness to "sink the whole of the past into oblivion," as a distinct possibility.

More than one hundred and twenty years later, black men and women, who participated in the continuing struggle for the "soul" of America in their fight for justice, continued to seek the welfare of the cities with a sense of hope. For example, the martyred civil rights leader Martin Luther King stated the following in his defense of young freedom riders in 1961, who were seeking to integrate segregated lunch counters in the South:

> These students are seeking to save the soul of America. They are taking our whole nation back to those great wells of democracy which were dug deep by the Founding Fathers in the formulation of the Constitution and the Declaration of Independence.

---

58. Walker, *David Walker's Appeal*, 89–90.

> In sitting down at the lunch counters, they are in reality standing up for the best in the American dream.[59]

In his defense of the freedom riders, he not only praises the Founding Fathers, but he also appeals to the nation to be faithful to its ideals. He expresses the desire for the welfare of the nation. In his iconic "I Have a Dream" speech in 1963, he affirmed the willingness of the African-American community to join with whites for the welfare of the nation:

> With this faith we will be able to work together, to pray together, to struggle together, to go to jail together, to stand up for freedom together, knowing that we will be free one day. This will be the day when all of God's children will be able to sing with new meaning—"my country 'tis of thee; sweet land of liberty; of thee I sing; land where my fathers died, land of the pilgrim's pride; from every mountain side, let freedom ring"—and if America is to be a great nation, this must become true.[60]

King had a vision of a moral life together, shared by the progeny of slaveholders and the descendants of slaves. It included faithfulness to the country's highest ideals, but with the assumption that we would act as children of God.

The grassroots civil rights activist Fannie Lou Hamer, who worked for the cause of black freedom from her own faith convictions, also indicates a desire to ensure the welfare of America:

> So we are faced with a problem that is not flesh and blood, but we are facing principalities and powers and spiritual wickedness in high places: that's what St. Paul told us. And that's what he meant. America created this problem. And we forgive America, even though we were brought here on the slave ships from Africa. Even though the dignity was taken away from the black men, and even though the black women had to bear not only their own kids but kids for the white slave owners. We forgive America for that. But we're looking for this check now, that's long past due, to let us have our share in political and economic power, so that we can have a great country together.[61]

She reckoned that the racial problem in America is, at its root, a spiritual problem that needs to be fought on spiritual grounds. One of the weapons

---

59. King, "The Time for Freedom Has Come (1961)," in *I Have a Dream*, ed. Washington, 81.

60. King, "I Have a Dream," in *I Have a Dream*, ed. Washington, 105.

61. Hamer, "Sick and Tired," in *Can I Get a Witness?* 180.

against evil is forgiving love. It is astonishing that she not only freely offers forgiveness, but posits a willingness to put the painful past behind, in the hope that sharing and reciprocity would lead to the spiritual and moral greatness of the country. Hamer, like Walker and King, had a hunger for the righteousness that is the foundation for communal living reminiscent of the reign of God. The eschatological vision that renders all earthly approximations pale in comparison informs the hopes and longings of those who love justice more than a life of ease and love peace more than their own personal welfare.

Singing songs of praise in exile is never easy. The memories of a former homeland invade the senses. Heartache over the loss of a treasured past can cut off one's breath. Songs of praise in exile can only be sung by grace through faith—a faith that has been sown and watered and tended with care. African Americans felt grace in exile and sang songs of praise that revealed why the caged bird sings.

HOW CAN PALESTINIAN REFUGEES SING?

As one reflects on the experience of African Americans in the United States and the current plight of the Palestinian refugees in the Middle East, the question arises as to whether Palestinians can possibly sing songs of praise in light of their lengthy experience of exile. As in the case of the Africans who were brought to the Americas as slaves, there would appear to be many reasons for Palestinians not to sing.

Nineteen forty-eight marks the year when the Palestinian refugee problem began. When David Ben-Gurion declared the birth of the State of Israel, what followed was the first round of what has been a protracted armed conflict between Arabs and Jews over the Holy Land. What Israelis have called the "War of Independence," Palestinians have called *An-Nakba*, "The Catastrophe." There are additional aspects about which Palestinians and Israelis fail to see eye-to-eye. They disagree about the root causes of the displacement of Palestinians as a result of the war in 1948. They also disagree about who can properly be categorized as a Palestinian refugee. Moreover, they disagree about how many refugees there are.[62] The periodical *Forced Migration Review* reports that three-quarters of the Palestinian people are displaced and more than half of them are displaced outside

---

62. Rempel, "Who Are the Palestinian Refugees?" *Forced Migration Review* 26, August 2006, Palestinian Displacement, at www.fmreview.org/FMRpdfs/FMR26/FMR2602.pdf, 1, 2; accessed on Feb 12, 2012.

the borders of their historic homeland.[63] The Palestinian people have the dubious distinction of being the largest single group of refugees, *and* their situation is the longest unresolved refugee case in the world today.[64] The Palestinians are indeed "a nation of forced migrants."[65]

What is not in dispute is that life in the refugee camps is precarious at best. For the majority of Palestinian refugees poverty plagues their existence. Like refugees in other contexts, the level of hardship varies for the refugees outside the Occupied Palestinian Territories, based on the economic, political, and perceived ethnically-motivated unrest in Jordan, Syria, and Lebanon, with the Palestinians in the latter country faring the worst. Most of the refugees have been unable to assimilate into their host country.[66] The largest age group in the refugee population is youth, with more than 50 percent of the refugees in the Occupied Territories younger than twenty-five years of age as of 2010.[67] Although the United Nations Relief and Works Agency for Palestine Refugees in the Near East (UNRWA) is mandated to provide protection and essential services to Palestinian refugees in the Gaza Strip, the West Bank, Jordan, Lebanon, and the Syrian Arab Republic, their resources are greatly stretched. To complicate matters, access restrictions placed on UNRWA by Israeli policy have adversely impacted the delivery system for healthcare.[68] The long-term health of the refugees is endangered because of malnutrition due to the inability to ensure an adequate food supply.[69] Health-wise, women, children, and adolescents are particularly vulnerable. Treatment for post-traumatic stress and other psychological and behavioral disorders has become a high priority. Gender-based violence has increased within the camps because of high unemployment and other economic and social difficulties.[70] Fam-

---

63. Ibid., 1.

64. Ibid. Rempel's figures are corroborated by *Salaam* at www.salaam.co.uk/themeofthemonth/may02_index.php?l=5; accessed on Feb 12, 2012.

65. Bolesta, "Socio-Economic Conditions of Palestinian Refugees in Jordan, Syria, and Lebanon," Transformation, Integration, and Globalization Economic Research, *Tiger Working Paper Series* No. 35, 2002, 3, at www.tiger.edu.pl/publikacje/TWPNo.35.pdf; accessed on Feb 12, 2012.

66. Ibid., 10.

67. WHO Sixty-Fourth World Health Assembly, Provisional Agenda Item 15, A64/INF.Doc./3, May 12, 2011, at http://apps.who.int/gb/ebwha/pdf_files/WHA64/A64_ID3-enpdf, 3; accessed on Feb 12, 2012.

68. Ibid., 7.

69. Ibid., 4.

70. Ibid.

ily violence, domestic abuse, and violence among children and youth is on the rise.[71] Though international aid is provided for the refugees, the aid has not been enough to change the miserable standard of living that Palestinian refugees face.[72]

Points of Resonance

The plight of the Palestinian refugees defies an easy comparison with that of African Americans in the United States, past or present. Although their contexts are vastly different, nevertheless African Americans can find points of resonance with the experience of Palestinian refugees, beyond their forcible removal from their respective ancestral homes. The Israeli settlements, which Israel began to establish in the Occupied Territories in the 1970s, severely limit the freedom of the refugees to move from one place to another.[73] Israeli settlements encircle Palestinian neighborhoods in East Jerusalem, isolating Palestinian neighbors from each other and cutting off East Jerusalem from the West Bank.[74] Similar settlements in the West Bank are established in ways that eliminate territorial contiguity for Palestinians: they separate town from town, village from village; and Palestinians cannot move from one Palestinian town to the next without passing through Israeli-controlled territory.[75] For African Americans, this severe restriction of movement harks back to the days after the Civil War when the South instituted the harsh Black Codes.[76] Such restrictions, with the attending humiliation that such a situation can evoke from the refugees, heighten the sense of longing for freedom that can foster the kind of desperation that fuels violent attempts to overthrow the yoke of one's oppressor. Just as black slaves in the United States resorted to revolts that proved unsuccessful, the Palestinians have had their own failures at seeking violent redress for their oppression as well.[77]

---

71. Ibid., 6.
72. Bolesta, "Socio-Economic Conditions of Palestinian Refugees," 14, 15.
73. Weaver, *What is Palestine-Israel?* 30.
74. Ibid., 31.
75. Ibid., 32.
76. The Black Codes were laws enacted to control the labor, migration, and other activities of the newly freed slaves.
77. In the nineteenth century there were three major, unsuccessful slave revolts in the United States: the revolt led by Gabriel Prosser in 1800, the revolt led by Denmark Vesey in 1825, and the Nat Turner rebellion of 1831. With regard to the Palestinians I

Zionism and Modern Christianity

The Tie That Binds

What ultimately connects African Americans with Palestinian refugees is the same theological tie that connects each and every human being. Each person has been created in the image of God (Gen 1:26–27). Although the biblical text does not reveal precisely in what way we image God, it is evident from biblical texts that human beings are the culmination of God's creative efforts (Gen 1:26–31 and Ps 8). As a consequence of this divine imprint, a measure of glory is imparted to each human being. I define this glory as "human dignity."[78] The gift of God's image, and the glory that arises from that image, is something that we all share. It is the spiritual tie that binds each of us to each other as well as to God.

Human dignity is given to *all* humans, regardless of abilities, capabilities, or disabilities. This dignity is not mitigated by our economic, social, or political status or our gender or national origin. This dignity is granted to us from the beginning of life and follows us to the grave. In fact, I would argue that, when attempts are made to assault that dignity, the cry of protest, whether vocal or muted, is indeed a staunch testimony to the ultimate indestructibility of this dignity. The plight of the Palestinians stands as an indictment of the global community because they have experienced the kind of maltreatment that belies their full humanity. While the leadership in the international community squabbles and dithers over the "Palestinian problem," men, women, and children continue to suffer needlessly. The Palestinians are crying out: "How long, O Lord, how long?" As Jean Zaru so eloquently concurs,

> In Palestine today you will hear the cry of every Palestinian, man, woman, and child. A cry. A cry from the depths. A cry of grief and lamentation. A cry with the hope that this grief might possibly penetrate the numbness of history and open a way towards newness.[79]

This indignant cry of protest from deep in the soul of the Palestinian people is a rebuke and a judgment against the attempted violation that reverberates in the heavens. African-American slaves and their progeny

---

have in mind the First Intifada from 1987 to 1993 and the Second Intifada from 2000 to 2005.

78. I define human dignity at length in both *Black Abolitionism*, 3–5, and *Plantations and Death Camps*, 39–45, 50–51.

79. Zaru, "Theologising, Truth, and Peacemaking," 175.

have known well this cry from the depths of their souls. This cry signals the presence of what I call "defacement."

Defacement is the assault on the dignity of another. To deface someone or a group is to deny them the respect and honor due to them by virtue of their full humanity. It is to fail to see their sacredness. It is to dismiss a person or persons as having no value or worth. It is to say that they do not matter, that they have no place in God's world. It is an attempt to erase their presence and a challenge to their right to exist. Defacement is too often a violent expression of sin in our day. What African Americans have experienced, historically, in the United States is defacement. Today's Palestinian refugees are being victimized by defacement as well. The contempt with which they are treated by their Israeli occupiers, as well as the lack of powerful national allies who advocate for them, compounds their physical suffering. It eats at their souls.

African Americans and the Palestinian refugees, however, are more than their suffering. As human beings created in the image of God, they experience the full range of human affect. There is the possibility of joy in the midst of sorrow. They are a people who belong to God, who—despite their present circumstances—have not been abandoned. By grace through faith, they, too, can experience God's presence and rehearse their own stories of God's faithfulness in the midst of their tribulations. Moreover, just as the slaves had those who were willing to agitate for their emancipation, the Palestinian refugees have those within the global community who see their suffering, hear their cries, and are moved to challenge this long season of occupation. There are voices being raised that recognize our interconnectedness to the refugees by virtue of sharing in that which makes us all human. There are those of us who understand that our welfare is tied to the welfare of the marginalized, the outcasts, and the dispossessed, and are committed to fight for the preservation of the dignity and the well-being of the Palestinian people. But *their* songs of lamentation and praise, frustration and hope, sorrow and joy, will be their own.

BIBLIOGRAPHY

Biblical quotations have been drawn from the New Revised Standard Version.
Angelou, Maya. *I Know Why the Caged Bird Sings*. 1970. Reprint. New York: Ballantine, 2009.
Bolesta, Andrzej. "Socio-Economic Conditions of Palestinian Refugees in Jordan, Syria, and Lebanon." In *Transformation, Integration, and Globalization Economic*

Research, Tiger Working Paper Series, No. 35, 2002. At www.tiger.edu.pl/publikacje/TWPNo.35.pdf. Accessed on Feb 12, 2012.

Bridges, Flora Wilson. *Resurrection Song: African-American Spirituality.* Maryknoll, NY: Orbis, 2001.

Comblin, José. *The Holy Spirit and Liberation.* Maryknoll, NY: Orbis, 1989.

Cone, James H. *The Spirituals and the Blues: An Interpretation.* Maryknoll, NY: Orbis, 1991.

Delk, Yvonne. "Singing the Lord's Song." In *Can I Get a Witness?: Prophetic Religious Voices of African American Women, An Anthology,* edited by Marcia Y. Riggs, 93–96. Maryknoll, NY: Orbis, 1997.

Dixon, Christa K. *Negro Spirituals: From Bible to Folk Song.* Philadelphia: Fortress, 1976.

Fisher, Miles Mark. *Negro Slave Songs in the United States.* New York: Carol, 1990.

Franklin, John Hope. *From Slavery to Freedom: A History of Negro Americans.* 5th ed. New York: Knopf, 1980.

Hamer, Fannie Lou. "Sick and Tired of Being Sick and Tired." In *Can I Get a Witness?: Prophetic Religious Voices of African American Women, An Anthology,* edited by Marcia Y. Riggs, 170–80. Maryknoll, NY: Orbis, 1997.

Harding, Vincent. *There is a River: The Black Struggle for Freedom in America.* New York: Harcourt Brace & Co., 1981.

The Holy Bible. New Revised Standard Version. Division of Christian Education of the National Council of the Churches of Christ in the U.S.A. Nashville, TN, and Burlingame, CA: Holman Bible Publishers for Cokesbury, 1989.

Lincoln, C. Eric, and Lawrence H. Mamiya. "The Religious Dimension: 'The Black Sacred Cosmos.'" In *Down by the Riverside: Readings in African American Religion,* edited by Larry G. Murphy, 32–37. New York: New York University Press, 2000.

Mitchell, Beverly Eileen. *Black Abolitionism, A Quest for Human Dignity.* Maryknoll, NY: Orbis, 2005.

———. "Black Abolitionists, Faithful Voices in Exile." In *Strangers in a Strange Land: A Festschrift in Honor of Bruce C. Birch upon his Retirement as Academic Dean of Wesley Theological Seminary,* edited by Lucy Lind Hogan and D. William Faupel, 105–12. Lexingon, KY: Emeth, 2009.

———. *Plantations and Death Camps: Religion, Ideology, and Human Dignity.* Minneapolis: Fortress, 2009.

Moltmann, Jürgen. *The Source: The Holy Spirit and the Theology of Life.* Minneapolis: Fortress, 1997.

———. *The Spirit of Life: A Universal Affirmation.* Minneapolis: Fortress, 1992.

Raboteau, Albert J. "The Black Experience in American Evangelicalism: The Meaning of Slavery." In *African American Religion: Interpretive Essays in History and Culture,* edited by Timothy E. Fulop and Albert J. Raboteau, 89–106. New York: Routledge, 1997.

———. *Slave Religion: The "Invisible Institution" in the Antebellum South.* Oxford: Oxford University Press, 1980.

Rediker, Marcus. *The Slave Ship: A Human History.* New York: Viking, 2007.

Rempel, Terry M. "Who Are the Palestinian Refugees?" *Forced Migration Review* 26 August 2006, "Palestinian Displacement." At www.fmreview.org/FMRpdfs/FMR26/FMR2602.pdf. Accessed on Feb 12, 2012.

Stewart, Carlyle Fielding, III. *Black Spirituality & Black Consciousness: Soul Force, Culture and Freedom in the African-American Experience*. Asmara, Eritrea: Africa World, 1999.

Thurman, Howard. *Deep River*. 1975. Reprint. Richmond, IN: Friends United, 1990.

———. *The Negro Spiritual Speaks of Life and Death*. 1975. Reprint. Richmond, IN: Friends United Press, 1990.

Walker, David. *David Walker's Appeal, To the Coloured Citizens of the World, but in particular, and very expressly, to those of the United States of America* (1830). Introduction by James Turner. Baltimore, MD: Black Classic, 1993.

Washington, James M., editor. *I Have a Dream: Writings and Speeches That Changed the World*. New York: HarperSanFrancisco, 1992.

Weaver, Sonia K. *What is Palestine-Israel? Answers to Common Questions*. Waterloo, ON: Herald, 2007.

WHO Sixty-Fourth World Health Assembly, Provisional Agenda Item 15, A64/INF. Doc./3, May 12, 2011. At http://apps.who.int/gb/ebwha/pdf_files/WHA64/A64_ID3-enpdf. Accessed on Feb 12, 2012.

Zaru, Jean. "Theologising, Truth, and Peacemaking in the Palestinian Experience." In *Speaking the Truth: Zionism, Israel, and Occupation*, edited by Michael Prior, 165–89. With foreword by Archbishop Desmond Tutu. Northampton, MA: Olive Branch, 2005.

5

Praiseworthy Intentions, Unintended Consequences

Why Krister Stendahl's Quest for "Healthy Relations" between Jews and Christians Ended Tragically

Paul H. Verduin

> American Jews have not created this situation by ourselves. We have been enabled by our Christian compatriots, who, because of their sense of responsibility for historical anti-Semitism, feel that they have no right to criticize any actions that Israel may take, even when these actions violate principles of human rights and justice cherished by Jews and Christians alike.
>
> — Mark Braverman,
> Jewish-American author, 2010[1]

> Get off the backs of the Jews, and leave them in the hands of God.
>
> — Krister Stendahl,
> noted Christian biblical scholar, 1993[2]

---

1. Braverman, *Fatal Embrace*, 7.
2. Stendahl, *Final Account*, 40.

Paul H. Verduin —*Praiseworthy Intentions, Unintended Consequences*

KRISTER STENDAHL (1921–2008)—RENOWNED LUTHERAN biblical scholar and theologian, iconoclastic New Testament author and lecturer, Harvard University Professor of New Testament (1954–84) and faculty dean (1968–79) at Harvard Divinity School, Bishop of Stockholm (1984–88) in his native country of Sweden, Professor of Christian Studies at an acclaimed Jewish institution, Brandeis University (1991–93), and finally from 1994 to 1998, co-director of Israel's Osher Center for Tolerance and Pluralism at the Shalom Hartman Institute in Jerusalem. On the occasion of this eminent Swedish-American luminary's death in 2008, just six days before his eighty-seventh birthday, the presiding bishop of America's leading Lutheran body, the Evangelical Lutheran Church in America (ELCA), justifiably called Krister Stendahl one of "the most distinguished biblical scholars, theological leaders and insightful churchmen of the 20th century."[3] Professor Stendahl's paradigm-shattering New Testament scholarship set down in his books, articles, and lectures, his patient but persistent advocacy of women's rights in church and society, his steadfast promotion of interfaith dialogue and mutual respect, and especially his unwavering devotion to building what he called "healthy relations"[4] between Christians and Jews won him near-universal praise throughout an influential academic career spanning five decades.

Indeed, more than anything else, it was Dr. Stendahl's lifelong efforts to mend relations between Jews and Christians, both theologically[5] and existentially, that had a pervasive and lasting influence toward reforming the attitudes held by mainline Christians toward Jews and Judaism, both in the United States and internationally. But tragically, Stendahl's tireless and unflinching efforts to promote positive Christian attitudes toward all things Jewish—even to the point of coaxing Christians into viewing themselves as "honorary Jews"[6]—unintentionally but inevitably contributed to a growing and pervasive attitude of acquiescence, especially in American mainline churches, toward the accelerating and ever more blatant viola-

---

3. Mark S. Hanson, quoted in "Krister Stendahl, Lutheran Bishop, Dean, Scholar and Teacher, Dies," ELCA News Service, Apr 17, 2008, found at http://www.elca.org/Who-We-Are/Our-Three-Expressions/Churchwide-Organization/Communication-Services/News/Releases.aspx?a=3842; accessed on Mar 15, 2012.

4. Stendahl, "Christian-Jewish Relations"; Stendahl, letter to Judith Banki, Mar 2, 1992. Both in unpublished Stendahl Papers, boxes 9 and 14, respectively. The term "Stendahl Papers" refers to the "Papers of Krister Stendahl, 1956–2007," Collection 2080402, in the Andover-Harvard Library, Harvard Divinity School.

5. Stendahl, "Paul Among Jews and Gentiles," 1, 3.

6. Ibid., 5.

tions of human rights and international law committed by the Jewish State of Israel against the Palestinian people, whether Muslim or Christian, particularly after 1967.

While throughout his long career these injustices on the part of the State of Israel were mounting and becoming ever more apparent, Stendahl was assiduously accelerating and intensifying his leadership and involvement in organizing and institutionalizing his well-intentioned but uncritical efforts in building and intensifying Jewish-Christian dialogue and fostering a concomitant sense of appreciation for Jewish religion, Jewish culture, and the Jewish people among a wide audience of American and European Christians. In his quest to create an atmosphere of unvarnished appreciation for all things Jewish, Stendahl's words, "Get off the backs of the Jews,"[7] his advice to Christians intended primarily in regard to theological issues, was easily and implicitly interpreted by Stendahl's hearers and readers to include political controversies concerning the State of Israel's actions as well.

But tragically, although by the turn of the twenty-first century he could no longer hide from his closest Jewish colleagues his sense of outrage and impatience at the cruelties and pervasive oppression he observed in the occupied Palestinian territories, Stendahl was somehow never able or willing to address publicly—even once—the injustices committed by Israel toward Palestinians that by now had become so obvious to him. This essay traces the development of Krister Stendahl's impressions of and involvement with the Jewish community—from his youth in Sweden during the Nazi era, during his years of teaching at Harvard and Brandeis, via his tireless lecturing at colloquia from Berkeley to Jerusalem, and culminating in the painful breach in his relations with his closest American Jewish colleague that occurred in 2002.

EARLY AWAKENING: COMING OF AGE IN HITLER'S THIRD-REICH EUROPE

It is often remarked that in military matters, the generals are always fighting the last war, a latter-day proverb that would seem to apply to modern theologians as well—particularly to theologians, biblical scholars, and church leaders of the post-World War II era of the twentieth century. The initial sense of relief that through total and unrelenting war the brutal, dictatorial Axis powers of Germany, Italy, and Japan had been utterly defeated

---

7. Stendahl, *Final Account*, 40.

gave way quickly to a profound and universal sense of guilt that so much death, destruction, and carnage had been carried out by both sides in the conflict, whether offensively or defensively, and mostly by the Christian nations of Europe and North America and their Christian populations. Was Christianity—the dominant religion and moral compass of Western civilization—somehow itself to blame for this unspeakably inhuman war?

The sense of collective guilt was particularly painful among Lutherans in Germany, Scandinavia, and the United States, for the Lutheran faith had arisen and been nurtured in Germany. Germany had been and continued to be the home or place of origin of most Lutheran theologians, hymn-writers, and thinkers. Moreover, at the time of World War II and during the post-war years the majority of the world's Lutherans lived in Germany. In view of this German heritage of Lutheranism and Lutherans, the question had to be asked: To what degree had attitudes of anti-Judaism among Lutheran theologians and pastors, from the great Martin Luther himself on down, contributed to German anti-Semitism as well as anti-Semitism in other countries? Had the cultural anti-Semitism so widespread among Catholics and Lutherans in Germany inevitably led to Hitler's malevolent plan for systematically annihilating Europe's Jews? To more than a few Lutheran scholars and church leaders around the world, the answer was yes. And if the answer was yes, what could be done to atone for this terrible wrong? For a young Swedish Lutheran New Testament scholar in his early thirties who emigrated to America in 1954, the place to start was a fresh look at the theology of the New Testament writers, particularly that of the Apostle Paul.

But how was it that Krister Stendahl developed his lifelong passion to rehabilitate Lutheran and mainline Christian attitudes toward the Jewish religion and all things Jewish? A definitive answer to this question seems beyond reach, but there are tantalizing hints in the circumstances of his upbringing in pre-World War II Sweden. At the time of his death, Brita Stendahl, Krister's widow, told the *New York Times* that her late husband's faith, as the *Times* paraphrased her, "grew out of extremely painful arthritis in his spine that started when he was 16 or 17. While traveling to other countries for treatments and spas, he learned several languages, including German."[8] Thus we learn that while he was still a teenager the young, impressionable future Harvard New Testament scholar spent time traveling

---

8. Martin, "Krister Stendahl, 86, Ecumenical Bishop, is Dead," *New York Times*, Apr 16, 2008.

in Germany and elsewhere on the European continent during the prewar Nazi era of the late 1930s.

It is to be noted that Stendahl turned sixteen in 1937, four years after Hitler and the Nazis came to power in Germany. Austria was apparently one of the countries Stendahl visited during his adolescence in the late 1930s, as Hitler's grip on Germany, Austria, and the Czech Sudetenland was intensifying. From an oblique account given by Stendahl himself, it seems he visited Vienna during this period, and that while in Vienna young Stendahl came into contact with members of a Swedish missionary unit operating there for the purpose of converting Jewish residents of Vienna to Christianity. Somewhat ironically, these Swedish missionaries seeking to bring spiritual salvation to Viennese Jews were among the first Christians in Austria to try desperately, out of a sense of Christian compassion, to save these Jews from intensifying Nazi persecution, according to Krister Stendahl's later account.[9] Whether any of these rescue efforts were witnessed by Stendahl himself has not been learned, and no other source has been found that would reveal the teenage Stendahl's impressions of the Nazi regime from this or other possible firsthand encounters. In any event, by the onset of World War II in September 1939, Stendahl had presumably returned to Sweden.

It is to be remembered that for nearly all of World War II, neutral Sweden was completely surrounded by lands the German armies had occupied: on the south, across the Baltic Sea, Denmark, Germany itself, and the conquered Baltic states; on the east, Finland, initially Germany's ally; and to the north and west, conquered Norway. In a word, the proud country of Sweden had become a ghettoized open-air prison of sorts, with very few people able to get in or out. Pro-Nazi agitators spied on fellow-citizens, and German U-boats patrolled its harbors. The Swedish government was forced to allow German shipments of supplies destined for the Third Reich's soldiers in occupied Norway to cross Sweden on Swedish railways. Until mid-1944, the outcome of the war seemed in doubt. This atmosphere of ominous gloom must have magnified the pain from Krister Stendahl's unrelenting spinal disability as he studied at Uppsala University for the Christian ministry in the Church of Sweden. Did Krister Stendahl's personal experiences of chronic pain and a kind of ghettoized existence as he entered his twenties create in his heart a sensitivity for the prolonged sufferings of Europe's Jews? One wonders. In 1944, the year before the war's end, Stendahl was ordained at the age of twenty-three

---

9. Stendahl, "Christian-Jewish Relations," 2–3, box 9.

for the Lutheran ministry in the Church of Sweden and accepted his first charge as a parish priest.[10]

When the war was over, young Stendahl once again resumed his travels abroad, this time going to Cambridge University in England and to Paris for further study. He also served as a chaplain at Uppsala before earning his doctorate there in 1954.[11] In 1947 he married Brita Johnsson, a fellow Swede and a scholar in Scandinavian and comparative literature,[12] who became his life partner for sixty-one years.

Although his Uppsala doctoral dissertation on the newly discovered Dead Sea Scrolls and his pioneering study of authorship issues in St. Matthew's Gospel awakened Krister Stendahl's probing mind to the enigmatic and complicated world of first-century Judaism, the road to international recognition as a biblical scholar opened much more fully for him when he was offered a professorship at Harvard University's divinity school in 1954. The young New Testament scholar and newly minted author seems to have jumped at the opportunity. He accepted the challenge of proving himself in this new milieu, and clearly threw himself into the task at hand, for just three years later he was offered tenure at this prestigious American Ivy League institution located in Cambridge, Massachusetts, just outside of Boston.

JEWS, GENTILES, AND THE APOSTLE PAUL: THE WEIGHT OF WESTERN GUILT

Though he had already proven his scholarly mettle in his first book, *The School of St. Matthew*, it was through his iconoclastic reinterpretation of the writings of the Apostle Paul that Stendahl was to achieve international attention and ultimately acclaim. Moreover, it was Stendahl's travels with Paul and the great apostle's theology-laden New Testament Epistles that rather quickly led the new Harvard academician into the world of Christian-Jewish dialogue and détente.

When he was securely tenured at Harvard Divinity School, Professor Stendahl waded into his re-examination of the New-Testament-era relationship between Jews and Gentiles cautiously, perhaps even hesitantly,

---

10. Joyner, "Krister Stendahl, 1921–2008," *Harvard Divinity School News and Events,* at http://www.hds.harvard.edu/news-events/2011/02/07/krister-stendahl-1921-2008; accessed on Mar 15, 2012.

11. Ibid.

12. "Krister Stendahl," ELCA News Service, Apr 17, 2008. See note 3.

as the 1960s approached. But once it was published two years later, his 1961 essay, "The Apostle Paul and the Introspective Conscience of the West," proved to be revolutionary. The issue that Stendahl attacked head-on as he rounded the age of forty was "the function and the manifestation of introspection in the life and writings of the Apostle Paul."[13] Stendahl proceeded by boldly challenging whether Paul's letter to the Romans was really primarily about "justification by faith," as Protestant Christianity had adamantly maintained since the time of Martin Luther and the Reformation. The Harvard professor audaciously asserted that he found no evidence in Romans or any of the apostle's other writings of a guilt-ridden conscience on the part of Paul, a previously unassailable paradigm of Pauline interpretation that, as Stendahl correctly maintained, "has its roots in Augustine and in the piety of the Middle Ages."[14] The Pauline awareness of sin, Stendahl went on to say, had been misinterpreted by Protestant scholars in the light of Luther's introspective struggle with his conscience.[15]

Totally contrary to the prevailing centuries-old view, Krister Stendahl overturned the tables of his scholarly predecessors with the assertion: "A fresh look at the Pauline writings themselves shows that Paul was equipped with what in our eyes must be called a rather 'robust' conscience." There is no indication, he maintained, that Paul had had any difficulties in fulfilling the Jewish religious laws as they were understood in his day. The New Testament professor reminded readers that in Phil 3:6 Paul boasted that he had been "flawless" as to "the righteousness required by the law."[16] While Stendahl, in adherence to orthodox Christian teaching, acknowledged Paul's position that "the old covenant, even with its provision for forgiveness and grace, is not a valid alternative any more [sic]," he quickly added the following rather provocative statement: "It is also striking to note that Paul never urges Jews to find in Christ the answer to the anguish of a plagued conscience."[17]

Having thus summarily dismissed the fifteen-hundred-year paradigm of a guilt-ridden Apostle Paul suffering unbearably from the pangs of a relentlessly unforgiving conscience, Stendahl bravely turned to the issues "with which he [Paul] actually deals." These he enumerated as follows:

13. Stendahl, "Apostle Paul and Introspective Conscience," 79.
14. Ibid., 79, 83.
15. Ibid., 79.
16. Ibid., 80.
17. Ibid., 81.

1. "What happens to the Law [the Torah, the law of Moses] ... when the Messiah has come?"
2. "What are the ramifications of the Messiah's arrival for the relation between Jews and Gentiles?"[18]

Thus, in his radically new paradigm for understanding Paul, one might say that for Krister Stendahl the central question for the apostle is no longer "how humanity as a whole gets right with God" (that is, "justification" as theologians have understood that term), but rather "how Jews and Gentile Christians are to relate to each other in their divergent but perhaps equally valid approaches to the same God" (that is, achieving co-existence as co-religionists who honor and worship the same Abrahamic God, but who have different understandings of what is required in order to be in right relationship with God).

Stendahl brushed aside yet another defining paradigm in his landmark essay on Paul and introspective conscience when he baldly stated that the great apostle did not experience a road-to-Damascus conversion event, but "only the call to the work among the Gentiles."[19] Moreover, Stendahl maintained that "we look in vain for a statement in which Paul would speak about himself as an actual sinner."[20] Although one does well to resist the temptation to lift such unconventional, unorthodox assertions by Stendahl out of their fuller context, it would be hard to understate their jolting effect on readers in the early 1960s—especially since Stendahl supplied a concluding caveat such as, "We should venture to suggest that the West for centuries has wrongly surmised that the biblical writers were grappling with problems [such as sin, guilt, justification, sanctification] which no doubt are ours, but which never entered their consciousness."[21] "The theologian," he added, "would be suspicious of a teaching and a preaching which pretended that the only door into the church was that of ever-more introspective awareness of sin and guilt. For it appears that the Apostle Paul was a rather good Christian, and yet he seems to have had little such awareness."[22]

---

18. Ibid., 84.
19. Ibid., 85. See also Stendahl, "Paul among Jews and Gentiles," 7.
20. Stendahl, "Apostle Paul and Introspective Conscience," 91.
21. Ibid., 94–95.
22. Ibid., 95–96.

"SOMETHING WRONG": THE HISTORIC SEPARATION OF JEWS AND GENTILE CHRISTIANS

While it was Krister Stendahl's paradigm-shattering 1961 essay, "The Apostle Paul and the Introspective Conscience of the West," that gained him wide attention and no little amount of notoriety, it was in his 1963 lecture "Paul among Jews and Gentiles," which followed closely on its heels just two years later (but available only on audiotape until 1976), that he clearly spelled out his radical reinterpretation of the first-century apostle's views on the relations between Jews and Gentiles, and, by extension, between Christians and Jews.[23]

"It will be my contention," Stendahl stated on this lengthy essay's very first page, "that the main lines of Pauline interpretation—and hence both conscious and unconscious reading and quoting of Paul by scholars and lay people alike—have for many centuries been out of touch with one of the most basic of the questions and concerns that shaped Paul's thinking in the first place: the relation between Jews and Gentiles."[24]

"The lost centrality of 'Jews and Gentiles' is most clearly to be felt in a study of Romans," Stendahl went on to say. For Paul, it was chiefly his concern about relations between Jews and Gentiles that led the apostle to employ as one of his arguments the idea of justification by faith, the Harvard Divinity School professor asserted. But in so doing, Stendahl denied the traditional view that Paul in Romans is chiefly addressing the question: "On what grounds, on what terms, are we to be saved?"[25]

Stendahl allows that part of Paul's purpose in Romans is to explain how his mission to the Gentiles fits into God's total plan, but the Harvard academic is quick to add, "Simultaneously he [Paul] sees that God has mysterious and special plans for the salvation of Israel." Stendahl maintains that for Paul the key question is the relationship between "the church and the Jewish *people*—not 'Christianity' and 'Judaism' . . . the relation between two communities and their coexistence in the mysterious plan of God."[26]

If these assertions by Krister Stendahl were not enough to make his Christian readers and listeners sit up and take notice, what he stated immediately following this would have positively riveted them bolt upright.

---

23. Stendahl, "Paul among Jews and Gentiles," Preface; Stendahl, *Final Account*, xi.
24. Stendahl, "Paul among Jews and Gentiles," 1.
25. Ibid., 3.
26. Ibid., 4. Emphasis is Stendahl's.

"It should be noted," Stendahl began, "that Paul does not say that when the time of God's kingdom, the consummation, comes Israel will accept Jesus as the Messiah. He says only that the time will come when 'all Israel will be saved' ([Rom] 11:26)." "It is stunning to note," Stendahl continued, "that Paul writes this whole section of Romans (10:18—11:36) without using the name of Jesus Christ. This includes the final doxology (11:33–36), the only such doxology in his writings without any christological element."[27] Stendahl intensifies his thesis on the real meaning of Romans by remarking, "Paul's reference to God's mysterious plan [for the Jews] is an affirmation of a God-willed coexistence between Judaism and Christianity in which the missionary urge to convert Israel is held in check."[28]

It is hard to escape the conclusion that for Christian New Testament scholar Krister Stendahl, the Jews, unlike the rest of fallen humanity, are not a people who have any need of, or can derive any benefit from, an acknowledgment of God's revelation in Jesus Christ. Indeed, quite sarcastically Stendahl adds this provocative statement: "Once this mystery [of God's unique and special plans for the Jews] became inoperative in the central thinking of the church . . . the road was ever more open for beautiful spiritualizations of Pauline theology. Romans became a theological tractate on the nature of faith. Justification no longer 'justified' the status of Gentile Christians as honorary Jews." "Paul," he adds, "was no longer seen 'among Jews and Gentiles' but rather as the guide for those perplexed and troubled by the human predicament."[29]

The New Testament's Pauline Epistles as interpreted by Stendahl portray a very different view of Paul's mission than that presented by Western, especially Protestant, theologians since Augustine of Hippo and Martin Luther. According to this Harvard Divinity School academic iconoclast, Paul's ministry is based on "the specific conviction that the Gentiles will become *part* of the people of God without having to pass through the [Jewish religious] law." "This," concluded Stendahl, "is Paul's secret revelation and knowledge."[30] The implication here, of course, is that those contemporaries of Paul who adhere to the Jewish religious laws already constitute "the people of God" by virtue of prior standing, and that their special standing with God has nothing to do with Jesus Christ, or if one prefers, with Jesus the Messiah. Viewing Jews and Christian-Jewish

27. Ibid.
28. Ibid.
29. Ibid., 5.
30. Ibid., 9. Emphasis added.

relations in any way that implies a judgmental Christian attitude toward Judaism, such as that which Stendahl thinks Paul perceives and combats in Rom 11, was, said the Harvard professor, "swallowed up in self-serving Christian anti-Judaism, if not anti-Semitism."[31] Indeed, one could easily infer from this statement that perhaps for Stendahl, any Christian critical analysis of Judaism is anti-Judaism and tantamount to anti-Semitism. The implied warning that Stendahl appears to be conveying to his twentieth-century Christian readers can hardly be missed.

Krister Stendahl ended his highly original and influential essay on "Paul among Jews and Gentiles" by confirming the apostle's writings as "indispensable to the Christian community," though on the Harvard academic's own revolutionary terms. He praises his Paul as "our champion," as "a Jew who by vicarious penetration gives to us Gentiles *the justification* for our claims to be God's children in Jesus Christ."[32] In case one misses the point, Stendahl clarifies his truly revolutionary notion of justification by adding: "He [Paul] came by God's call of a Jew, justifying the right of us Gentiles by a unique argument of faith."[33] Through faith in Jesus the Jewish Messiah, the Harvard professor clearly maintains, God's grace allows the world's Gentiles to become "honorary Jews." Christians, it seems, are by implication obliged to place the world's Jews on a pedestal of honor, and to be by theological conviction highly disinclined to make judgments concerning the collective behavior of any of their number. After all, their place in God's plan is, for Stendahl and his adherents, categorically mysterious, beyond knowing, and beyond judgment.

COVENANT THEOLOGY: ONE COVENANT, PARALLEL COVENANTS, OR "GOD'S TRAFFIC PLAN"?

Krister Stendahl's foray into the controversial question of the place of the Jews in Christian theology and consequent Christian approaches to Jewish-Christian relations had been spectacularly launched with his landmark essays and lectures of the early 1960s. But this was to be just the beginning. The Ivy League professor was not about to limit his audience to his academic peers, but enthusiastically shared his paradigm-shattering ideas with his theological students at Harvard Divinity School as well. By all accounts, the tall, handsome Swedish-American professor was

31. Ibid., 16.
32. Ibid., 76. Emphasis added.
33. Ibid.

throughout his long career immensely popular with his students,[34] and presumably his revolutionary ideas about Paul and Christian-Jewish relations were popular and thought-provoking among them as well.

In a February 15, 1967, lecture, for example, Stendahl reflected "on how and why Judaism and Christianity separated."[35] Stendahl proceeded by introducing three models of the relation between the two faiths, apparently graphically representing each model on a chalkboard or perhaps employing a series of projected slides.[36] Calling the first model the "Jewish model," he sketched it out for his students as a long vertical line beginning with the "Old Testament" and continuing unwaveringly into the future as "Judaism," but with a second line representing "Christianity" branching off tangentially at roughly its halfway point "[a]round 70 or 80 C.E." Dubbing his second model "the orthodox Christian point of view," Stendahl laid it out in a similar way, except that now the vertical line, labeled on one end as the "Old Testament" line, continued straight on from its midpoint as "Christianity." But in the case of this second model it is now the line of "Judaism," not Christianity, that veers off in a tangential direction at 70 CE. Christianity, Stendahl explained, became in this model "the legitimate and full heir to the promises and all that is worthwhile and best in the Old Testament." Finally, in the third model—which "the speaker always believes in," Stendahl transparently admitted—both "Judaism" and "Christianity" veer off at equal tangential angles from the straight-up "Old Testament" line at the point in time that begins in 70 CE, the year the second Jewish temple was destroyed by the Romans, and Temple Judaism came to an abrupt end.[37] Thus in this third model, which Krister Stendahl "believe[d] in," Christianity and Rabbinical Judaism are simultaneous departures from Second Temple Judaism that are represented as being equal in validity and status.

The great enigma about Krister Stendahl is whether he viewed the fateful though equitable fork in the road represented by his third model—the model which by his own admission he "believe[d] in"—simply as a way of dispassionately representing an obvious historical development, or rather, and much more provocatively, as a way of arriving at an important and highly revolutionary theological point of view. The statements of his

---

34. University Lutheran Church, "Guest Book for Krister Stendahl."
35. Stendahl, "Course in Jewish-Christian Relations," 1, box 9.
36. Ibid., 1, 2.
37. Ibid.

that follow within the text of this same 1967 lecture provide considerable insight into this question.

"When one looks at the separation between Judaism and Christianity . . . one might even say that something went wrong," Stendahl ruefully remarked in his lecture. "I'm very serious when I say that I really think that something went wrong in the first century," he lamented once again. "Something went wrong, *and we are not bound to this wrongness,* because we are not really, when it comes down to it, discussing abstract ideas or ideologies . . . [such as] law on the one side and gospel on the other, faith on the one hand and peoplehood on the other."[38] Instead, Stendahl asserted vehemently, Christians and Jews "should primarily understand that we are two people [sic], *or two branches* of the people of God."[39] The agonized ambiguity of this latter statement can hardly escape notice. Which is it—two peoples, or two branches of just one people of God?

In reference to the terms of admission into what one might call this blended family of the people of God, Stendahl, speaking now as a Christian, invites the ire of some of his readers by abjectly asserting that "we are the ones who have to beg to be recognized," and that it is "we Christians who are the thieves." "We are the ones who have claimed to be heirs to the promises of Israel," Stendahl continues. "We are the wild olive branch, to speak with Paul, who claim to have the right to be engrafted on the good old tree. We are the beggars. We are the ones who have to plead with our Jewish friends to recognize our claim to be children of God, yes, children of Abraham, through Jesus Christ, our Lord."[40]

Little wonder that, with lectures such as this one in his quiver of ammunition, Krister Stendahl was able to pierce the consciences and evoke and expose deep and remorseful feelings of profound guilt and shame in the hearts and minds of a whole generation of mostly liberal, mainline Christian hearers, readers, theological protégés, and admirers throughout the United States and Europe. The pervasive Christian conviction of guilt and shame elicited by Stendahl's revolutionary views moved many of their number throughout the last four decades of the twentieth century and beyond, in places high and low, to reassess soberly and contritely their emotional and intellectual attitudes toward the Jewish people, the Jewish religion, and—perhaps most of all—toward the Jewish State of Israel.

---

38. Ibid., 5. Emphasis added.
39. Ibid., 6. Emphasis added.
40. Ibid.

Equally, lectures by Stendahl such as this one opened many thoughtful and broadminded liberal Christian minds to the possibilities afforded by the kind of parallel covenant theology at which the New Testament scholar seemed to be hinting. No wonder also, that this Harvard professor found himself facing the charge of "representing a two-covenant model, or two ways of salvation, one for Jews and one for Gentiles."[41] Throughout the remaining decades of his career, and particularly in his 1993 work, *Final Account: Paul's Letter to the Romans,* Stendahl summarily brushed aside this accusation with little in the way of explanation or elaboration, except to remark that the "two-covenant" model was unacceptable since in his words it was an expression of "misplaced concreteness"[42] (whatever that esoteric term might mean). But Stendahl's critics persevered, accusing him of teaching "two ways of salvation, one for Jews and one for Christians."[43] "But I do no such thing," the Harvard Divinity School professor emeritus demurred in 1993. Somewhat disingenuously, he maintained that God's mysterious plan for Israel (which he claimed he perceived in Paul's letter to the Romans) was what he would call God's "traffic plan."[44]

"God is running this strange show," Krister Stendahl opined in the pages of *Final Account,* and he imagined for his readers that the great Apostle Paul might have said it today as follows: "The Jews are in the hands of God and at the mercy of God, and the promises of God are irreversible. God does not go back on his promises. . . . The only thing you [Gentile Christians] have to do is be faithful, and this is a mystery." Stendahl succinctly summarizes this thought with a short, pithy string of words he imaginatively interprets Paul to be saying, but which clearly constitute his own message for his own modern audiences: "Get off the backs of the Jews, and leave them in the hands of God."[45]

ANTI-SEMITISM, THE HOLOCAUST, AND THE CHRISTIAN CULPABILITY QUESTION

Not content merely to promote a Christian "hands-off" theology in reference to the Jewish people, the decades following his landmark study of Paul's views concerning the Jews saw Krister Stendahl intensifying his

---

41. Stendahl, *Final Account,* "Preface," x.
42. Ibid.
43. Ibid., 7.
44. Ibid.
45. Ibid., 40.

efforts to convince thoughtful and sensitive twentieth-century Christians of the culpability of the whole Christian tradition in an unbroken history of anti-Semitism that inexorably culminated in the European Holocaust of the 1930s and 1940s. For example, in an October 1963 article in the *Harvard Divinity Bulletin* Stendahl, in a sweeping generalization, asserted that an alleged first-century cutting-off of debate between the Roman Empire's Christian and Jewish communities "transformed into an unusually grim history of everything ugly from name-calling to pogroms and holocaust."[46] Christianity, he seemed to imply, was the institution in Western history most responsible for anti-Semitism and persecution of the Jews throughout the world.

Yet, Krister Stendahl believed, significant progress was being made in combating this virulent and deeply ingrained Western Christian prejudice toward the Jews and their ancient religion. By 1981 he was able to report in a lengthy *Christian Science Monitor* interview that he was somewhat cheered by the progress made in the previous three decades. Stendahl shared with *Monitor* reporter Richard M. Harley that in virtually every major American city there was now "some form of Jewish-Christian dialogue or joint social welfare action, a development totally unprecedented in American history." (Stendahl might well have added that he had participated in and been instrumental in organizing a good number of these.) Since World War II, Stendahl revealed, the Protestant and Catholic churches had "made sweeping audits of their doctrines to eliminate anti-Semitic stereotypes." He added that consultations with Jewish scholars had led to many revisions in educational materials.[47] And for his role in rooting out anti-Semitism in American society and the Christian community, Stendahl was being recognized and presented with awards by the American Jewish community, the *Christian Science Monitor* article revealed.[48]

Yet all was not going well in mid-1981, the Harvard Divinity School professor feared. New strains of anti-Semitism had emerged, he believed. Flaws in the early building of Jewish-Christian bridges had now widened, he told *Monitor* readers. "As we Christians did our rethinking of Jewish-Christian relations after World War II, we tried to achieve action on the basis of a guilt trip about the treatment of Jews in the war," he said. While admitting that that strategy had brought some quick results, "it is my experience," he added, "that that approach, in the long run, comes back to

---

46. Stendahl, "Judaism and Christianity, Then and Now," 3.
47. Harley, "Anti-Semitism," *Christian Science Monitor*, June 4, 1981, B28.
48. Ibid.

haunt us. You should do what you do not because of guilt, but because of what is right."⁴⁹ Ironically, subsequent statements by Krister Stendahl make clear that in the years following 1981 he was quite willing to employ guilt-tripping when it seemed effective for defending and advancing his own point of view.

Take, for example, a point of view shared by Stendahl in this same 1981 *Christian Science Monitor* article. In the *Monitor* reporter's words, the Harvard professor revealed that high on his "personal list of anti-Semitic dragons is one of the most formidable and slippery of all: increasing misuse of the term 'Zionism.'" What did Professor Stendahl mean by this? Apparently Stendahl told his interviewer, in so many words, that "this term—meaning the political ideology behind formation of the Jewish State of Israel—has often been linked narrowly with alleged Israeli abuses of Arab Palestinians, and turned into a catchword *for racism or for anti-Israel propaganda*."⁵⁰ "A popular Christian perception today identifies Judaism with Zionism as a gimmick for engaging in anti-Semitism," the *Monitor* reporter quotes Stendahl as saying. "We have very little bona fide 'anti-Semitism' any more under that name," Stendahl continues. "It tends to come now in the language of 'anti-Zionism.' There's a language game going on. You can see it even in materials circulated by some Christian peace groups." Stendahl then pointed out for the interviewing reporter a leaflet "recently distributed by a prominent Christian peace group." The leaflet apparently showed linked bayonets forming a Star of David, while a peace dove was depicted perching on an Arab Crescent.⁵¹

The sixty-year-old professor, approaching the height of his career, must have felt quite relaxed in this interview with a highly regarded Boston-based national newspaper, for he seemed to hold nothing back in sharing his candid views about what he took to be the strong linkages between the Jewish community, Israel, and the Jewish religion. The interviewer reported that Stendahl emphasized the impossibility of dialogue with Jews without a recognition that 95 percent of the Jewish community identified with Israel and its survival.⁵² "All Jews do not identify, of course, with everything that is *done* in the name of Zionism," Stendahl elaborated, "but you have to at least recognize that the survival of Israel is part of Jewish religion." Anticipating the objections of American readers to such

49. Ibid.
50. Emphasis added.
51. Ibid., B30–31.
52. Ibid., B32.

a close linkage between faith and country, Stendahl admonished, "If we try to impose a framework of the separation of church and state, we make our own little definition and break the first rule of dialogue: Listen to how the other party defines itself."[53]

LEGITIMIZING TRIUMPHANT POLITICAL ZIONISM: ISRAEL, JUDAISM, AND THE SIX DAY WAR

One might well wonder whether Krister Stendahl's apparent approval (as portrayed in the popular press) of what he took to be Judaism's melding of state and religion is consistent with his scholarly writings on the subject. Indeed, it is, and Stendahl's well-considered lead article in the Autumn 1967 issue of the *Harvard Divinity Bulletin*—published in the wake of Israel's triumphant Six Day War the previous June—makes this abundantly clear. Listen to the following statements in the pages of this influential essay, which was reprinted that same fall in the journal *Cross Currents*, to amplify its impact:

> It is clear enough from what we have said already that current events and theological work are not unrelated. . . . The relation between Judaism and the State of Israel is naturally quite complex. It would be wrong to identify the two [as one and the same]. . . . But it would be equally wrong to consider Israel a purely secular state. . . . Israel is a Jewish state and its religion is Judaism. Without getting involved in the difficulties of defining "Jew," "Judaism," and "Israel," it is important for Christians and Westerners to realize that a certain kind of "clean thinking" does not work here, although it would be convenient. . . . The driving forces which made Palestine—rather than Uganda—the goal for Zionism are reason enough for the intertwining of Jewish faith and the State of Israel. That force was rooted in the Scriptures and the tradition. Our evaluation of the present situation [the Israeli conquests in the Six Day War] must take that into account. Whether we like it or not, when we speak and think about the State of Israel, we are speaking about a very substantial element of Judaism . . . in terms of Jews who see the State of Israel as the fulfillment of God's promises.[54]

---

53. Ibid.
54. Stendahl, "Judaism and Christianity II," 6–7.

Paul H. Verduin —*Praiseworthy Intentions, Unintended Consequences*

Obviously, in these carefully weighed observations, the Rev. Dr. Stendahl is baptizing—legitimizing—the expansionist objectives of political Zionism. Secondly, he is making equally clear that it is necessary for the Christian church "to grant to Judaism its right to work out its own problems according to its own understanding of its Scripture and tradition." It is not for Christians, Stendahl admonishes insistently, "to prescribe for Judaism that its religious aspirations should not be tied to a land or a city"—by which he means, of course, the land between the Jordan River and the Mediterranean, and the city of Jerusalem, which, as a result of Israel's 1967 war of conquest, have come into the full possession of the State of Israel. "Judaism as we know it today," Stendahl asserts with an air of finality, "is related to the Land, the *Eretz*."[55]

While thus granting to Judaism the complete freedom to work out its own problems and its own destiny regarding the State of Israel and the conquered Palestinian lands without Christian interference, in the same breath Krister Stendahl gives evidence of his determination to nip-in-the-bud any negative criticism of Israel's 1967 conquests and its concomitant military occupation of Palestinian, Egyptian, and Syrian territory. He issues the stern warning that "all of us should watch out for the ways in which the ancient venom of Christian anti-Semitism might enter in." In an inscrutable way he then ominously intensifies his warning by making an oblique reference to "a threatened Jewish people in danger of its second holocaust"—meaning, probably, the danger he surmises a beleaguered Israel had narrowly averted in the run-up to the Six Day War. But then Stendahl equivocates just slightly in his warning against resurgent anti-Semitism with the following disclaimer: "That does not mean that Israel is always right or that its political behavior and demands should always be supported by all who as Christians would like to be considered honorary Jews for Jesus Christ's sake."[56] Is the Harvard luminary beginning to have a few doubts about his blanket admiration and support for all things Jewish and for perceiving the boogeyman of anti-Semitism in every criticism of Israel?

Perhaps yes, perhaps no, but there are at least some scattered signs of a few ruminations in that direction, however infrequent. In October 1982, four months into Israel's invasion and occupation of southern Lebanon, and in the midst of international outrage at the Israeli-instigated atrocities committed there against the Palestinian refugee camps of Sabra and

55. Ibid.
56. Ibid., 7.

Shatila on September 16, Krister Stendahl was quoted in the *Boston Globe* as seeing growing signs of anti-Semitism, which had by then become more socially acceptable, he said, "than it has been for a long period of time." Stendahl told the *Globe* that up till then, a "well-deserved guilt" about the Holocaust was a reason for a general improvement in Christian-Jewish relations. But, Stendahl began to equivocate, the "appeal to guilt . . . came to haunt us when we realize[d] we forgot a homeless Palestinian people." It begins to appear that the Harvard professor who had built a national reputation through his broad and unconditional defense of all things Jewish was beginning to have a few second thoughts. "The question is what is right, and not action born out of guilt," he told his interviewer.[57]

Whatever glimmer of sympathy Krister Stendahl may have felt for the Palestinians in 1982 was to be relegated to the recesses of his mind for another dozen years. Always devoted to his teaching and his students at "Harvard Div," he concentrated on his New Testament lectures, his promotion of the acceptance and advancement of women and of gays and lesbians in the clergy and in society, and, as always, his assiduous efforts to build bridges and mutual appreciation between the Christian and Jewish communities in the United States and internationally. Stendahl found time to serve on the council of the World Union of Jewish Studies, and between 1975 and 1985 he was honored to chair the World Council of Churches' prestigious and influential Consultation on the Church and Jewish People (CCJP). From 1968 to 1979 he had served as dean of Harvard Divinity School's faculty, during the turbulent decade of anti-war and anti-establishment student unrest at Harvard and elsewhere in the nation. Throughout this period, and up until his retirement from the Harvard Divinity School faculty in 1984, Stendahl continued to participate frequently in conferences for Jewish-Christian dialogue throughout the United States, from coast to coast and from north to south.[58]

Then somewhat unexpectedly, at the age of sixty-three, Krister Stendahl was called back to his native Sweden to become the Bishop of Stockholm in the Church of Sweden, the Lutheran state church in that nation. Stendahl had always kept up his contacts with his native land and had continued to publish his scholarship in the Swedish language for the benefit of students, laypeople, and professional peers in that Scandinavian country. While in Sweden from 1984 to 1988, Bishop Stendahl continued

---

57. Franklin, "Workshop to Re-examine Jewish-Christian Relations," *Boston Globe*, Oct 21, 1982, 35.

58. "Krister Stendahl," ELCA News Service, Apr 17, 2008. See note 3.

his work in Jewish-Christian relations, and promoted dialogue and linkages between the Swedish people and the Jewish people in Europe and elsewhere. An outgrowth of Stendahl's efforts in this regard led to the creation in Jerusalem of Lund University's Krister Stendahl Chair in Theology of Religion, located at Jerusalem's Swedish Theological Institute. Stendahl's unceasing efforts to root out anti-Semitism and foster worldwide appreciation for the Jewish religion and the Jewish people won him the second Ladislaus Laszt International Ecumenical Award from an Israeli academy, Ben Gurion University of the Negev.[59]

Perhaps flushed by his successes and heightened stature gained from his efforts to build positive and productive relations between Christians and Jews in Europe during his interim sojourn there, Stendahl, upon returning to the United States in 1988, redoubled his stateside activities in the Christian-Jewish realm. Harvard Divinity School was happy to have him return to their fold as its first official chaplain, on the basis, no doubt, of his legendary skills in relating to the institution's budding theologs. As a dean and professor at Harvard Divinity School, Krister Stendahl had been widely appreciated for his "wry humor and his enormous gift for listening," which were said to be part of "a complete, and consistent, pastorly presence." And after all, because of his support for the role of women in the present and future church, Harvard Div's female students had come to call him "Sister Krister."[60]

A FORMIDABLE ASSIGNMENT: COMBATING INTOLERANCE IN ISRAEL AND OCCUPIED PALESTINE

Besides his award from Israel's Ben Gurion University—and perhaps, in part, as a consequence of it—seventy-year-old Professor Emeritus/Bishop Emeritus Krister Stendahl was offered in 1991 a professorial chair at one of America's paramount Jewish institutions of higher learning, Brandeis University, and Stendahl no doubt relished the opportunity and the honor of becoming the Boston-area university's first Myra and Robert Kraft and Jacob Hiatt Distinguished Professor of Christian Studies. Stendahl seems to have greatly enjoyed this chance to share with Jewish and other Brandeis students his particular take on Christianity, on the New Testament and its relationship to the Hebrew Scriptures, and on the commonalities and

59. Ibid.
60. Joyner, "Krister Stendahl, 1921–2008"; see note 10. Martin, "Krister Stendahl, 86, Ecumenical Bishop, is Dead"; see note 8.

divergences between the two closely-related Abrahamic faiths of Judaism and Christianity. But Stendahl's popularity in his new chair among both students and faculty led to yet one more formidable assignment. Although this was to be a part-time tenure, in many ways it would prove to be the most challenging one that Stendahl would face, for it would eventually force him to re-examine some of his most dearly held premises. This last and most challenging assignment was his appointment in 1994 as co-director of the Israel-based Osher Center for Tolerance and Pluralism, a part of the Shalom Hartman Institute in Jerusalem.[61]

The Bernard and Barbro Osher Center for Tolerance and Pluralism (name later modified to the Osher Jerusalem Center for Religious Pluralism) had been established as one of the programmatic divisions of the Shalom Hartman Institute, a high-profile, private-sector Israeli institution founded in 1976 by Brooklyn-born, Jewish-American academician and rabbi David Hartman in honor of his father, Shalom Hartman.[62] Educated and ordained at Yeshiva University in New York, Rabbi Hartman had earned his Ph.D. at McGill University in Montreal before joining the faculty at Hebrew University in Jerusalem. Professor Hartman had been introduced to Krister Stendahl in 1981[63] by Jerusalem's longtime mayor Teddy Kollek, with whom Professor Stendahl had somehow made an earlier acquaintance, during the years (1975–85) when Stendahl was chairing the Jewish-Christian dialogue efforts of the World Council of Churches.[64]

However they met, Mayor Kollek had appointed Stendahl to his prestigious Jerusalem Committee, an international group of notables with whom the mayor consulted from time to time on matters related to the promotion of tolerance in the ancient multicultural city, with an eye toward the promotion of Jerusalem tourism as well. For example, Krister Stendahl traveled to Jerusalem from his Cambridge, Massachusetts, home in August 1990 for the Jerusalem Committee's meeting to begin planning a festive event to be held in 1996 to commemorate what Mayor Kollek said would be the three-thousand-year anniversary of the biblical King David's establishment of Jerusalem as his kingdom's capital.[65] Many years later,

61. "Krister Stendahl," ELCA News Service, Apr 17, 2008. See note 3.

62. Shalom Hartman Institute brochure, circa 2002. Stendahl Papers, box 7.

63. "The Muskegon Debate" (undated loose papers). Stendahl Papers, box 17.

64. Abbey, "Krister Stendahl, Theologian, Former Hartman Institute Director, Dies at 86," *Shalom Hartman Institute News*, Apr 16, 2008, at http://www.hartman.org.il/SHINews_View.asp?Article_Id=100&Cat_Id=303&Cat_Type=SHINews; accessed on Mar 15, 2012.

65. Kollek, letters to Krister Stendahl: Oct 6, 1989; Feb 19, 1990; Mar 5, 1990; Aug

Hartman fondly recalled, "I met him and was overwhelmed by his passion and his keen mind in thinking about contemporary theological issues." Rabbi Hartman also said of Stendahl, "He together with the late Paul Van Buren, first director of the [Shalom Hartman] Institute's Center for Contemporary Theology, was committed to enriching and giving a new spirit to Jewish-Christian relations in the modern world."[66]

David Hartman and Krister Stendahl quickly became close friends and collaborators, and very soon began to appear together at Jewish-Christian colloquia around the United States.[67] When Professor Paul Van Buren left the Shalom Hartman Institute in the early 1990s, Hartman persuaded Stendahl to resign his teaching post at Brandeis University and join him in 1994 as part-time co-director of the Institute's new Osher Center for Tolerance and Pluralism.[68] Thus, beginning in 1993, a year before he assumed his new position, Krister Stendahl and his wife Brita spent usually four weeks every year—usually around the month of February—residing in Jerusalem and teaching at the Shalom Hartman Institute. In addition, as one would fully expect, they began traveling throughout portions of Israel and the occupied Palestinian territories and making acquaintances with various people as they traveled, including Palestinian Christians and Palestinian Muslims as well as Israeli Jews. The Stendahls' annual excursions to Jerusalem and "the Holy Land" continued past the year 1998, when Professor Stendahl completed his four years as co-director at the Osher Center, and into the first decade of the twenty-first century.[69]

But what septuagenarian Krister Stendahl might have anticipated as the crowning glory of his career turned out to be fraught with difficulty. For one thing, once on board at the Osher Center he quickly learned that what David Hartman primarily had in mind by the Center's promotion of "tolerance and pluralism"—as its name called for—was the promotion of harmony and mutual respect among the several components of Israel's *Jewish* community, for example among Ashkenazi, Sephardic, Mizrahi, Yemeni, Iranian, and Ethiopian Jews, and among the Orthodox, Conservative, Reform, Reconstructionist, and other varieties of Judaism. It was to *these* activities that the Shalom Hartman Institute was directing most

---

15, 1990; Aug 24, 1990. Stendahl Papers, box 8.

66. Abbey, "Krister Stendahl." See note 64.

67. *National Dialogue Newsletter* 7/1 (Fall 1991) provides one example of Stendahl-Hartman collaboration.

68. Abbey, "Krister Stendahl." See note 64.

69. Interview with the Rev. John Stendahl, Boston, MA, July 12, 2011.

of its efforts while Hartman was its director and also the Osher Institute's co-director. David Hartman, it turned out, saw the promotion of dialogue and the building of harmony between Jews and Palestinian Arabs in Israel, and between Jews and Palestinians in the conquered territories, as only a secondary concern. Likewise, he seemed to have only a minor interest in fostering positive relations among the Jewish and indigenous Muslim and Christian populations inhabiting Israel and the Palestinian territories under Israel's military occupation. And certainly, he was hardly about to try to promote harmonious relations between the religiously fundamentalist Jewish settlers in East Jerusalem, the West Bank, and Gaza, and their alarmed and intimidated Palestinian Christian and Muslim neighbors.[70] Nonetheless, while Krister Stendahl was its co-chair, the Osher Center's Annual International Theology Seminar was always careful to include Muslim and Christian scholars among its presenters and in its audience, a practice that continued well past the end of Stendahl's tenure there.[71]

BELATED AWAKENING: MEETING PALESTINIANS FOR THE FIRST TIME IN THEIR OCCUPIED HOMELAND

While in Jerusalem and environs every year the ever-curious and inquisitive Krister Stendahl took full advantage of his opportunities to make acquaintances in the Palestinian community. Chief among these was the Rev. Dr. Mitri Raheb, a fellow Lutheran who was pastor of Bethlehem's Christmas Lutheran Church and general director of the International Center in Bethlehem, a community development enterprise; and of course he met and talked with fellow Lutheran Munib Younan, Bishop of the Evangelical Lutheran Church in Jordan and the Holy Land. Another individual in the Palestinian Christian community who became a friend was the Quaker author Jean Zaru, based at the Friends Center in Ramallah. Stendahl also made the acquaintance of the Rev. Dr. Naim Ateek, a Palestinian Anglican priest, author, and Israeli citizen who directed the Sabeel Ecumenical Liberation Theology Center in Jerusalem, an entity with an international reach that he had founded a dozen years earlier to promote justice for the Palestinians, to be achieved through grassroots education and nonviolent

---

70. See *A Word from Jerusalem: Bulletin of the Shalom Hartman Institute*, Oct 1997, 1–4. Stendahl Papers, box 7.

71. Shalom Hartman Institute brochure, circa 2002. Stendahl Papers, box 7. (See Shalom Hartman Institute mission statement, and description of the Osher Center's activities.)

resistance. Another Bethlehemite whom Stendahl met was Zoughbi Zoughbi, director of the Palestinian Conflict Resolution Center. And he met Mustafa Abu-Sway, an Associate Professor of Philosophy and Islamic Arts at Jerusalem's Al-Quds University. Also at Al-Quds was another new acquaintance, Professor Khuloud Khayyat Danjani, director of the International Cooperation Department who also taught community health there. An Israeli Arab who became an acquaintance was Abdessalam Najjar, the development director at the ethnically integrated Israeli village of Neve Shalom/Wahat al-Salam, a unique experiment in co-existence that would have interested Krister Stendahl greatly. Stendahl's press contacts included Israeli author/commentator Tom Segev, and Cordelia Edvardson of the *Svenska Dagbladet,* a Swedish paper. The list of Palestinians, Israelis, internationals, and academics of every stripe whom Stendahl met and whose calling cards he kept includes several dozen other individuals of position and rank in their respective fields of endeavor. It is noteworthy that the great majority of these were men and women who were passionate about the urgent need for a just peace between Palestinians and Israelis, to be achieved sooner rather than later.[72]

Even more noteworthy is that, beginning in the early 1990s, Krister Stendahl was no longer solely dependent on—and one might say, solely a captive of—his Jewish-American colleagues and friends to supply him with the empirical and historical narrative data and modes of theological and philosophical analysis he needed to comprehend and interpret the tragic realities of Jewish-Palestinian and Israeli-Palestinian relations. He was now, for the first time, seeing and hearing these realities through the lens of his own experience, as a follower of Jesus of Nazareth and his teachings about what constitutes the kingdom of God. And more and more, he didn't like what he saw and heard.

But in order to preserve his hard-won achievements in the struggle to create a new paradigm in New Testament interpretation and Christian theology for the advancement of positive, mutually respectful, and "healthy" relations between the Jewish and Christian communities, and in defense of his attempts to redefine Gentile Christians as "honorary Jews," Krister Stendahl hesitated. Moreover, in light of his uniform insistence since the 1960s that the "Land of Israel" properly and inextricably plays an essential role in the Jewish religion—a role that Christians are obliged to respect—the gentle and humane former Harvard professor kept strictly silent, at

---

72. Business and calling cards retained by Krister Stendahl while in Jerusalem, 1990s. Stendahl Papers, box. 7.

least in the public realm, about the flagrant and unconcealed human rights abuses visited on the Palestinians that he had heard about from credible sources and seen with his own eyes. There is absolutely no evidence, in the record left by his voluminous writings and extensive personal papers, that Krister Stendahl ever—even once—publicly spoke out or put anything in print about the injustices being suffered by Palestinians at the hands of Israeli Jews, aided and abetted by their American supporters in the Jewish and Christian communities. After the end of his tenure at the Osher Institute in 1998, Stendahl seems to have maintained his cordial if somewhat tested friendship with Shalom Hartman Institute director David Hartman, and continued to visit Jerusalem and the Institute annually.[73]

THE SECOND INTIFADA: VERBAL VIOLENCE AND A DISENCHANTING ESTRANGEMENT

Finally, however, a noteworthy incident of verbal violence occurred that tore at eighty-year-old Krister Stendahl's heart and for several years interrupted his deep friendship with his former colleague, Rabbi David Hartman. In early March of 2002, at the height of the Second Palestinian Intifada with its attendant suicide bombings by Palestinian militants, Stendahl, then at his comfortable home on a shady, tree-lined street near the Harvard campus, got the e-mail from Jerusalem. It was from the Revs. Susan and Michael Thomas, an American married couple who were at the time serving as co-pastors of the venerable Lutheran Church of the Redeemer in Jerusalem's historic Old City. Stendahl knew Susan and Michael well; Michael had studied at Harvard Divinity School and been in campus ministry at Boston University, and Susan had been an M.I.T. campus pastor as well as pastor at the University Lutheran Church in Cambridge, where the Stendahls were members. Besides these earlier contacts, Dr. Stendahl had probably seen the Thomases in Jerusalem on recent visits.[74]

What Stendahl read in his March 3, 2002, e-mail from the Thomases shocked him. They told him that in that morning's issue of the *International Herald Tribune*, in an article by Lee Hockstader of the *Washington Post*,

73. Stendahl's unwillingness to speak out concerning injustices suffered by the Palestinians is confirmed by both his widow Brita and his son John. Telephone interviews with Brita Stendahl: July 7, 2011; July 8, 2011; and Sept 7, 2011; and interview with the Rev. John Stendahl, Boston, MA, July 12, 2011.

74. Our Savior Lutheran Church and Student Center, Hanover, NH, website at http://www.dartmouth.edu/~lutheran/from-the-pastors/remembering-krister-stendahl/; accessed on Mar 15, 2012.

Paul H. Verduin —*Praiseworthy Intentions, Unintended Consequences*

Stendahl's old friend David Hartman was quoted as saying the following: "Which population in the world would allow itself to be intimidated and terrified as this whole population [Israel] is, where you can't send your kid out for a pizza at night without fear he'll be blown up?" In his article, reporter Hockstader positively identified the man he interviewed as "David Hartman, a rabbi and philosopher who runs a think tank in Jerusalem." But what Rabbi Hartman was quoted as saying next about the Palestinians (according to the Thomases), was what really upset Krister Stendahl: "'Let's really let them understand what the implication of their actions is,' he said of the Palestinians. 'Very simply, wipe them out. Level them.'"[75]

Krister Stendahl lost little time in reacting. The following day, March 4, he photocopied a printed copy of the damning e-mail and carefully mounted it on the center of a blank sheet of paper, carefully scissoring off the portions of the e-mail that gave the Thomases' names, address, and contact information at the Lutheran Church of the Redeemer in Jerusalem, thus leaving only the body of the printed e-mail. Then, in his clear and legible hand, Stendahl prefaced the hateful sentiments conveyed in the body of the e-mail letter with a handwritten message to Rabbi Hartman, scrupulously dated March 4, 2002: "Dear, dear David: How to answer this e-mail we received?" Then, immediately below the e-mail's printed text, Stendahl continued: "If this is true, it puts much stress and pain on one of the most precious friendships I have been given. . . . We will be in Sweden [contact phone number supplied] March 9–13. Then back in C–e [Cambridge]. Yours Krister."[76] Even though he obviously was profoundly saddened and emotionally wounded by Rabbi Hartman's hateful, intemperate public remarks, and deeply disappointed with him, in his characteristic kindness Stendahl left the door open for reconciliation and future communication.

It would seem likely that Stendahl faxed this composite message to Hartman the same day, though he might also have mailed it via the Postal Service. There can be virtually no doubt that he indeed sent it to Hartman, however. Both Stendahl's widow, Brita Stendahl, and, independently, their son, John Stendahl, have confirmed that Krister Stendahl's relationship

---

75. Susan and Michael Thomas, e-mail to Krister Stendahl, Mar 3, 2002. Stendahl Papers, box 7. These words of David Hartman are also quoted in a *Washington Post* article by Lee Hockstader of Mar 1, 2002 ("Seeds of Dissent Take Root in Israeli Army as Reservists Sign Protest Statement"), found at http://www.washingtonpost.com/wp-srv/world/articles/israel030102.htm; accessed on Mar 14, 2012.

76. Stendahl, letter to David Hartman (probably faxed), Mar 4, 2002. Stendahl Papers, box 7.

with his old partner in the business of building "tolerance and pluralism," being strained to the breaking point, was substantially interrupted for several years.[77]

David Hartman's ill-considered outburst in the pages of the widely read *Herald Tribune* was very probably the last straw in a relationship where significant strains had very likely been simmering and building for several years. In an interview given to this writer on July 12, 2011, Krister's son, the Rev. John Stendahl, remembered that in private conversations with Jewish colleagues his father "started speaking and conversing against Israel." "This cost him in friendships," especially his friendships with Jewish theologians with whom his thinking was closely allied, John Stendahl said. On the consequences of these fallings-out for his father's deep, longstanding relationship with David Hartman, Krister's son remarked, "Their relations were strained, even though he [Krister] wanted to keep the relationship going." "So he was restrained" in what he said and how he said it, John Stendahl confirmed. Krister's widow, Brita, in telephone interviews given to this writer in July and September 2011, maintained that communication between her late husband and David Hartman was cut off completely around the time of the 2002 *Herald Tribune* episode, though there was a partial restoration near the end of Krister Stendahl's life, she recalled.[78]

STENDAHL'S LEGACY: A TRIPLE TRAGEDY OF UNINTENDED CONSEQUENCES

It would seem to this writer to be singularly tragic that Krister Stendahl was never able to overcome his "restraint" and speak out vocally and publicly to Jews and Christians, Israelis and Americans, concerning the oppression endured by the Palestinian people living under a harsh and unjustifiable Israeli military occupation for multiple decades: injustices that Palestinian men, women, and children, Christian and Muslim alike, have to this day been forced to endure, injustices that Stendahl himself sometimes personally observed in the occupied Palestinian territories at military checkpoints and elsewhere,[79] injustices completely contrary to the

---

77. Telephone interviews with Brita Stendahl: July 7, 2011; July 8, 2011; Sept 7, 2011; and interview with the Rev. John Stendahl, Boston, MA, July 12, 2011.

78. Ibid.

79. In a telephone interview the Rev. Susan Thomas recalled an incident at the checkpoint between Bethlehem and Jerusalem when Stendahl, a passenger in the

most deeply cherished moral values of Jews and Christians alike. It is laudable that Krister Stendahl spoke out so eloquently against the prejudice and atrocities that Jews had to endure for many centuries in Christian lands, and guarded so vigilantly during his years of maturity against any perceived sign of a resurgence of such damaging prejudice at their expense. Yet, is it not tragic that Stendahl, despite a few small signs of an uneasy conscience, declined to do anything whatsoever in the public arena to combat the truly heinous atrocities and acts of prejudice committed, so ironically, by a segment (Israelis) of that same Jewish community that he had sought so valiantly for so many decades to honor and protect?

Secondly, it would seem doubly tragic that, for all his patient and forbearing "restraint," Krister Stendahl was rewarded only with the loss of "one of the most precious friendships" he had been given, his friendship with David Hartman.

Thirdly and finally, it is especially tragic that the unintended consequence of Stendahl's highly influential admonition to fellow Christians throughout the United States, Europe, and elsewhere to "get off the backs of the Jews," to defer to God's "mysterious and special plans" for them, and to let the Israelis and their religious leaders decide what to do about the Palestinians, has proven to be a major, substantial contribution on Stendahl's part to the high level of fear, moral laxity, and disinclination on the part of American Christians and the American churches to speak out and effectively advocate against such obvious and longstanding injustices as those visited on the Palestinians by the "Jewish" State of Israel. This last unintended consequence is by far the greatest tragedy of Krister Stendahl, the one that people of faith in the U.S. and elsewhere must get to work to undo.

On the day following Stendahl's death in 2008, the Shalom Hartman Institute published a lengthy tribute to the venerable Harvard scholar, in which David Hartman was quoted as saying, among other things, "The passing of Krister Stendahl is a sad moment for all human beings who celebrate diversity and appreciate the significance and dignity of the other."[80] An ironic tribute indeed.

Thomases' car, called David Hartman on a cell phone and angrily complained about the inspection delays, which were greatly imposing on his time and comfort as well as on those of so many other people, including the Palestinians, and which would cause him to miss an engagement at the Shalom Hartman Center. Telephone interview with the Rev. Susan Thomas, Sept 8, 2011.

80. Abbey, "Krister Stendahl." See note 64.

BIBLIOGRAPHY

Unpublished Sources

Business and calling cards retained by Krister Stendahl while in Jerusalem, 1990s. Stendahl Papers (uncataloged), box 7. Andover-Harvard Library, Harvard Divinity School.

Interviews with Brita Stendahl. Telephone: July 7, 2011; July 8, 2011; Sept 7, 2011.
Interview with the Rev. John Stendahl. Boston, MA, July 12, 2011.
Interview with the Rev. Susan Thomas. Telephone: Sept 8, 2011.
Kollek, Teddy. To Krister Stendahl. Letters: Oct 6, 1989; Feb 19, 1990; Mar 5, 1990; Aug 15, 1990; Aug 24, 1990. Stendahl Papers (uncataloged), box 8. Andover-Harvard Library, Harvard Divinity School.
"The Muskegon Debate." Undated loose papers. Stendahl Papers (uncataloged), box 17. Andover-Harvard Library, Harvard Divinity School.
Stendahl, Krister. "Christian-Jewish Relations: A Protestant View." May 15, 1981. Stendahl Papers (uncataloged), box 9. Andover-Harvard Library, Harvard Divinity School.
———. "A Course in Jewish-Christian Relations." Feb 15, 1967. Faculty Writings File: Stendahl/Writings of Krister Stendahl (bms 13001), box 5, folder 1. Andover-Harvard Library, Harvard Divinity School.
———. To Judith Banki, American Jewish Committee. Letter: Mar 2, 1992. Stendahl Papers (uncataloged), box 14. Andover-Harvard Library, Harvard Divinity School.
———. To David Hartman. Letter: Mar 4, 2002. Stendahl Papers (uncataloged), box 7. Andover-Harvard Library, Harvard Divinity School.
Thomas, Susan, and Michael, to Krister Stendahl. E-mail: Mar 3, 2002. Stendahl Papers (uncataloged), box 7. Andover-Harvard Library, Harvard Divinity School.

Published Sources

Abbey, Alan D. "Krister Stendahl, Theologian, Former Hartman Institute Director, Dies at 86," *Shalom Hartman Institute News*, Apr 16, 2008. At http://www.hartman.org.il/SHINews_View.asp?Article_Id=100&Cat_Id=303&Cat_Type=SHINews. Accessed on Mar 15, 2012.
Braverman, Mark. *Fatal Embrace: Christians, Jews, and the Search for Peace in the Holy Land*. Austin, NY: Synergy, 2010.
Franklin, James L. "Workshop to Re-examine Jewish-Christian Relations." *Boston Globe*, Oct 21, 1982.
Harley, Richard M. "Anti-Semitism: 'Christians Have a Responsibility.'" *Christian Science Monitor*, June 4, 1981.
Hockstader, Lee. "Seeds of Dissent Take Root in Israeli Army as Reservists Sign Protest Statement." *Washington Post*, Mar 1, 2002. At http://www.washingtonpost.com/wp-srv/world/articles/israel030102.htm. Accessed on Mar 14, 2012.
Joyner, Will. "Krister Stendahl, 1921–2008." *Harvard Divinity School News and Events*. At http://www.hds.harvard.edu/news-events/2011/02/07/krister-stendahl-1921-2008. Accessed on Mar 15, 2012.

Paul H. Verduin —*Praiseworthy Intentions, Unintended Consequences*

"Krister Stendahl, Lutheran Bishop, Dean, Scholar and Teacher, Dies." ELCA News Service, Apr 17, 2008. At http://www.elca.org/Who-We-Are/Our-Three-Expressions/Churchwide-Organization/Communication-Services/News/Releases.aspx?a=3842. Accessed on Mar 15, 2012.

Martin, Douglas. "Krister Stendahl, 86, Ecumenical Bishop, is Dead." *New York Times*, Apr 16, 2008.

National Dialogue Newsletter 7.1 (Fall 1991). Stendahl Papers (uncataloged), box 8. Andover-Harvard Library, Harvard Divinity School.

Our Savior Lutheran Church and Student Center, Hanover, NH. At http://www.dartmouth.edu/~lutheran/from-the-pastors/remembering-krister-stendahl/. Accessed on Mar 15, 2012.

Shalom Hartman Institute. Brochure, circa 2002. Stendahl Papers (uncataloged), box 7. Andover-Harvard Library, Harvard Divinity School.

Stendahl, Krister. "The Apostle Paul and the Introspective Conscience of the West." Paper given at the American Psychological Association Annual Meeting, Sept 3, 1961, and first published in *Harvard Theological Review* 56 (1963), as a revised edition of the article, "Paulus och Samvetet" published in Sweden in *Svensk Exegetisk Arsbok* 25 (1960) 62–77. In *Paul among Jews and Gentiles and Other Essays*, 78–96. Minneapolis: Fortress, 1976.

———. *Final Account: Paul's Letter to the Romans*. Minneapolis: Fortress, 1995. First published by University Lutheran Church, Cambridge, MA, 1993.

———. "Judaism and Christianity II—After a Colloquium and a War." *Harvard Divinity Bulletin. New Series* 1.1 (1967) 2–8. Article subsequently published in *Cross Currents* 17.4 (1967) 445–58.

———. "Judaism and Christianity, Then and Now." *Harvard Divinity Bulletin* 28.1 (1963) 1–9.

———. "Paul Among Jews and Gentiles." Based on lectures given at Austin Presbyterian Theological Seminary (Currie Lectures) in 1961 and 1963, and at Colgate Rochester Divinity School (Ayer Lectures) in 1964. In *Paul among Jews and Gentiles and Other Essays*, 1–77. Minneapolis: Fortress, 1976.

———. *Paul among Jews and Gentiles and Other Essays*. Minneapolis: Fortress, 1976.

———. *The School of St. Matthew, and its Use of the Old Testament*. Uppsala: Gleerup, Lund, 1954. Reprinted, with new Introduction by Stendahl, Philadelphia: Fortress, 1968. Reprinted in paperback, Mifflintown, PA: Sigler, 1991.

University Lutheran Church, "Guest Book for Krister Stendahl." At www.unilu.org/memories/stendahl_guestbook.html. Accessed on June 30, 2011.

A Word from Jerusalem: Bulletin of the Shalom Hartman Institute. October 1997. Stendahl Papers (uncataloged), box 7. Andover-Harvard Library, Harvard Divinity School.

6

Catholic Social Teaching and Vatican Relations with Israelis and Palestinians

Bernard Sabella

CATHOLIC SOCIAL TEACHING IS both specific, as it is addressed to the faithful, and universal, since it is also addressed to the women and men of good will. The "humanistic" aspect or dimension of Catholic social teaching, described in a Vatican document of 2006, is a reflection of "God's plan of love in history." It is "an integral and solidary humanism capable of creating a new social, economic, and political order, founded on the dignity and freedom of every human person, to be brought about in peace, justice, and solidarity."[1]

The Ten Commandments, according to the Church, are "the indispensable rules of all social life," as they set the "universal human morality" with its essential duties imperative to preserve "the fundamental rights of the human person."[2] These commandments, the Decalogue, necessitate not only fidelity to the Lord, our God, but also determine "the social relations among the people of the Covenant."[3] They are described as follows:

---

1. *Compendium of the Social Doctrine of the Church*, 2006, #19. For internet access information for this and all other references, please see the Bibliography, below.
2. Ibid., #22.
3. Ibid., #23.

> All of this applies also to strangers: . . . "The stranger who sojourns with you shall be to you as the native among you, and you shall love him as yourself; for you were strangers in the land of Egypt; I am the Lord your God" (Lev 19:33–34). . . . The gift of freedom and the Promised Land, and the gift of the Covenant on Sinai and the Ten Commandments are therefore intimately linked to the practices which must regulate, in justice and solidarity, the development of Israelite society.[4]

The covenant with the Jewish people demands a "moral existence" as a response to the "Lord's loving initiative."[5] The Church highlights the words of Jesus regarding the moral commandments given to Israel:

> To the scribe who asks him, "Which commandment is the first of all?" (Mk 12:28), Jesus answers: "The first is: 'Hear, O Israel: the Lord our God, the Lord is one; and you shall love the Lord your God with all your heart, and with all your soul, and with all your mind, and with all your strength.' The second is this: 'You shall love your neighbor as yourself.' There is no other commandment greater than these" (Mk 12:29–31).[6]

THE CHURCH'S SOCIAL DOCTRINE: RELIGIOUS AND MORAL ORDER

The intent of the Church's social doctrine is of the religious and moral order addressed to "man in his concrete reality as sinful and righteous."[7] It is moral because the Church aims at a "full-bodied humanism,"[8] that is to say, at the "liberation from everything that oppresses man"[9] and "the

---

4. Ibid.

5. Ibid., #22.

6. Ibid., #40.

7. John Paul II, *Centesimus Annus*, #53. Various encyclical letters and other papal communications since 1931 stress the religious and moral nature of the social doctrine of the Church, such as Pius XI's encyclical letter *Quadragesimo Anno*, 1931, for the fortieth anniversary of *Rerum Novarum* (Leo XIII, 1891); Pius XII's radio message for the fiftieth anniversary of *Rerum Novarum*, in 1941; the Second Vatican Council, Pastoral Constitution *Gaudium et Spes*, 1966; John Paul II, encyclical letter *Sollicitudo Rei Socialis*, 1988; and the Congregation for the Doctrine of the Faith, Instruction *Libertatis Conscientia*, of 1987.

8. Paul VI, *Populorum Progressio*, #42.

9. Paul VI, *Evangelii Nuntiandi*, #9.

development of the whole man and of all men."[10] Pope John Paul II promulgated *Centesimus Annus* on the first of May 1991 to commemorate the hundredth anniversary of *Rerum Novarum*; in this encyclical letter he "demonstrates how the Church's social teaching moves along the axis of reciprocity between God and man: recognizing God in every person and every person in God is the condition of authentic human development."[11] This theme of reciprocity is also emphasized in *Sollicitudo Rei Socialis*, John Paul II's encyclical letter in commemoration of the twentieth anniversary of *Populorum Progressio* (Paul VI). John Paul II sees a "prophetic role" for the Church that includes condemning "evils and injustices. . . . But it should be made clear that proclamation is always more important than condemnation, and the latter cannot ignore the former, which gives it true solidity and the force of higher motivation."[12]

The relationship hence with God of the covenant is not simply bilateral but necessarily trilateral: God, the believer, and the "Other." This triangular relationship is imperative if we are to subscribe to God's revelation, teaching, and wisdom in history. The 1971 Synod of Bishops document, *Justice in the World,* declared, "Action on behalf of justice and participation in the transformation of the world fully appear to us as a constitutive dimension . . . of the Church's mission for the redemption of the human race and its liberation from every repressive situation."[13]

The Church is affirmative on issues of justice and basic human rights and links its theological position, among other linkages, to the experience of the Israelites as they were liberated from the oppression of Egypt: "Israel understood itself as having been born as a nation out of the experience of the Exodus, that is, liberation from the personal, religious, social, political, and economic oppression of Egypt. The meaning of the Exodus for Israel (and for us) is that God reveals himself as God in the liberation of an oppressed people."[14] But this saving divine act requires a commitment on the part of the Israelite society for justice:

---

10. Paul VI, *Populorum Progressio,* #42.

11. See also *Centesimus Annus,* #11, in which Pope John Paul II reemphasizes the "correct view of man with God's image and likeness imprinted on man," as originally presented in *Rerum Novarum.*

12. John Paul II, *Sollicitudo Rei Socialis,* #41.

13. *Justice in the World,* Synod of Bishops, 1971, #6.

14. Australian Catholic Social Justice Council, "Social Justice in Everyday Life," 5–6.

God brings justice to the oppressed, champions the poor and heeds the cry of the defenseless (Ps 76:9; 103:6; 9:10–12; Ezek 34:27 and many others). The prophets continually remind Israel that what God desires most is justice. Prominent among them are Isaiah, Jeremiah, Amos, Hosea and Micah. (Is 1:23; 3:14–15; Jr 21:12; 22:3, 13; Ho 4:1–2; Am 5:7–17; Mi 6:2–12 and many others).[15]

It is relevant to emphasize here that the idea that man and woman are created in the image of God is an idea that was first introduced by Judaism, as mentioned in the Intervention of Special Guest Rabbi David Rosen, Advisor to the Chief Rabbinate of Israel and Director of the Department for Interreligious Affairs, at the Special Assembly for the Middle East of the Synod of Bishops. Rabbi Rosen remarked, "To begin with, . . . Judaism brought the recognition to the world that every human person is created in the Divine Image; and . . . accordingly, as the sages of the Talmud teach, any action of disrespect for another person, is an act of disrespect for the Creator himself."[16]

THE COMPLEXITY OF CHURCH RELATIONS WITH THE JEWISH PEOPLE

But whereas the Church draws on the history of the religious experience of the Hebrews and acknowledges the relevance and importance of their religious experience to applying universal rules of justice and morality, regardless of context, the relationship of the Church with the Jewish people proved to be extremely complex, if not problematic, throughout the two millennia since the rise of Christianity.

While it is not within the scope of this essay to go through the complexities and problematic of these relationships, it is important to consider these complexities as they have a strong bearing on how the Jewish people and the State of Israel, in particular, view the positions and proclamations of the Holy See and Vatican officials on the practices of the Israeli occupation in the Palestinian Territories; the rights of the Palestinian people; the issue of Jerusalem and the other thorny issues that prevent a just and lasting resolution of the conflict, in keeping with U.N. resolutions.

---

15. Ibid. Within Israel itself.

16. Rosen, Intervention, Special Assembly for the Middle East, Synod of Bishops, 2010.

According to Aharon Lopez, Ambassador of Israel to the Holy See between 1997 and 2000, *Nostra Aetate,* the *Declaration of the Relation of the Church to Non-Christian Religions,* proclaimed by Pope Paul VI in 1965,[17] delegitimized the deicide accusation and rejected the doctrine that there is a collective indictment against the Jews because of Christ's crucifixion.[18] He nevertheless stressed that "the attitude of the Holy See toward Israel was, from the very beginning, negative and even hostile. . . . some people raise, first and foremost, considerations of a theological nature."[19] According to Toni Johnson, the Senior Editor and Senior Staff Writer of the Vatican's Council on Foreign Relations, *Nostra Aetate* in a conciliatory gesture to the Jewish people acknowledged that the Church "received the revelations of the Old Testament through the people with whom God in His inexpressible mercy concluded the Ancient Covenant. . . . Although the Church is the new people of God, the Jews should not be presented as rejected or accursed by God . . ."[20] But *Nostra Aetate* did not make specific reference to the State of Israel, and recognition came only in 1993. On the Jewish side, anger and mistrust still linger on in spite of strong gestures undertaken by the various Popes since Pope John XXIII, who ordered the expression "perfidious Jews" to be deleted from prayer books on Good Friday. The absence of diplomatic relations between the Holy See and the State of Israel was perceived as being a "serious obstacle in the dialogue between the Catholic Church and the Jewish people, as well as to the improvement of the relationship."[21]

DIPLOMATIC TREATY, VATICAN AND ISRAEL, 1993

It was in December of 1993 that the Vatican and Israel signed a diplomatic treaty with an exchange of ambassadors a few months later. This treaty normalized relations, furthered Jewish-Catholic dialogue, and helped establish a path for regularizing the Church's legal status in Israel.[22] Pope John Paul II visited a Rome synagogue in April of 1986—the first visit ever for a Pope—where he declared: "You are our brothers and, in a certain

---

17. Paul VI, *Nostra Aetate, The Declaration of the Relation of the Church to Non-Christian Religions.*
18. Lopez, *Jerusalem Letter* No. 401.
19. Ibid.
20. Johnson, "Vatican-Israel Relations."
21. Lopez, *Jerusalem Letter* No. 401.
22. Johnson, "Vatican-Israel Relations."

way, our dearly beloved older brothers." It was the first time any Pope had made such a gesture of fraternity. The distance separating Vatican City from the Great Synagogue in Rome is a few hundred meters, but many centuries had to go by before it was crossed.[23] Referring to Jewish-Catholic relations as "a blessed transformation in our times," Rabbi David Rosen, in his Intervention at the 2010 Vatican synod addressing the Middle East, saw the visit of Pope John Paul II to the Western Wall in 2000 as stunning and overwhelming: "For Israelis to see the Pope at the Western Wall, the remnant of the Second Temple, standing there in respect for Jewish tradition and placing there the text that he had composed for a liturgy of forgiveness that had taken place two weeks earlier here at St. Peter's, asking Divine forgiveness for sins committed against the Jews down the ages, was stunning and overwhelming in its effect."[24]

The basic disagreement or conflict with the Jewish people is theological and not political. True, as Johnson argues, Vatican relations with Israel, following the 1993 treaty, are based on international law and not on theology.[25] But theology figured prominently in how the Church, and the Holy See specifically, saw the creation of the State of Israel back in 1948. The refusal of the Jewish people to accept Jesus Christ and the transformation from the Old Testament to the New Testament, which makes the Church "the new people of God," as *Nostra Aetate* has stated, posed serious theological considerations within the Catholic Church in its relations not only with the Jewish people but also with the new Jewish state. Even the connection of the Jewish people to the land was cast in doubt when the State of Israel was declared in 1948: "[M]odern Israel is not the heir to biblical Israel."[26] The complexities and horrors of the *Shoah* (the Holocaust) also played a role in the mistrust and anger that characterized Jewish relations with the Vatican. In particular the role of Pope Pius XII during the Holocaust and the prospects of his canonization, which is clearly a Church matter, raised some questions on Jewish-Catholic relations.[27]

---

23. Lopez, *Jerusalem Letter* No. 401.

24. Rosen, Intervention, Special Assembly for the Middle East, Synod of Bishops, 2010.

25. Johnson, "Vatican-Israel Relations."

26. *L'Osservatore Romano*, May 14, 1948, as quoted by Johnson, "Vatican-Israel Relations."

27. See Gerstenfeld's 2003 interview with Lopez, "The Possible Beatification of Pius XII and Other Unresolved Issues."

THE VATICAN AND THE RIGHTS OF THE PALESTINIAN PEOPLE

But in spite of the highly sensitive theological and practical matters that characterize the relations of the Vatican with Israel and the Jewish people, the Holy See has followed a consistent "political" position with respect to the plight of the Palestinian people and their rights and legitimate aspirations. While the recognition of Israel came only in 1993, following international developments, in particular the Madrid Peace Conference of 1991, the Holy See since 1948 has recognized the rights of the Palestinian people, a majority of whom became dispersed as refugees.

> Pope Pius XII established the Pontifical Mission for Palestine in 1949 in direct response to the tragedy of the Palestine refugees in the aftermath of the war in 1948. What began as a temporary agency of the Holy See to provide the beleaguered Palestine refugees with food, clothing, shelter, and education became a permanent expression of the Vatican's concern for the well-being and the rights of Muslims and Christians in the region.[28]

It is appropriate to mention here that up to 60,000 of the 726,000 Palestinian refugees were indigenous Palestinian Christians. In fact, the whole Christian population of West Jerusalem, estimated in 1945 at 31,330, became refugees in 1948, except for a handful of families.[29]

The position of the Holy See on the conditions of life of Palestinian refugees is expressed annually at the United Nations General Assembly through the Intervention of its Permanent Observer Mission on the UNRWA (United Nations Relief and Works Agency) Report to the Assembly. On October 31, 2011, Archbishop Silvano Maria Tomasi, the Representative of the Holy See to the U.N., pointed "to a very crucial fault line that is developing in the region." He was referring to the fact, given the global economic crisis, that UNRWA, as well as other NGOs working with Palestinian refugees, is "fast approaching a breaking point. Resources are

---

28. "Israeli-Palestinian Conflict: A Brief Overview," Education for Justice, Center of Concern.

29. In 2011, the estimated number of Palestinian Christians in Jerusalem did not stand at more than 12,000 Christians at the most generous enumeration, many of whom are descendants of refugees from West Jerusalem. For statistics on Christians and other communities in Jerusalem and Palestine in 1945 see *A Survey of Palestine*, prepared in December 1945 and January 1946 for the Anglo-American Committee of Inquiry. For more current statistics see the more recent issues of Statistical Yearly Abstracts of both the Palestinian Central Bureau and the Israeli Central Bureau of Statistics.

shrinking as demands are increasing."[30] As Archbishop Tomasi insisted on the urgency "to find a just and lasting resolution" to the situation of Palestinian refugees, he also stressed the conviction of his delegation that "the two-state solution has the best chance of resolving the suffering of refugees." Reflecting on the stalled peace process, he noted:

> To postpone endlessly the resolution of this conflict by indecision or by a willingness to maintain the status quo, by a refusal to negotiate and to compromise reasonably, is to perpetuate a situation that should have been resolved with justice long before now; instead it has caused violence which impacts on innocent people and entire families, both Israeli and Palestinian.[31]

In his Intervention Archbishop Tomasi could not but reflect, using the following quotation from Archbishop Dominique Mamberti, Secretary for Relations with States, on the September 2011 request presented by the Palestinian President Mahmoud Abbas to the U.N. for recognition of Palestine as a member state:

> [T]he Holy See considers this initiative in the perspective of the attempts to find a definitive solution, with the support of the international community.... It is necessary that the competent organs of the United Nations make a decision that helps to get underway effectively the final objective, namely, the realizations of the right of Palestinians to have their own independent and sovereign State, and the right of the Israelis to security, both States being provided with borders that are recognized internationally.[32]

On the question of Jerusalem, Archbishop Tomasi once again reaffirmed the position of the Holy See on the need "to guarantee that the status of the City of Jerusalem will respect religious freedom and access to the Holy Sites." The Holy See "renews its support for 'internationally guaranteed provisions to ensure the freedom of religion and conscience of its inhabitants, as well as permanent, free and unhindered access to the Holy Places by the faithful of all religions and nationalities' (A/RES/ES-10/2)."[33]

30. Tomasi, Intervention in response to the 2011 UNRWA Annual Report to the U.N. General Assembly.

31. Ibid.

32. Mamberti, General Debate of the 66th Session of the U.N. General Assembly, September 27, 2011, as quoted in Tomasi's Intervention.

33. Tomasi, Intervention, 2011, quoting U.N. General Assembly Resolution ES-10/2 of April 25, 1997.

POPE BENEDICT XVI AND THE PREDICAMENT OF PALESTINIAN REFUGEES

The predicament of the Palestinian refugees continues to hold the attention and concern of the Holy See. Pope Benedict XVI made it a point to visit the Aida Refugee Camp during his visit to Bethlehem in May of 2009. In his address at the camp, in the presence of Mrs. Karen Abu Zayd, Commissioner General of UNRWA, the Pope expressed his "solidarity with all the homeless Palestinians who long to be able to return to their birthplace, or to live permanently in a homeland of their own." The Pope spoke to the hearts of Palestinians by telling them that he knows that "many of your families are divided—through imprisonment of family members, or restrictions on freedom of movement—and many of you have experienced bereavement in the course of the hostilities. My heart goes out to all who suffer in this way."[34]

Aida Refugee Camp, in the northwestern part of Bethlehem, is situated in the shadow of the Separation Wall, built by Israel since 2002.[35] The Pope has seen the Wall and in his speech alluded to it as

> a stark reminder of the stalemate that relations between Israelis and Palestinians seem to have reached—the wall. In a world where more and more borders are being opened up—to trade, to travel, to movement of peoples, to cultural exchanges—it is tragic to see walls still being erected. How we long to see the fruits of the much more difficult task of building peace! How earnestly we pray for an end to the hostilities that have caused this wall to be built![36]

The Pope reminded his audience that the long-term solution to the conflict can only be a political one, and he appealed to the international community to bring their influence "to bear in favor of a just and lasting solution, respecting the legitimate demands of all parties and recognizing their right to live in peace and dignity, in accordance with international law."[37]

In his farewell speech at the Presidential Palace in Bethlehem, the Pope expressed his belief that "walls do not last forever." The Pope

---

34. *Washington Report on Middle East Affairs* (July 2009) 16–17. Also, Benedict XVI, "Visit to the Aida Refugee Camp," Catholic News Agency.

35. For an overview of the Separation Wall or Barrier and a map of its route in the West Bank, see the website of B'Tselem, a prominent Israeli human rights organization.

36. *Washington Report* (July 2009) 16–17. Also, Benedict XVI, "Visit to the Aida Refugee Camp," Catholic News Agency.

37. Ibid.

reassured President Abbas that he will use every opportunity to urge those involved in peace negotiations,

> to work towards a just solution that respects the legitimate aspirations of Israelis and Palestinians alike. As an important step in this direction, the Holy See looks forward to establishing shortly, in conjunction with the Palestinian Authority, the Bilateral Permanent Working Commission that was envisioned in the Basic Agreement, signed in the Vatican on 15 February 2000.[38]

The implication of the Pope's reference to the Bilateral Working Commission is to indicate to the Palestinians that they are on a par with other nation-states, Israel in particular, when it comes to relations with the Vatican. The Palestinian President did indeed follow up on the Pope's suggestion, and the first meeting of the Bilateral Working Commission did take place in January of 2011. The *Basic Agreement between the Holy See and the Palestine Liberation Organization,* signed in 2000, was very similar to the *Basic Agreement* signed between the Vatican and Israel back in 1993, with one noticeable exception. The preamble of the *Basic Agreement* with the PLO was criticized by Israel since it declared "that an equitable solution for the issue of Jerusalem, based on international resolutions, is fundamental for a just and lasting peace in the Middle East, and that unilateral decisions and actions altering the specific character and status of Jerusalem are morally and legally unacceptable."[39] The preamble also called for a special statute for Jerusalem to be internationally guaranteed in order to secure the freedom of religion; the equality before the law of the three monotheistic religions; the proper identity and sacred character of the city and its universally significant religious and cultural heritage; the freedom of access to the Holy Places and of worship in them; and finally, respect for the Regime of the "Status Quo" where it applies.[40]

THE VATICAN AND THE QUESTION OF JERUSALEM

The questions of Jerusalem as well as freedom of religion and access to the Holy Places have not been easy questions in the relations between the Vatican and Israel. In October 1998, Archbishop Jean Luis Tauran, then

---

38. Benedict XVI, "Farewell Ceremony," Catholic News Agency. See also *Basic Agreement between the Holy See and the Palestine Liberation Organization,* art. 9.

39. *Basic Agreement between the Holy See and the Palestine Liberation Organization.*

40. Ibid.

Secretary for Relations with States, gave a presentation in Jerusalem on the occasion of a conference held at the invitation of the Latin Patriarch, Michel Sabbah, and attended by presidents or delegates of worldwide Catholic Bishops' Conferences (Americas, Asia, Europe, and Africa).[41] Archbishop Tauran characterized the situation in Jerusalem in this way: it "has been brought about and is maintained by force. The Holy See has spoken out on this and will continue to speak out clearly, without mincing words, and consistently adhering to the position of the majority within the international community, as expressed above all in the pertinent United Nations Resolutions." Tauran emphasized that East Jerusalem is illegally occupied: "Since 1967, a part of the city has been occupied militarily and subsequently annexed. In that part of the city are to be found most of the Holy Places of the three monotheistic religions..." The Holy See, according to Tauran, is not interested solely in the religious aspect of the city as it considers also the political and territorial aspects. "The Holy See is indeed interested in this aspect and has the right and duty to be, especially insofar as the matter remains unresolved and is the cause of conflict, injustice, human rights violations, restrictions of religious freedom and conscience, fear and personal insecurity. In the case of Jerusalem, both aspects, the religious and the political and territorial are closely linked..."[42]

Quoting the book of Archbishop Edmond Farhat on the papal documents on the position of the Holy See on Jerusalem between 1887 and 1986, Tauran shows how the Holy See has been consistent "on the need to protect the physical integrity of the Holy Places and on the needs of all the inhabitants of Jerusalem," for the period until 1947. In the second phase, between 1947 and 1964, "the stress is on safeguarding the Holy Places, on freedom of access for all the faithful of the three religions and the right of each of the three religions to have control of its own holy sites." In the third phase, from 1964 to the present, "the emphasis moves to Jerusalem in a global context and to the preservation of its identity and vocation: the Holy Places; the areas surrounding them; guarantees for everybody of their own cultural and religious identity; freedom of religion and conscience for the inhabitants and the pilgrims; the cultural dimension."[43]

Tauran then proceeds to characterize Jerusalem

> as a treasure of the whole of humanity.... In view of a situation of evident conflict and considering the rapid transformation of

---

41. Tauran, "The Holy See and Jerusalem," 1998.
42. Ibid., III.
43. Ibid., II.

the Holy City, any unilateral solution or one brought about by force is not and cannot be a solution at all. It is the view of the Holy See that every *exclusive* claim—be it religious or political—is contrary to the logic proper to the very city itself.... Exclusive claims cannot be backed up by numerical or historical criteria.[44]

THE FUTURE OF PEACE: AN ADEQUATE SOLUTION TO THE QUESTION OF JERUSALEM

The future of peace between Israelis and Palestinians depends on having an "adequate solution" to the question of Jerusalem. Archbishop Tauran calls on both Palestinians and Israelis to reach an agreement that responds to their respective "legitimate and reasonable aspirations" and that "respects the principles of justice." The Holy See seeks to have "a special internationally guaranteed Statute" that would protect Jerusalem in its various characteristics and would offer equality of rights and freedom to all of its communities in their different pursuits and would ensure the preservation and the freedom of religion and worship, with access to residents and pilgrims alike. Paramount in Tauran's view, which reflects that of the Holy See, is the "protection of the identity of the city in its entirety.... The identity of the city includes a sacred character which involves Jerusalem in its entirety, its holy places and its communities with their schools, hospitals, cultural, social and economic activities."[45]

Tauran reminds both Israelis and Palestinians, as they search for peace and a political settlement, that Jerusalem "has aspects which go far beyond their legitimate national interests," and that they should consider these aspects as well as "the efforts and demands of all legitimately interested parties."[46] The Holy See has been consistent on maintaining this position throughout the years, even after having established diplomatic relations with Israel. The question, however, is whether the position of the Holy See can go beyond signaling to both Israelis and Palestinians the perspective of the Vatican on the Jerusalem question and can proceed to working actively to promote this position at different levels.

---

44. Ibid., IV.
45. Ibid.
46. Ibid.

JERUSALEM HEADS OF CHURCHES: THE SIGNIFICANCE OF JERUSALEM FOR CHRISTIANS

The Tauran presentation emphasized what the thirteen heads of churches in Jerusalem had earlier on proclaimed in an important document of November 14, 1994, entitled "The Significance of Jerusalem for Christians." The church leaders insisted that the local Christians should have the same fundamental rights as all others in the city. These rights include the following: the human right of freedom of religion and conscience; civil and historical rights that would enable them to carry out religious, educational, and other duties; and the right to have their own institutions and to run them freely. But the most important point made in the November 1994 statement was the consensus of the church leaders on the need to have a special statute for Jerusalem. Such a statute, according to the document, would "satisfy the national aspirations of all its inhabitants," and would enable the faithful of the three monotheistic religions to feel "at home" in the city. Included in the promotion of a special statute is a call for the international community to be "engaged in the stability and permanence of this statute."[47]

The universal Church does not always adopt positions synchronized with all of what local church leaders and the faithful in the Holy Land propose. An example is the *Kairos Palestine* document entitled *A Moment of Truth: A Word of Faith, Hope, and Love from the Heart of Palestinian Suffering*, which was issued by a group of Palestinian Christians in December of 2009, modeled on the well known South African *Kairos* document of 1985.[48] The document, which was referred to in some Interventions during the Special Synod on the Middle East held in October 2010 at Vatican City, was not acknowledged in the last document of the Synod, *Message to the People of God*. This silence was due to sensitivity to the possibility that the inclusion might not be helpful to the relations of the Vatican with Israel and Jewish groups. Christians were hoping for at least a certain reference to and support for the main message of the document, which was the commandment of love, to be lived in the conflict, and the call to Christian Palestinians to develop consciousness of their duty towards peace and justice in their country. But nothing was said. The call of the *Kairos* document to support "divestment and . . . an economic and com-

---

47. "On the Significance of Jerusalem for Christians," Memorandum of Patriarchs and Heads of Christian Communities, 1994.

48. For the full text of the Palestinian *Kairos* document, see website in the bibliography, below.

mercial boycott of everything produced by the occupation"[49] could be one primary reason for non-acknowledgment, and perhaps there were some other practical considerations that precluded the Vatican from giving any sign of recognition to this document.

THE SPECIAL SYNOD FOR THE MIDDLE EAST: THE MESSAGE TO THE PEOPLE OF GOD AND THE *LINEAMENTA*

In the *Message to the People of God*, which was the concluding statement of the Special Synod for the Middle East of October 2010, the Synod Fathers stated that they "have taken account of the impact of the Israeli-Palestinian conflict on the whole region, especially on the Palestinians who are suffering the consequences of the Israeli occupation: the lack of freedom of movement, the wall of separation and the military checkpoints, the political prisoners, the demolition of homes, the disturbance of socio-economic life and the thousands of refugees." They also referred to the question of Jerusalem and expressed their anxiety about "unilateral initiatives that threaten its composition and risk to change its demographic balance."[50]

At the same time, the Synod Fathers addressed the Israelis by acknowledging "the suffering and insecurity" in which they live, and addressed the Jewish people as united with Christians in the same Scriptures, the Old Testament, which is "the Word of God . . . for both you and us," and reminded them that Abraham is "our common father in the faith, Father of Jews, of Christians, and of Muslims." There was an appeal for peace with an invitation "to listen to the voice of God, 'who speaks of peace': 'Let me hear what God the Lord will speak, for he will speak peace to his people, to his holy ones' (Ps 85:9)."[51]

The Synod Fathers highlighted the need to avoid recourse to biblical positions in order to "wrongly justify injustices. . . . On the contrary, recourse to religion must lead every person to see the face of God in others and to treat them according to their God-given prerogatives and God's commandments, namely, according to God's bountiful goodness, mercy, justice, and love for us."[52] This statement was in keeping with the teachings

49. *Kairos Palestine*, 4.2.6.
50. *Nuntius: Message to the People of God*, Special Assembly for the Middle East, Synod of Bishops, 2010, I #3.2.
51. Ibid., IV #8.
52. Ibid., VI #8.

of the Catholic Church, in particular the social teachings, which see in others the image of God and necessitate that the fulfillment of the covenant with God is through how we treat others.

Realizing that the intervention of the international community is imperative to secure peace in the region, the Synod Fathers appealed to the United Nations to "conscientiously work to find a peaceful, just and definitive solution in the region, through the application of the Security Council's resolutions and taking the necessary legal steps to put an end to the occupation of the different Arab territories." The fruit of such a solution would be twofold: on the one hand, the Palestinian people would have "an independent and sovereign homeland where they can live with dignity and security; on the other, the state of Israel will be able to enjoy peace and security within their internationally recognized borders."[53]

On the city of Jerusalem, the Synod Fathers called for the city to "acquire its proper status, which respects its particular character, its holiness, and the religious patrimony of the three religions, Jewish, Christian, and Muslim." The Interventions within the Synod were generally in line with the *Lineamenta,* which specified some of the difficulties that Christians and other Palestinians living under Israeli occupation go through.[54] These Interventions did not please some Israeli officials, who hurriedly accused the Synod of having become an anti-Israel platform.[55]

THE *LINEAMENTA* AND ISRAELI OCCUPATION: FEASIBILITY OF RELIGIOUS DIALOGUE WITH JUDAISM

The term *Lineamenta* refers to the collection of the Pastoral Letters of the Council of Catholic Patriarchs of the Middle East. The *Lineamenta* states:

> The Israeli occupation of the Palestinian Territories makes daily life difficult with regard to freedom of movement, the economy, and religious life (access to the Holy Places is dependent on military permission, which is granted to some and denied to others on security grounds). Moreover, certain Christian fundamentalist theologies use Sacred Scripture to justify Israel's

---

53. Ibid., VII #11.

54. *Lineamenta,* Special Assembly for the Middle East, Synod of Bishops, 2009.

55. For example, Mr. Danny Ayalon declared that the Synod was "hijacked by an anti-Israel majority"; see "DFM Ayalon Criticizes Vatican Synod Communiqué."

occupation of Palestine, making the position of Christian Arabs even more sensitive.[56]

The confusion that arises out of this Christian fundamentalist position is the misperceived labeling of the Western countries as Christian in opposition to Islam. The *Lineamenta* wants to set the record straight on this point as it reminds Muslims that Western countries today "have secular regimes and governments and are far from being inspired in their politics by the Christian faith." There is fear among the Synod Fathers that this confusion may seriously damage the churches in our region. Accordingly, the Synod Fathers think it important "to explain what 'secular' really means, and to remind people in our countries of the non-existence of a *League of Christian States* as compared to the *Organisation of the Islamic Conference (OIC)*."[57]

The fact that Christian fundamentalists, and those who define themselves as Christian Zionists, put their weight, both political and financial, in support of Israel and its annexationist and illegal building of settlements in the occupied Palestinian Territories, specifically in the West Bank, makes religion appear ever stronger as a reference point that pits Jews and Christians against Muslims. This problem is certainly worrisome for the Synod Fathers and for many of the Catholic and other churches around the world who insist, out of principle, that Christianity does not condone the use of biblical accounts or narratives to justify the kind of injustice going on under Israeli occupation of Palestinian lands.

The Synod Fathers have a practical reason to worry about the continuing Israeli-Palestinian conflict, which they see as a cause of the emigration of their faithful: "Today, emigration is particularly prevalent, because of the Israeli-Palestinian conflict and the resulting instability throughout the region and culminating with the war in Iraq and the political instability of Lebanon."[58] While some may argue that developing dialogue between Catholic churches and their followers and the Jewish communities and their faithful would be one way to defuse the tense political environment, with its injustices, the fact of the conflict constrains most of the churches in the Middle East from undertaking such an action.

The churches of Jerusalem, because of their geographic location and access to Jewish believers and institutions, are naturally more available for such a task. The *Lineamenta* observes:

56. *Lineamenta*, #18.
57. Ibid., #76.
58. Ibid., #25.

> A number of associations for Jewish-Christian dialogue exist in Palestine and Israel. Similar initiatives in dialogue also involve Jews, Christians, and Muslims, the most important of which is the "Interreligious Council of Religious Institutions," dating back to 2001 (including the Chief Rabbinate, the Chief *qāḍi* and the Minister of *Waqf*, and the thirteen Patriarchs or Heads of Churches in Jerusalem).[59]

These associations, however, and even the meetings and initiatives at the level of the Interreligious Council remain limited both in concrete results and in wider diffusion to the faithful of the three monotheistic religions.

While more work is needed, it is worth mentioning that in a 2006 survey of local Christians conducted under the auspices of the Sabeel Ecumenical Liberation Theology Center in Jerusalem, the response to a question on religious dialogue between Jews and Christians showed that 50 percent of local Christian respondents in Israel and the West Bank favored dialogue and that 60 percent said that such a dialogue cannot take place without discussing also the historic injustice that befell the Arab Palestinian people.[60]

THE *LINEAMENTA* AND THE PASTORAL LETTERS OF THE COUNCIL OF CATHOLIC PATRIARCHS OF THE MIDDLE EAST

Since the establishment in the early 1990s of the Council of Catholic Patriarchs of the Middle East, its Pastoral Letters, that is, the *Lineamenta*, have addressed, among other issues, the issue of relations with Judaism. These relations, according to the Pastoral Letter of 2009, are viewed on the human, religious, and political levels. On the human level, the Council reiterates the teachings of the Church that "each of us sees the face of God in others in recognising their dignity and giving them respect, no matter what their religion or nationality." On the religious level, the Patriarchs recall that "religions are invited to meet, engage in dialogue, and act to bring people together, especially in times of crisis and wars." On the political level, the hostility that exists between the Palestinians and the Arab world, on the one hand, and Israel, on the other, is seen by the Council as caused by "Israel's occupation of the Palestinian Territories and some Lebanese and Syrian territory." The Catholic Patriarchs of the Middle East

59. Ibid., #61.
60. Sabella, *Sabeel Survey*, 39–93.

see that the necessary political decisions are those of the concerned political leaders who, "with help from the international community, have the responsibility to make the necessary decisions in accord with the resolutions of the United Nations."[61]

The two-state solution is endorsed by the Council of Catholic Patriarchs as they make reference to the statements of the Holy Father during the welcoming ceremonies both in Bethlehem and at Ben Gurion Airport in 2009. In Bethlehem, the Pope addressed the Palestinian President: "Mr. President, the Holy See supports the right of your people to a sovereign Palestinian homeland in the land of your forefathers, secure and at peace with its neighbours, within internationally recognised borders." At Ben Gurion Airport, the Holy Father offered his wish that "both peoples might live in peace in a homeland of their own, within secure and internationally recognised borders."[62]

The Church Fathers are worried that in spite of the religious link between the Old and New Testaments—the link that *Nostra Aetate* stipulates when it addresses "the religious bond between Judaism and Christianity"—politics may in fact "spoil" relations. Accordingly, they insist on the "distinction between politics and theology" and that the "Bible should never be used for political purposes nor politics for theological ends."[63]

THE PALESTINIAN BID FOR FULL MEMBERSHIP IN THE UNITED NATIONS

On the more recent development of the Palestinian bid to gain full membership in the United Nations, which was submitted by the Palestinian President, Mahmoud Abbas, on September 23, 2011, Federico Lombardi, spokesman for the Holy See, has stated: "We have nothing to say on the subject; we will respect any decision made by the United Nations." Palestinian Christians and their church leaders, as well as some national episcopates, such as the French, support wholeheartedly the Palestinian membership bid. In a declaration to SIR news agency, Father Jamal Khader, a Latin Patriarchate priest and Professor of Peace and Strategy Studies on Conflict Resolution at the Pontifical University of Bethlehem, in the Palestinian Territories, himself one of the promoters of the *Kairos Palestine* document,

---

61. *Lineamenta*, #62 and #63.

62. Ibid., #64. See also Benedict XVI, "Farewell Ceremony" and "Address at Ben Gurion," both from the Catholic News Agency.

63. *Lineamenta*, #67, citing *Nostra Aetate*, #4.

said: "What we want from the family of Nations, is for it to recognise us as a people that deserves a State, so that it can be a nation among nations. We are experiencing the longest military occupation of modern times, and the time has come for us to be recognised."[64]

SOCIAL TEACHINGS OF THE CHURCH AT THE CORE OF THE VATICAN POSITION ON THE PLIGHT OF PALESTINIANS

The social teachings of the Church remain at the core of its position on the plight of Palestinians and their aspirations for a Palestinian State. The Vatican again and again has insisted on the relevance of the U.N. Resolutions to the Palestinian-Israeli conflict and its solution. While the complexities and intricacies of Catholic-Jewish relations throughout the centuries have added a heavy weight on the Vatican's approach to issues of human rights infractions, to restrictions on movement and access to holy sites, and to the question of Jerusalem, among others, it is nevertheless clear that the Vatican cannot accept the status quo with continuing Israeli occupation of Palestinian lands, including East Jerusalem. Most important, the Vatican, like a majority of world states and countries, sees the two-state solution as imperative for achieving a lasting and just resolution of the conflict.

But the Vatican is not like other states, since its primary preoccupation remains theological and spiritual. True, there are practical concerns with the State of Israel and with the Palestinian Authority that necessitate arriving at mutually agreeable accords on practical and mundane matters, but the power of the Vatican is not political; rather, it is ethical and spiritual. Accordingly, both in the Western world, which has relegated spirituality to the side, and in the Middle East, where religion continues to play a defining communal role that supersedes individual choices and wills, the religious and spiritual message of the Vatican does have a place and needs to be considered seriously, especially by the followers of Judaism, Christianity, and Islam.

64. Galeazzi, *Vatican Insider*, Sept 20, 2011.

POPE BENEDICT XVI'S INTERVENTIONS IN THE HOLY LAND: INSISTENCE ON PALESTINIAN ASPIRATIONS

In his speech at President Shimon Peres' residence, Pope Benedict eloquently spoke to the role of religions in bringing about peace and oneness of purpose:

> Religious leaders must therefore be mindful that any division or tension, any tendency to introversion or suspicion among believers or between our communities, can easily lead to a contradiction which obscures the Almighty's oneness, betrays our unity, and contradicts the One who reveals himself as "abounding in steadfast love and faithfulness" (Ex 34:6; Ps 138:2; Ps 85:11).[65]

Referring to Jerusalem, the Pope described it as "a crossroads for peoples of many different origins . . . which affords Jews, Christians and Muslims both the duty and the privilege to bear witness together to the peaceful coexistence long desired by worshippers of the one God." The Pope emphasized the role of religion as that of bringing different communities together: "Let us resolve to ensure that through the teaching and guidance of our respective communities we shall assist them to be true to who they are as believers, ever aware of the infinite goodness of God, the inviolable dignity of every human being, and the unity of the entire human family."[66]

Pope Benedict XVI in this speech addressed the question of equality with the "Thou" as a basis for justice and lasting peace and security:

> [L]asting security is a matter of trust, nurtured in justice and integrity, and sealed through the conversion of hearts which stirs us to look the other in the eye, and to recognise the "Thou" as my equal, my brother, my sister. In this way does not society itself become the "fruitful field" (Is 32:15) marked, not by blocks or obstructions, but by cohesion and vibrancy? Can it not become a community with noble aspirations where all are willingly afforded access to education, family housing and the opportunity for employment, a society ready to build upon the lasting foundations of hope?[67]

---

65. Benedict XVI, "Speech at Shimon Peres' Residence," 2009.
66. Ibid.
67. Ibid.

In the welcoming ceremony at Ben Gurion Airport, Pope Benedict XVI bemoaned the fact that "[e]ven though the name Jerusalem means 'city of peace,' it is all too evident that, for decades, peace has tragically eluded the inhabitants of this holy land." He pleaded with the political authorities "to explore every possible avenue in the search for a just resolution of the outstanding difficulties, so that both peoples may live in peace in a homeland of their own, within secure and internationally recognised borders."[68]

CONCLUSION

Pope Benedict XVI's 2009 visit to the Holy Land, together with the 2010 Special Synod for the Middle East, reemphasized the consistent policies of the Holy See on the political and human rights issues that plague Israeli-Palestinian relations. The position of Pope Benedict XVI and that of the Synod Fathers are in keeping with the social doctrine of the Catholic Church as it is expounded in the various papal encyclicals and messages throughout the ages. In particular, Pope Benedict XVI during his pilgrimage visit to the Holy Land used "proclamation" rather than "condemnation"[69] to convey to Israelis the position of the Holy See on the rights of the Palestinians and on the status of the city of Jerusalem, among other things. This could be the preferred method of the Catholic Church to make its positions known on various issues, not simply those pertaining to the Middle East and the Arab-Israeli conflict. Proclamation can indeed be a method to convey messages and positions. The expectations and anticipations of Palestinians, however, and of all those who work for justice and an end to the Israeli occupation of Palestinian lands are based on implementation by Israel of the relevant international resolutions and conventions. The Vatican as a moral and religious power has much to say on implementation. It needs to reiterate again and again its positions that are in keeping with international resolutions and that call for the respect of the basic human rights and political aspirations of Palestinians. As a moral and spiritual power, the Vatican has the responsibility to see to it that its various proclamations on behalf of the Palestinians are seriously considered in international fora and, most importantly, by Israel itself.[70]

68. Benedict XVI, "Address at Ben Gurion," 2009, Catholic News Agency.

69. See John Paul II, *Sollicitudo Rei Socialis*, #41, as in note 12, above.

70. Thanks are owed to His Beatitude Monsignor Michel Sabbah, Emeritus Latin Patriarch of Jerusalem, who kindly commented on the first draft of this paper.

BIBLIOGRAPHY

Australian Catholic Social Justice Council. "Social Justice in Everyday Life." 1990. Reprint, 1992. Website, 2003. At http://www.socialjustice.catholic.org.au/content/publications/documentation/social_justice_in_everyday_life.html. Accessed on Feb 24, 2012.

Basic Agreement between the Holy See and the Palestine Liberation Organization. Feb 15, 2000. At http://www.vatican.va/roman_curia/secretariat_state/2000/documents/rc_seg-st_20000215_santa-sede-olp_en.html. Accessed on Feb 25, 2012.

Benedict XVI. "Address of His Holiness Benedict XVI at Ben Gurion International Airport in Tel Aviv (Welcoming Ceremony)." May 11, 2009. Catholic News Agency. At http://www.catholicnewsagency.com/holyland09/resource.php?res_id=1142. Accessed on Feb 25, 2012.

———. "Farewell Ceremony in the Courtyard of the Presidential Palace, Address of the Holy Father." May 13, 2009. Catholic News Agency. At http://www.catholicnewsagency.com/holyland09/resource.php?res_id=1155. Accessed on Feb 25, 2012.

———. "Speech of Pope Benedict XVI at Shimon Peres' Residence." May 11, 2009. Catholic News Agency. At http://www.catholicnewsagency.com/resource.php?n=1145. Accessed on Feb 25, 2012.

———. "Visit to the Aida Refugee Camp in Bethlehem, Address of the Holy Father." May 13, 2009. Catholic News Agency. At http://www.catholicnewsagency.com/holyland09/resource.php?res_id=1154. Accessed on Feb 25, 2012.

———. "What He Said: Pope Benedict XVI's Address at the Aida Refugee Camp in Bethlehem." *Washington Report on Middle East Affairs* (July 2009) 16–17.

The Catholic Church in the Middle East: Communion and Witness, Lineamenta. Synod of Bishops, Special Assembly for the Middle East. Vatican City: The General Secretariat of the Synod of Bishops and Libreria Editrice Vaticana, 2009. At http://www.vatican.va/roman_curia/synod/documents/rc_synod_doc_20091208_lineamenta-mo_en.html. Accessed on Feb 25, 2012.

Compendium of the Social Doctrine of the Church Pontifical Council for Justice and Peace. To His Holiness Pope John Paul II Master of Social Doctrine and Evangelical Witness to Justice and Peace. May 26, 2006. At http://www.vatican.va/roman_curia/pontifical_councils/justpeace/documents/rc_pc_justpeace_doc_20060526_compendio-dott-soc_en.html. Accessed on Feb 24, 2012.

"DFM Ayalon Criticizes Vatican Synod Communiqué." Oct 24, 2010. At http://www.dannyayalon.com/News/262/. Accessed on Feb 25, 2012.

Galeazzi, Giacomo. "Palestine Should Become a Permanent Non-Member Observer State." *Vatican Insider,* Sept 20, 2011. At http://vaticaninsider.lastampa.it/en/homepage/the-vatican/detail/articolo/onu-un-palestina-palestine-vaticano-vatican-8227/. Accessed on Feb 25, 2012.

Gerstenfeld, Manfred. "Jewish-Vatican Relations: The Possible Beatification of Pius XII and Other Unresolved Issues. An Interview with Aharon Lopez." Jerusalem: Jerusalem Center for Public Affairs, 2003. At http://www.jcpa.org/phas/phas-lopez.htm. Accessed on Feb 25, 2012.

"Israeli-Palestinian Conflict: A Brief Overview of Vatican Relations with the Palestinian People." Education for Justice. Center of Concern. At http://www.educationforjustice.org/pdfs/ej/history.pdf. Accessed on Feb 25, 2012.

John Paul II. Encyclical Letter *Centesimus Annus*. May 1, 1991. At http://www.vatican.va/holy_father/john_paul_ii/encyclicals/documents/hf_jp-ii_enc_01051991_centesimus-annus_en.html. Accessed on Feb 24, 2012.

———. *Sollicitudo Rei Socialis*. December 30, 1987. At http://www.vatican.va/holy_father/john_paul_ii/encyclicals/documents/hf_jp-ii_enc_30121987_sollicitudo-rei-socialis_en.html. Accessed on Feb 24, 2012.

Johnson, Toni. "Vatican-Israel Relations." Updated May 12, 2009. Council on Foreign Relations. At http://www.cfr.org/vatican/vatican-israel-relations/p19344. Accessed on Feb 25, 2012.

Justice in the World. Synod of Bishops. Second General Assembly, November 30, 1971. At http://www.vatican.va/roman_curia/synod/index.htm. Accessed on Feb 24, 2012.

Kairos Palestine. A Moment of Truth: A Word of Faith, Hope and Love from the Heart of Palestinian Suffering. English text at http://www.kairospalestine.ps/sites/default/Documents/English.pdf. Accessed on Feb 25, 2012.

Lineamenta. The Catholic Church in the Middle East: Communion and Witness. Special Assembly for the Middle East of the Synod of Bishops. Vatican City, 2009. At http://www.vatican.va/roman_curia/synod/documents/rc_synod_doc_20091208_lineamenta-mo_en.html. Accessed on Feb 25, 2012.

Lopez, Aharon. *Jerusalem Letter* No. 401. March 1, 1999. "Israel's Relations with the Vatican." Jerusalem Center for Public Affairs. At http://www.jcpa.org/jl/jl401.htm. Accessed on Feb 25, 2012.

Nuntius: Message to the People of God, Oct 23, 2010. Special Assembly for the Middle East of the Synod of Bishops, October 10–24, 2010. Synodus Episcoporum Bulletin. Holy See Press Office. Full text at http://www.vatican.va/news_services/press/sinodo/documents/bollettino_24_speciale-medio-oriente-2010/02_inglese/b23_02.html. Accessed on Feb 25, 2012.

"On the Significance of Jerusalem for Christians." Memorandum of their Beatitudes the Patriarchs and of the Heads of the Christian Communities in Jerusalem. November 14, 1994. At http://www.al-bushra.org/hedchrch/memorandum.htm Accessed on Feb 25, 2012.

Paul VI. Apostolic Exhortation *Evangelii Nuntiandi*. December 8, 1975. At http://www.vatican.va/holy_father/paul_vi/apost_exhortations/documents/hf_p-vi_exh_19751208_evangelii-nuntiandi_en.html. Accessed on Feb 24, 2012.

———. Encyclical Letter *Populorum Progressio* (*On the Development of Peoples*). March 26, 1967. At http://www.vatican.va/holy_father/paul_vi/encyclicals/documents/hf_p-vi_enc_26031967_populorum_en.html. Accessed on Feb 24, 2012.

———. *Nostra Aetate: The Declaration of the Relation of the Church to Non-Christian Religions*. October 28, 1965. At http://www.vatican.va/archive/hist_councils/ii_vatican_council/documents/vat-ii_decl_19651028_nostra-aetate_en.html. Accessed on Feb 24, 2012.

Rosen, David. Intervention of the Special Guest, October 13, 2010. Special Assembly for the Middle East of the Synod of Bishops, October 10–24, 2010. Synodus Episcoporum Bulletin. Holy See Press Office. At http://www.vatican.va/news_services/press/sinodo/documents/bollettino_24_speciale-medio-oriente-2010/02_inglese/b08_02.html. Accessed on Feb 24, 2012. Also at http://www.zenit.org/article-30645?l=english. Accessed on Feb 24, 2012.

Sabella, Bernard. "Palestinian Christians: Historical Demographic Developments, Current Politics and Attitudes Towards Church, Society and Human Rights." In *The Sabeel Survey on Palestinian Christians in the West Bank and Israel. Summer 2006*, 39–93. Jerusalem: Sabeel, 2007. Online text at http://www.sabeel.org/pdfs/the%20sabeel%20survey%20-%20english%202008.pdf. Accessed on Feb 25, 2012.

"The Separation Barrier." B'Tselem. At http://www.btselem.org/separation_barrier. Accessed on Feb 25, 2012.

"The Separation Barrier in the West Bank: February, 2008" (map). B'Tselem. At http://www.btselem.org/download/separation_barrier_map_eng.pdf. Accessed on Feb 25, 2012.

A Survey of Palestine. Prepared in December 1945 and January 1946 for the Anglo-American Committee of Inquiry. 3 volumes. Beirut: Institute for Palestine Studies, 1991. Also at http://www.mideastweb.org/angloamerican.htm. Accessed on Feb 25, 2012.

Tauran, Jean Luis. "The Holy See and Jerusalem." Address October 25, 1998. Published by the Vatican, November 4, 1998. Full text at http://www.christusrex.org/www1/ofm/jub/jerus2.html. Accessed on Feb 25, 2012.

Tomasi, Silvano Maria. Intervention in response to the UNRWA Annual Report to the U.N. General Assembly. October 31, 2011. The Permanent Observer Mission of the Holy See to the United Nations. At http://www.holyseemission.org/statements/statement.aspx?id=337. Accessed on Feb 25, 2012.

7

The New Jerusalem
A Personal Perspective

DAVID W. GOOD

ON THE SUBJECT OF "Jerusalem"—given the centuries of conflict that have taken place in that geographical location—I think it especially important not to pretend objectivity or detachment, but to allow one's own hermeneutic to be seen. While one might be tempted to offer a more academic exposé on this subject, I would prefer to offer a more personal perspective. We all look at life through different lenses, and sometimes, just like a person walking around in the dark with his or her sunglasses on, wondering why it's so dark, we all sometimes forget that our view of reality is filtered, maybe sometimes even distorted, by whatever those lenses might be.

When Jesus entered Jerusalem on that first "Palm Sunday," he wept and said, "Would that even today you knew the things that make for peace" (Luke 19:42). Those lamentations are as appropriate today as they were at the time of Jesus, as the city of Jerusalem is still a location for considerable conflict. Indeed, it has proven to be a flashpoint for the wider conflicts in the Middle East, a region where there have been far too many wars. The city of Jerusalem itself, perched as it is on a plateau between the Jordan River to the east and the Mediterranean to the west, is a place of conflicting identities—not just Jewish, Muslim, and Christian—but also within each of these faith traditions, there are competing identities, with some in each claiming inviolable authenticity, each staking claim to that geographical location, with too many in each faith tradition oblivious to their own subjectivity. Perhaps one of the things that "make for peace" is to understand the lens by which we see reality.

Elias Chacour, author of *Blood Brothers* and *We Belong to the Land*, and an archbishop of the Melkite Greek Catholic Church, is the founder of Mar Elias, a school and a university near Nazareth in the Galilee.[1] In his lectures he often describes himself in these or similar words: "I was born a baby. I wasn't born a Christian; I wasn't born a Jew; I wasn't born a Muslim. I was born a baby."[2] This existentialist perspective is an affirmation of our common humanity, a perspective sorely needed in this badly divided world and especially the Holy Land. All need to be honest about their own identities and the subjective perspectives that come with those identities, for it is only in knowing and acknowledging our own identities (as we remember ancient Greek wisdom: "know thyself" and "the unexamined life is not worth living") that little-by-little we can peel back the layers to discover our common humanity.

Here, then, is my own personal perspective on Jerusalem and its significance to my own Christian faith.

In offering my own perspective, I do not pretend to speak for all Christians, for if there are differences between our Jewish, Christian, and Muslim perspectives, so it is within Christianity also. Indeed, it's safe to say that if one were to ask ten different people representing ten different Christian denominations about the significance of Jerusalem to our Christian faith, one would end up with at least that many different opinions. So I do not speak for Roman Catholics or Greek Orthodox, Lutherans or Anglicans, or a variety of other denominations, each of which has a presence, maybe even a stake, in the city of Jerusalem today. Although I am an ordained Protestant minister in the United Church of Christ and serve a New England Congregational church in that denomination, neither do I speak for all Congregationalists on this matter either. Nevertheless, what you read

1. Chacour and Hazard, *Blood Brothers*; Chacour, *We Belong to the Land: The Story of a Palestinian Israeli Who Lives for Peace and Reconciliation*.

2. See, for example, the following websites: http://www.satodayscatholic.com/052009_chacour.aspx; http://worldmethodistcouncil.blogspot.com/2011/08/archbishop-chacour-of-galilee.html; http://www.comeandsee.com/view.php?sid=501. All were accessed on Feb 4, 2012.

here is no doubt heavily influenced by my own Pilgrim/Puritan/Protestant tradition.

As such, for me, the actual city of Jerusalem itself has very little significance. Historically, architecturally, culturally, archeologically, and politically, I find it a fascinating and sometimes a troubling place to visit, but with regard to my Christian faith, it has no centrality, no significance. It has no more theological importance than New York City; Johannesburg, South Africa; Indianapolis, Indiana; or Old Lyme, Connecticut. It is insignificant.

For some, that may seem a fairly outrageous statement and may strike some as strange, maybe even ludicrous, given all the history that Christians have in that place. Walk around the ancient walls of that city, and one will see numerous reminders of our Christian heritage. There is of course the Via Dolorosa with the Stations of the Cross, the route through the cobbled streets of Jerusalem that Jesus would have walked on the way to the Crucifixion. This, and this alone, is enough for thousands of Christian pilgrims who visit the city of Jerusalem every year. Also, every year, these foreign pilgrims visit the Church of the Holy Sepulcher—the place historically associated with both the crucifixion and the burial of Jesus. In this church, there are six different Christian altars—Roman Catholic, Greek Orthodox, Syrian Orthodox, Coptic Orthodox, Armenian Orthodox, and Ethiopian Orthodox, each one fiercely defending its own sacred space. Because of the conflicts over control of the Church of the Holy Sepulcher that sometimes have taken place, Muslim families have been chosen to be the keepers of the keys, and more than a few times in both the Church of the Holy Sepulcher and the Church of the Nativity (in Bethlehem), violence has broken out between representatives of different Christian traditions.

Given all the places associated with the Christian faith—the Mount of Olives, the Kidron Valley, and the Garden of Gethsemane—and the passionate grip that Christians and Christian churches have on these places, how can one possibly be of the persuasion that the city of Jerusalem is "insignificant" to the Christian faith? Furthermore, one might say, what about the Crusades? If Jerusalem was or is "insignificant," why the tremendous investment of time and blood in defending that city against the so-called "infidels"?

When I visit Jerusalem, which I now do on a yearly basis, sometimes I have stayed in a place called the "Knights Palace," situated inside the ancient city, between the New Gate and the Jaffa Gate. It is owned by the Latin Patriarchate, and it is called the "Knights Palace" because part of it was built by the Crusaders. Whenever I'm there, I say a prayer, asking forgiveness for the brutality and bigotry of my Crusader ancestors, remembering how in their diaries, some of them bragged about the depth of the Muslim blood flowing in the streets of Jerusalem, whether ankle-deep for humans or knee-deep for the horses.[3] So when I return home, I visit our local mosque, where I ask forgiveness of my Muslim brothers and sisters for the damage done by a Christian theology that perceived "Jerusalem" to be a place that could be found on a map, a physical place with geographical coordinates.

Likewise, we need to be reminded of the centuries, indeed millennia, of anti-Jewish bigotry for which the Christian church has been responsible, and Jerusalem has been right at the epicenter of that disease. With Judaism itself being blamed for the crucifixion of Jesus, there were years when Jews were not allowed in the city of Jerusalem; these were years during which Christians were in possession of the city.[4] This Christian anti-Semitism—like an insidious malignancy—spread from there throughout the world, resulting ultimately in the Holocaust itself. So, whenever I'm in Jerusalem, I try to remember this painful part of my Christian heritage, and when I return home I visit with my Jewish neighbors and ask forgiveness for the damage done by a Christian theology that thought of "Jerusalem" as a possession and propagated the seeds for the Holocaust.

So maybe it's only wishful thinking when I speak of Jerusalem's "insignificance." Maybe if all three of our Abrahamic faiths had less of a stranglehold on the city of Jerusalem, maybe we would have less of a stranglehold on each other. A sense of entitlement has done terrible things to the human family.

Indeed, even within Christianity today, there is what is called "Christian Zionism," a notion propagated by such Christian ministers as John C. Hagee and Pat Robertson. Sadly, in my estimation, it is one that has influenced far too many politicians. If you were to ask Christian Zionists about the significance of Jerusalem to their faith, they would say that Jerusalem is absolutely significant, and they would argue that for the Second Coming of Christ to take place, all the land of promise, from the Mediterranean to the far side of the river Jordan, from the Trees of Lebanon all the way

---

3. See, e.g., chapter 27 in the twelfth-century account by Fulcher of Chartres, reprinted in *Readings*, ed. Geary, 417; here the blood is ankle-deep. Paul Halsall's Internet Medieval Sourcebook reproduces a letter from three Crusaders to the Pope, describing the tide of blood as rising to the horses' knees; www.fordham.edu/Halsall/source/cde-letters.asp; accessed on Feb 2, 2012.

4. Armstrong, *Jerusalem*, 196, 215.

down to the Gulf of Aqaba, will have to be restored to the people of Israel. It's not that these Christian Zionists care about Jews and Judaism; it's just that from their perspective this is the precondition for the apocalyptic Second Coming of Christ. So, according to this theology, Jerusalem is of absolute significance.

But not for me. Fortunately, Christianity, like all the other religious traditions, is not monolithic, and even though I am clearly not in the majority, I'd like to share with you why the city of Jerusalem, for me, does not have the same significance as it may have for others.

To clarify what I mean, I'd like to share four illustrations: a fairly recent movie entitled *Kingdom of Heaven*, two hymns from our church's hymn book, a poem by William Blake, and the names of some of the towns here in New England. I will then close with what I have called, "A Bible Story I Used to Love."

KINGDOM OF HEAVEN

The movie *Kingdom of Heaven* is graphically violent, but so were the Crusades themselves.[5] In order to drive the so-called "infidels" out of the Holy Lands, droves of Christian Crusaders came down from Europe for this purpose, and in this movie, just when there is about to be a cataclysmic battle with the overwhelming forces of Saladin, the hero of this movie peacefully turns the keys of Jerusalem over to the Muslim leader Saladin, and he does so because he has come to the realization that the kingdom of heaven does not have geographical coordinates, that the temple of God is not in Jerusalem, but rather in the temple of the human spirit, and once he came to that realization, or perhaps I should say, "revelation," Jerusalem was no longer so important.

Now, there is much about this movie that is fictional, but there is something about it that resonates with the teachings of Jesus, the founder of our faith. Jesus and most of the disciples were from the northern communities of Galilee. From my perspective, Jesus was a Jew—through and through—and as such he was in the great prophetic tradition of Judaism. So, when he decided to go to Jerusalem—the center of religious and political authority—he was following in the great tradition of the prophet Jeremiah, who reminded the people of Jerusalem that what was really important was not the sacrificial offerings in the temple, but rather the

---

5. *Kingdom of Heaven*, dir. Ridley Scott, Twentieth-Century Fox Corp., 2005.

building of a good and decent society that would be characterized by justice.[6] So, when the disciples were acting like tourists, gawking at the magnificent temple in Jerusalem, we find a rather cavalier Jesus, saying, "You see all these [great buildings], do you not? Truly, I say to you, there will not be left here one stone upon another, that will not be thrown down" (Matt 24:2).

One must remember that Jesus was a Jew, and in this instance, he wasn't saying anything that many of the prophets hadn't already said before him, namely, that the Spirit of God is not in a building in Jerusalem, but rather in the temple of the human spirit and our capacity to establish communities of justice and kindness, wherever we may be. St. Paul would later subscribe to this idea by saying, "[Y]ou are God's temple" (1 Cor 3:16).

TWO DIFFERENT HYMNS: WHERE IS JERUSALEM?

My second illustration has to do with the language, the poetry, of two hymns from my own Congregational tradition. In these hymns are two quite different understandings of "Jerusalem." The first is entitled, "Jerusalem the Golden."

> Jerusalem the golden, with milk and honey blest,
> Beneath thy contemplation sink heart and voice opprest.
> I know not, O I know not, what joys await us there,
> What radiancy of glory, what bliss beyond compare.
>
> They stand, those halls of Sion, all jubilant with song,
> And bright with many an Angel, and all the Martyr throng;
> The Prince is ever in them, the daylight is serene:
> The pastures of the blessed are deck'd in glorious sheen.
>
> O sweet and blessed country, the home of God's elect!
> O sweet and blessed country that eager hearts expect!
> Jesu, in mercy bring us to that dear land of rest;
> Who art, with God the Father, and Spirit, ever blest![7]

Although the author of this hymn has appropriated—my Jewish friends might say "misappropriated"—the story of the Israelites and their

---

6. See Jer 7:1–26. In verse 11 the prophet called the Temple "a den of robbers"—words that would later be echoed by Jesus (Matt 21:13, Mark 11:17, Luke 19:46).

7. Stanzas 1, 2, and 4 of Hymn 309, "Jerusalem the Golden," in *The Pilgrim Hymnal*, written by St. Bernard of Morlas, *Urbs Sion aurea* [*Zion, the Golden City*], from *De Contemptu Mundi*, c. 1145; trans. Rev. John Mason Neale.

quest for the "land of milk and honey," "Jerusalem the Golden" is not an actual place, this hymn would suggest, but rather the celestial city as envisioned by John in the book of Revelation, the heavenly place where God and humanity would be in perfect harmony. This is referred to as the "New Jerusalem."

From this Christian perspective, the actual city of Jerusalem, located in the Holy Land, is not what is significant. What is significant is the "New Jerusalem," far beyond this earthly realm. For many Christians, and especially Christians of the first century, those who suffered terribly from poverty and persecution, one can see why this remythologizing of Jerusalem, this repositioning of the "kingdom of heaven" in some celestial order, would have been so compelling and a source of comfort for them.

My own theology, however, is much more at home in a very different vision of where the "holy city" is, and it is one suggested by yet another hymn, entitled, "O Holy City, Seen of John":

> O holy city, seen of John, where Christ, the Lamb, doth reign,
> Within whose four-square walls shall come no night, nor need, nor pain,
> And where the tears are wiped from eyes that shall not weep again.
> O shame to us who rest content while lust and greed for gain
> In street and shop and tenement wring gold from human pain,
> And bitter lips in blind despair cry, "Christ hath died in vain!"
> Give us, O God, the strength to build the city that hath stood
> Too long a dream, whose laws are love, whose ways are brotherhood,
> And where the sun that shineth is God's grace for human good.[8]

In these two hymns one can see radically different perspectives on the city of Jerusalem, neither of which is to be identified with the place called "Jerusalem" that is so much at the center of the current conflict in the Middle East. In the first hymn, Jerusalem is the after-life, a place far removed from the injustices of the here-and-now, but in the second hymn, the New Jerusalem is taken out of the supernal, celestial heights, and is now a Vision, an architectural rendering of how all of our cities should be. The land of promise, the land of milk and honey, at first a geographical location on the far side of the river Jordan, and then in Christian mythology a heavenly place far removed from this earthly realm, is now brought back to earth as a vision not only for the city of Jerusalem in the Middle East, but also a vision for how each of our communities should be:

> Give us, O God, the strength to build the city that hath stood

---

8. Stanzas 1, 3, and 4 of Hymn 420, "O Holy City, Seen of John," in *The Pilgrim Hymnal*, written by Walter Russell Bowie, 1909.

> Too long a dream, whose laws are love, whose ways are brother-
> hood . . .[9]

One should also notice that there is now a change in voice, now no longer the passive voice. Jerusalem, the New Jerusalem, is now no longer something that happens to us, something bestowed upon us, something with which we are rewarded, but something we build, using all of our God-given abilities.

This perspective is sometimes referred to as Christian Humanism; this is the theology that waxes and wanes in many of our churches. The abolitionist movement, the struggle for civil rights and human rights, the Underground Railroad, the Social Gospel articulated by Walter Rauschenbusch, the peace movement, and those leaders such as Washington Gladden who helped our American churches to see the injustices in the unfair and unsafe working conditions of the New England mills and the coal mines of Appalachia all would have resonated with this hymn and its clarion call for social justice.

WILLIAM BLAKE'S JERUSALEM

Yet another illustration of this theological perspective is a poem by William Blake. During the time of the Industrial Revolution in England, Blake witnessed not only the desecration of the earth by what he called "the dark satanic mills" (made vivid by the movie trilogy *The Lord of the Rings*),[10] but also he saw the damage, the poverty, the injustices that unbridled greed can inflict on the human community. And so in this poem he says:

> I will not cease from Mental Fight,
> Nor shall my Sword[11] sleep in my hand:
> Till we have built Jerusalem,
> In England's green & pleasant Land.[12]

---

9. Ibid., stanza 4. And I would add "sisterhood" as well.
10. *The Lord of the Rings* trilogy, dir. Peter Jackson, New Line Cinema, 2001–3.
11. We must remember that for Blake the "sword" was both a pen and a paintbrush.
12. William Blake, preface to "Milton: A Poem" in *The Prophetic Books* (1804–8), printed by Blake in an edition that survives in just four copies; collected in *The Poetry and Prose of William Blake,* ed. Erdman, 95. The poem had been largely forgotten until it was resurrected as a World War I patriotic anthem, "Jerusalem," set to music by Sir Hubert Parry in 1916. It was rescored for orchestra by Sir Edward Elgar in 1922. Today it is often sung as an alternative British national anthem, so to speak.

Once again, we see Jerusalem, not as an actual place situated in the Middle East, but rather as an idealized city, a vision of how all of our communities should be.

THE NEW PROMISED LAND AND THE NEW ISRAELITES: MY PURITAN HERITAGE

For my fourth illustration, I would share something of my own Puritan Congregational heritage.

South of where I live in Old Lyme, Connecticut, and a little to the west is a town called "New Canaan," and a few miles to the north is a community by the name of "Hebron." Also, if one were to look at a map of Connecticut, one would find within close proximity such towns as Jericho, Salem, and Bethlehem. Over in Rhode Island, directly opposite a town called Galilee, there's a small town by the name of Jerusalem, with a population of eight hundred.

One should ask why the Pilgrims and the Puritans—my Congregational ancestors—named their communities after these biblical places. Once again, they appropriated—some might say "misappropriated"—that ancient story of the Israelites. The woodlands of New England were the new promised land. The Christian settlers were God's elect, and they would demonstrate to the rest of the world what it meant to be a "light to the nations" (Isa 42:6). Before they disembarked from the ship *Arabella* (or *Arbella*), their leader, John Winthrop, told them that they would be like a "Citty upon a hill. The eies of all people are uppon us. . . . wee must be willing to abridge our selves of our superfluities for the supply of others' necessities."[13]

In those early New England—Pilgrim/Puritan—communities, frequently the members would build their Meetinghouse, their place of worship, up on a hill. This was done not only, and not even especially, for the sake of security, to protect them from hostile forces; but primarily that hilltop location was chosen for a theological reason. Just as the ancient city of Jerusalem was built upon a hill, so the New England communities would also be a "city set upon a hill" (Matt 5:14). Each and every community would be a living manifestation of the New Jerusalem, a city of

---

13. John Winthrop, "A Modell of Christian Charity," 1630, a lay sermon written aboard the *Arabella*, or *Arbella*, the flagship for the fleet of eleven vessels carrying the "Great Migration" of some seven hundred colonists across the Atlantic to Massachusetts Bay. *The Winthrop Papers*, vol. II, 282–95.

Shalom. It was a noble experiment, to be sure, but of course one doesn't need to know too much about the early history of our country to know how quickly they betrayed that vision.

In Salem, Massachusetts, a place that was envisioned to be a community of Shalom, as the name "Salem" would seem to suggest, women were persecuted and hung as witches. In the male chauvinism, if not misogyny, of its leaders, strong women such as Anne Hutchinson were excommunicated from that "Citty upon a hill."

Rather quickly, the Mohegans, the Pequots, the Lakota, the Cherokee, and all the other indigenous tribes, like the Canaanites and the Jebusites before them, were victimized by "manifest destiny," a theological mandate for ethnic cleansing, a theological exceptionalism that manifested itself in bigotry and violence. Congregational Christian missionaries were commissioned to go out to the plains, and in their efforts to expand the "New Jerusalem," they denigrated and demonized Native American spirituality. Young children were stripped of their traditional Native American dress, their long braids were cut, and they were punished if they did not speak the language of the occupier. One should never underestimate the role that this corrupt theology had in these injustices. The Israelites' conquest of the promised land became my spiritual ancestors' template for their own exploitations and conquests.

The Puritans took the story of the Israelites and superimposed it on their own experience, with the theology of the "chosen people" becoming the doctrine of "election." It's hard for us to imagine, but for them the journey across the Atlantic was not only *like* the Israelites' forty-year journey through the wilderness; it was one and the same. Beyond mere emulation, the Puritans sincerely believed that they *were* the "New Israel," that their cities would be the "New Jerusalem," and that they had been chosen by God to be a "light to the nations."

Of course, the world has seen this dangerous theology of exceptionalism in other places as well. In Apartheid South Africa, a building was constructed on the road from Johannesburg to Pretoria—the Voortrekker Monument, a museum that celebrates the victory of the Voortrekkers in the Battle of Blood River, where a small number, about five hundred white Christian Afrikaners, circled their wagons (the *laager*) and defeated over ten thousand Zulus, and this victory was "irrefutable" evidence for that Christian minority that God was on their side.

Zionism and Modern Christianity

A BIBLE STORY I USED TO LOVE

When I was a student at Yale Divinity School, I would often go down to Battell Chapel on the old campus of Yale University to hear William Sloane Coffin preach, and on one occasion I heard him preach a sermon based upon the story of Caleb, which I found absolutely riveting. Like all good stories, it seems to catch the human spirit at its best and at its worst, and throughout my ministry, I have seen its relevance to a number of different situations. Like all good stories, it could be adapted for a multiplicity of different purposes, and I have used it as a text for sermons on countless occasions over the thirty-five years of my own ministry.

Now, as I reflect on the role that theology played in the establishment of Apartheid South Africa, and as I contemplate the damage done to our Native American neighbors by my own Protestant Puritan ancestors who thought of themselves as the "New Israel," and as I travel to Israel and the occupied territory of the Palestinians and the Syrians and witness the injustices being done, the land and the water confiscated by more and more illegal and immoral settlements, I am inexorably brought back to this Bible story that seems to be the source of what I would call an arrogant and aberrant theology.

Here is a summary of that story. The people of Israel had been captives in Egypt. Moses set them free, and for forty long years Moses led them on a circuitous route through the wilderness in pursuit of the promised land, which for them was on the west side of the Jordan River. There were twelve tribes of Israelites, and it's a testament to Moses' leadership that he was able to keep all these people moving, and moving in the same direction, for forty years. Periodically, there were those who groaned about the "good old days" back in Egypt. They might have been slaves, but certainly life was easier for them back then, some of them argued. One can see how pregnant this story is as an analysis of human psychology. We yearn for freedom, but there's also that all-too-human tendency to escape from our freedom, even if that means going back to whatever it was that enslaved us.

Be that as it may, the people of Israel were just on the verge of crossing over the river Jordan to take possession of the promised land, but the people were fearful of making that last leg of the journey. They had heard rumors about how dangerous that place was.

And so, being prudent, Moses did what any good leader might do. He appointed a committee, a "feasibility study," if you will, a scouting expedition. Practicing participatory democracy at its best, he took a representative from each of the twelve tribes and charged them to cross over the Jordan River and then to bring back a report. When they came back, there were both a majority report and a minority report.

The majority came back with what initially seemed like a very promising report. The land, they said, was exceedingly beautiful. They had visited the hill country around Hebron; perhaps it was a clear day, enabling them to see the Mediterranean in all its beauty. Perhaps they traveled up north and saw the Sea of Galilee and the magnificent trees of Lebanon. Up in the Jezreel valley, maybe they dug a few holes and saw how wonderfully rich the soil was, and maybe it was in the spring of the year, and so they saw almond trees in bloom and an abundance of dates and grapes and other produce.

But then they said, "[I]t flows with milk and honey. . . . Yet the people who dwell in the land are strong, and the cities are fortified and very large" (Num 13:27–28). They went on to name the Amalekites, the Hittites, the Jebusites, the Amorites, and the Canaanites—people whom they perceived as the "Other," as unlike themselves. Furthermore, they seemed huge: "The land . . . is a land that devours its inhabitants, and all the people that we saw in it are men of great stature . . . and we seemed to ourselves like grasshoppers, and so we seemed to them" (Num 13:32–33).

And so they said to the people of Israel, "Let us choose a captain, and go back to Egypt" (Num 14:4). Think of it: forty long years in the desert, looking for the promised land, and now they're being advised to give up on their hopes and dreams for the future and go back to where they had come from.

But just in the nick of time, a young man by the name of Caleb steps forward to offer the minority report.

I love the fact that Caleb was a young man, unafraid and uninhibited. I love the fact that despite what his elders had said, despite what the majority had said, he had the gumption and the bravado to offer a much more optimistic report. I love him for having the courage of his convictions. I love him for being able to look twelve tribes of angry Israelites in the eye and offer a very different vision for the future. I love him for the "can-do" spirit he exemplified, and, as such, Caleb has always been for me something of a patron saint for those who look to the future and say, "We have what it takes to do what has to be done," and, "The only thing you have to fear is fear itself," and, "Yes, there are challenges, to be sure, but the spirit that God has given us is a very good spirit, and we are very capable of overcoming whatever our challenges might be."

So, for over thirty-five years, Caleb, for me, has been the voice of that humanistic spirit, the voice of those who remind us that we are better and stronger than we sometimes think we are.

According to this great story, "Caleb quieted the people before Moses, and said, 'Let us go up at once, and *occupy* it; for we are well able to overcome it'" (Num 13:30).[14] That little word "occupy" is now, for me, a huge stumbling-block in the context of what I have seen in our church's annual journeys to Israel and the *occupied* territory of Palestine. I have seen how Caleb was exactly right in his assessment. Far from being "grasshoppers," the descendants of those Israelites have proven themselves to be more than equal to the Bedouin tribes that lived in that land.

I have seen how the successors to the Hittites, the Jebusites, the Amorites, and the Canaanites now live imprisoned by a twenty-eight-foot concrete wall. I have seen and I have met with their children, some of whom have had to drop out of university because their parents cannot afford to pay for their tuition because the occupation has all but destroyed their economy. I have stayed in the home of an elderly woman who speaks very little English but every morning greeted me with Arabic coffee and a warm smile and said, "Sabaah al-khair," which means, "Good morning," or "Salaam aleikum," which means, "Peace be upon you." She is a woman whose ancestors were Bedouin, one whose forefathers and foremothers have lived in the land of Canaan for many generations. This gracious and gentle Christian woman has holes in her proud dining room wall where the descendants of Caleb fired their weapons indiscriminately into her home, and if she had been in the wrong place at the wrong time, her dining room might very well have been her dying room.

I have met with the classmates of Christine Sahadeh. One of those classmates, Rola—the daughter of a Greek Orthodox priest in Beit Sahour—is now a proud student, studying mathematics in Amman, Jordan. When I see Rola, I am reminded of her friend, Christine, the daughter of the principal of the Greek Orthodox Shepherd's Field School. By "mistake," when she was twelve years of age, Christine Sahadeh was shot through the head and killed by Israeli soldiers, the descendants of Caleb, when she and her family were at a checkpoint in Bethlehem.

Over the years, I have gotten to know the family of George and Areeg Kassis, a Christian family that lives in a beautiful home, a home in which they are virtually held as prisoners. Areeg would love to travel to tell others

---

14. Author's emphasis added.

about the work that she does with the Arab Women Union,[15] but because of the leadership she exemplifies in this organization, the Israeli government, the descendants of Caleb, will not allow her to leave. She cannot get a visa; she cannot even get a permit to exit from Bethlehem to go to Jerusalem to apply for a visa. When I look at George and Areeg, I think of their predecessors, the Hittites, the Jebusites, the Amorites, and the Canaanites.

When I think of the Canaanites, I think also of my friend Daoud Nassar of the Tent of Nations, a farm south of Bethlehem where this Christian man lives and teaches non-violent resistance to the occupation. Even though surrounded by illegal settlements, even though his buildings have been demolished and the road to his farm blockaded, even though he's been threatened with violence, Daoud yearns for the day when all can live in peace with one another.

"Caleb quieted the people before Moses, and said, 'Let us go up at once, and *occupy* it; for we are well able to overcome it.'"

Having once loved the story of Caleb, I'm now haunted by its implications. Stories—however seemingly innocent—have a way of becoming mythology, and mythology has a way of becoming a part of one's own narrative. I have seen the damage that this narrative has done to those who live in the land of Canaan, on the west side of the Jordan River—not only the damage done to those who are occupied, but also the damage done to the occupier as well, for, ultimately, the occupation is terrible for everyone, because, even as it imprisons the people of Palestine and Syria, it also dehumanizes those in a position of power.

How I wish that this great, great story about Caleb had a different sort of ending! How I wish this story had created a very different mythology and a very different narrative! How I wish Caleb had quieted the people of Israel and said something like this:

> I have seen the land of promise, and it is very promising indeed. I have seen the snow on Mount Hermon, and I have floated upside down in the Dead Sea, and I have tasted the fish in the Sea of Galilee, and I have stretched out beneath the beautiful branches of an olive tree.
>
> But what you have heard from the others is not true. The tribes that live in that land: they are not some subhuman species that "devours its inhabitants," as you have been told. They are not giants that made me feel like a grasshopper by comparison. They're just ordinary people, just like you and me, wanting to

---

15. http://www.arabwomenunion.org/; accessed on Mar 7, 2012.

Zionism and Modern Christianity

> provide for their children. They are proud of their heritage, and I want you to know that I met with them and they extended unbelievable hospitality. Even though they lived in tents, these Bedouins invited me inside, and we sat down on their long and beautifully woven rugs, and they shared with me some tea and other refreshments. I shared with them how we had all been slaves in the land of Egypt, how we were tired from traveling for all these many years, and how we were hoping to find a new home for ourselves on this side of the Jordan River.
>
> They smiled and they said, "*Salaam aleikum*—may the peace of God be upon you." "The land of Canaan is indeed the land of promise," they said, "and it is large enough and rich enough for all of us to share. Bring your families, your tribes, your customs, and let's make the Holy Land a place that we can all be proud of."

And I wish that when Caleb had gone back to the Israelites to share his report, he had said:

> There will be challenges, to be sure, but based upon what I have seen, I have no doubt that the descendants of the Israelites, the Hittites, the Jebusites, the Amorites, the Canaanites, and the Amalekites all can live in peace and prosperity with one another. Let us go up at once and live together in this land of promise. It is not the promised land, but the land of promise. It is not land or real estate that God has given exclusively to us, but it is indeed a land of tremendous promise. We are God's chosen people, to be sure, but so are the Hittites, the Jebusites, the Amorites, the Canaanites, the Amalekites, and all the other tribes that belong to the human family. We are all God's chosen people, for we are all God's children, and the spirit that God has given us is a good and noble spirit. There is nothing we cannot do. We can overcome our tribalism. We can learn to live in peace with one another. We can make this land of promise the place that God created it to be, a beacon of hope for all humanity.

That for me would be the New Jerusalem.

BIBLIOGRAPHY

Biblical quotations have been drawn from *The Oxford Annotated Bible: Revised Standard Version*.

Literature

Armstrong, Karen. *Jerusalem: One City, Three Faiths*. New York: Ballantine, 2005.
Blake, William. Preface to "Milton: A Poem." In *The Prophetic Books* (1804–8), printed by Blake. Collected in *The Poetry and Prose of William Blake*. Edited by David V. Erdman, 94–95. Garden City, NY: Doubleday, 1965.
Chacour, Elias. *We Belong to the Land: The Story of a Palestinian Israeli Who Lives for Peace and Reconciliation*. South Bend, IN: University of Notre Dame Press, 2001.
Chacour, Elias, and David Hazard. *Blood Brothers*. Grand Rapids: Chosen, 1984.
Fulcher of Chartres. *A History of the Expedition to Jerusalem*. In *Readings in Medieval History*, 3rd ed., edited by Patrick J. Geary, 407–17. Toronto: University of Toronto Press, 2003.
"O Holy City, Seen of John." Hymn 420 in *The Pilgrim Hymnal*. 27th printing. Cleveland, OH: Pilgrim, 1987. Used by permission.
"Jerusalem the Golden." Hymn 309 in *The Pilgrim Hymnal*. 27th printing. Cleveland, OH: Pilgrim, 1987. Used by permission.
Medieval Hymns and Sequences. Translated by Rev. John Mason Neale. 2nd ed. London: Masters, 1863.
The Oxford Annotated Bible. Edited by Herbert G. May and Bruce M. Metzger. New York: Oxford University Press, 1962.
Winthrop, John. "A Modell of Christian Charity." 1630. In *The Winthrop Papers*, vol. II. Boston: Massachusetts Historical Society, 1931.

Films

The Lord of the Rings Trilogy. Directed by Peter Jackson. New Line Cinema, 2001–3.
Kingdom of Heaven. Directed by Ridley Scott. Twentieth-Century Fox Corp., 2005.

Websites

www.arabwomenunion.org. Accessed on Mar 7, 2012.
http://www.comeandsee.com/view.php?sid=501. Accessed on Feb 4, 2012.
www.fordham.edu/Halsall/source/cde-letters.asp. Accessed on Feb 2, 2012.
http://www.satodayscatholic.com/052009_chacour.aspx. Accessed on Feb 4, 2012.
http://worldmethodistcouncil.blogspot.com/2011/08/archbishop-chacour-of-galilee.html. Accessed on Feb 4, 2012.

www.ingramcontent.com/pod-product-compliance
Lightning Source LLC
Chambersburg PA
CBHW070254230426
43664CB00014B/2529